# Freedom Inc.

# Freedom Inc.

## *Gendered Capitalism in New Indian Literature and Culture*

Mukti Lakhi Mangharam

BLOOMSBURY ACADEMIC
LONDON • NEW YORK • OXFORD • NEW DELHI • SYDNEY

BLOOMSBURY ACADEMIC
Bloomsbury Publishing Plc
50 Bedford Square, London, WC1B 3DP, UK
1385 Broadway, New York, NY 10018, USA
29 Earlsfort Terrace, Dublin 2, Ireland

BLOOMSBURY, BLOOMSBURY ACADEMIC and the Diana logo
are trademarks of Bloomsbury Publishing Plc

First published in Great Britain 2023
Paperback edition published 2025

Copyright © Mukti Lakhi Mangharam, 2023, 2025

Mukti Lakhi Mangharam has asserted her right under the Copyright, Designs and Patents Act, 1988, to be identified as Author of this work.

For legal purposes the Acknowledgments on pp. ix–x constitute an extension of this copyright page.

Cover image © Andrew Holbrooke/Contributor

All rights reserved. No part of this publication may be reproduced or transmitted in any form or by any means, electronic or mechanical, including photocopying, recording, or any information storage or retrieval system, without prior permission in writing from the publishers.

Bloomsbury Publishing Plc does not have any control over, or responsibility for, any third-party websites referred to or in this book. All internet addresses given in this book were correct at the time of going to press. The author and publisher regret any inconvenience caused if addresses have changed or sites have ceased to exist, but can accept no responsibility for any such changes.

A catalogue record for this book is available from the British Library.

A catalog record for this book is available from the Library of Congress.

ISBN: HB: 978-1-3502-0081-4
PB: 978-1-3502-0085-2
ePDF: 978-1-3502-0082-1
eBook: 978-1-3502-0083-8

Typeset by Newgen KnowledgeWorks Pvt. Ltd., Chennai, India

To find out more about our authors and books visit www.bloomsbury.com and sign up for our newsletters.

*For my mother Lajwanti Daryani Lakhi, my mother-in-law Kavita Mangharam, my second mother Nirmala Lakhi, and my Philadelphia mother Jagir Kaur.*
*You each inspire me more than you know.*

# Contents

| | |
|---|---|
| List of Figures | viii |
| Acknowledgments | ix |
| | |
| Introduction: Pirated Freedoms | 1 |
| 1  Working Women and the Quest for Freedom in Bildung Narratives | 39 |
| 2  Dalit Women and the Quest for Freedom in Ambedkarite Life-Writing | 71 |
| 3  Underemployed Young Men and the Quest for Freedom in the Self-Help Novel | 99 |
| 4  Chasing Freedom through Romantic Love in Popular and Literary Fiction | 129 |
| Coda | 161 |
| | |
| Bibliography | 169 |
| Index | 179 |

# Figures

| | | |
|---|---|---|
| 1 | Individual freedom in Dalit life-writing | 9 |
| 2 | The *New York Times* page for "Young Rural Women in India Chase Big-City Dreams" | 43 |
| 3 | A still from the dance finale in *The Great Indian Kitchen* | 67 |
| 4 | Still from the DICCI website showing the organization at an event with PM Modi | 76 |
| 5 | Photograph of a statue of Ambedkar atop a model of the Indian Parliament | 81 |
| 6 | Shilpa talks about her sister Kavya in *Daughters of Destiny*, Season 1, Episode 3 | 92 |
| 7 | Cover image of *The Monk Who Sold His Ferrari* | 104 |
| 8 | Aparna's criteria | 144 |
| 9 | Modi and *Raksha Bandhan* | 162 |

# Acknowledgments

This book was written during the pandemic, which meant that the usual avenues of fruitful conversation and feedback were fewer than usual. Nevertheless, I am blessed to be a member of the Rutgers English Department, which provided me with the year-long sabbatical that made this research possible and with gracious and helpful interlocuters and friends who kept me going. I am thankful for this wider Rutgers community, including Abigail Zitin, Sarah Novacich, Anjali Nerlekar, Meheli Sen, and Preetha Mani. The English Department's wonderful graduate students gave me invaluable feedback when I presented sections of the book during my graduate seminar. Brad Evans's and Jeffrey Lawrence's Pragmatism Working Group at the Rutgers Center for Cultural Analysis got me interested in the influence of John Dewey's Pragmatism on B. R. Ambedkar. This led to beneficial conversations with Scott R. Stroud that eventually culminated in the research in Chapter 2. Portions of Chapter 1 have appeared in *ARIEL: A Review of International English Literature* and in Audrey Jaffe and Sarah Winters's edited collection, *From Political Economy to Economics through Nineteenth-Century Literature: Reclaiming the Social*. I am thankful for the permission to reprint them here. Thanks also to Anusha Goossens and Nidhi Lakhi for providing me with a much needed second opinion on sections of the manuscript.

I am also thankful to Ben Doyle at Bloomsbury for acting as a necessary spur to productivity when the world closed down around us and for encouraging me to turn this latent research into a full-fledged book. My wish for this book was that it would be as accessible to an Indian audience as a US or UK one and I am grateful that Ben pushed to make this happen with Bloomsbury India.

During the pandemic, I found myself homeschooling and working at the same time. The fact that this book happened anyway is largely due to my wonderful husband, Rahul, to Jagir Kaur, whose home-cooking and childcare kept us going, and to my two children, Pari and Param, who are spirited in the best possible of ways. My New York family—Prakash uncle, Nirmala aunty, Vivek, Vipul, Puneet, and Nushie, Roshni, and Nitya—provided weekends of entertainment and care. My sister Nidhi and my brother Prabhu, though far away, were necessary phone buddies. Silvanio Reis made sure there was always delicious food, beautiful piano music, and caring company around when I needed it. Danielle Haque, Virginia Kennedy, Aparna Kumar, Tania Khanna, Goju, Jobi, Lounie, the members of Chai Pe Hai and the Philly Girls Gang (you know who you are) kept my spirits up with weekend lunches, cat dates, and nights out when Covid numbers allowed it.

As always, my parents, Motiram Lakhi and Lajwanti Daryani Lakhi, are models of love, sustenance, and stimulation—their sensibility is infused into every part of this book. Their unconditional love powers much of what I do.

Much of this research is inspired by the women in my life—my mother, my mother-in-law, and my aunt. Thank you for being such great female role models.

# Introduction: Pirated Freedoms

In the cover photo of this book, a young street peddler holds Walter Isaacson's biography of Steve Jobs up to a closed car window. The boy's look of desperation starkly contrasts with the quiet, calm confidence on Steve Jobs's face. His other hand balances a tower of literary novels, popular fiction, and self-help books. He has been on the streets all day, selling pirated bestsellers through the closed windows of vehicles stopped briefly at traffic lights, in the heat and diesel fumes. If he is lucky, one of these windows will open, allowing a rush of cool conditioned air to soothe his furrowed brow, and a hand will reach out for one of those books, handing over a few currency notes in exchange. If he is not, he will need to keep moving to sell his wares to the occupants of temporarily stopped cars. The cover photograph positions us along with the passenger of the vehicle as the possible buyers of these books, looking out at the peddler. We sit in our air-conditioned spaces consuming stories about the masculine success of entrepreneurs, like Steve Jobs or the heroes in Chetan Bhagat's potboiler novels, who overcome social obstacles to become rich and marry the girls of their dreams.

Many of the street peddler's books have in common their engagement with a discourse that I will henceforth refer to as Freedom Inc., which is defined by the idea that it is possible to achieve complete autonomy from one's restrictive life circumstances. Within this discourse, freedom from caste if you are a Dalit entrepreneur, from gender restrictions if you are a woman who works for a wage, and from poverty if you are a man who embodies an enterprising masculinity, are all achievable. All you need to do is embrace free market capitalism. Since the 1990s when the Indian economy was liberalized, these dreams of freedom have been marketed to Indians by the government, by popular culture, by big corporations, and by international organizations like the World Bank. For instance, in 2019, the World Bank began its "Working for Women in India" campaign for gender equality, telling Indian women that they could be free of patriarchy if they worked for a wage in the global economy or accepted one of their start-up loans;[1] countless news articles in the Indian media celebrate the claim that the free market is liberating Dalits from centuries of caste-based oppression; and the Indian government continues to launch efforts to free youth from poverty through Prime Minister Modi led campaigns like "Start Up India."[2]

The ubiquity of Freedom Inc. means that the idea of individual freedom, once capacious enough to include notions of political sovereignty, individual agency, and social and economic liberty, has contracted to mean market freedoms tied to the spread of global capitalism and to the endless consumer choice it makes possible. "Freedom Inc." is not just a discourse that encompasses a set of free market principles but also an organization of subjectivity, personhood, and consciousness within which people think of themselves as free when they can: (1) compete in a free market shorn of any regulations; (2) sell their labor for a wage and consume whatever they desire with those wages; (3) choose, with choice reduced to consumer choice; and (4) freely make and remake themselves endlessly in an entrepreneurial pursuit of profit.

I begin with this photograph because it neatly encapsulates what participating in global capitalism really looks like for those who cannot hope to embody these four markers of Freedom Inc.'s autonomous self. The fourth book in the street peddler's pile, *The Steve Jobs Way,* is written as a universal parable for how to achieve such a freedom. Yet that "universal" freedom is denied to the very man who sells it. He can only participate in free market capitalism illegally, never truly reaping its benefits. This reality means that as the potential readers in this photograph, we are separated from the street peddler in more ways than just that

---

[1] World Bank, "Working for Women in India," March 8, 2019, https://www.worldbank.org/en/news/feature/2019/03/08/working-for-women-in-india (accessed April 8, 2021). Similarly, in 2016, in another bid to free women from patriarchy by participating in the market economy, the online consumer giant, Amazon India, launched its "Mom, Be a Girl Again!" advertising campaign. The campaign suggested that women could liberate themselves from their self-sacrificing roles as mothers or wives through exercising their consumer choice and buying hobby related items from the Amazon.in website.

[2] Ivanka Trump, speaking at the Global Entrepreneurship Summit in 2017, endorsed these ideas of freedom through entrepreneurship, claiming that India has lifted millions of "people out of poverty by promoting entrepreneurship under the leadership of Prime Minister Modi." "Complete Text of Ivanka Trump's Hyderabad Speech," NDTV India, November 28, 2017, https://www.ndtv.com/india-news/complete-text-of-ivanka-trumps-hyderabad-speech-1781045 (accessed January 5, 2021). In 2020, the Indian government shifted their focus from freeing youth from poverty to freeing farmers. In support of a move to lift state protections on agricultural prices, Modi claimed that "farmers will now be masters of their own will." Agricultural sectors would be "freed from many shackles" because farmers would have the "freedom to sell not only fruits and vegetables, but anything that they grow like rice, wheat, mustard, sugarcane, to anyone paying a better price. As endless mass protests continued to show, farmers disagreed that the free market has freed them from anything. "Mann Ki Baat: Farmers Will Now Be Masters of Their Own Will, Says PM Modi on Farm Bills," September 27, 2020, https://www.youtube.com/watch?v=FyLz-LAPQ9Q (accessed February 1, 2021).

of the closed car window. We read in the hope of living the stories of freedom we consume, or of hoping to imbibe the truths about the human condition that they contain. The street peddler, meanwhile, only sells them, embodying a state of being that is a far cry from the alpha-masculinity portrayed in many of the books he sells. The books are pirated—he can never hope to rightfully own the freedoms they speak of.[3] They, and the dreams of freedom they contain, are only meant to pass through his hands, never to rest in them. You could even say that the freedoms contained in these pirated books come at his expense. For they form their entrepreneurial myths on the basis of an imagined universality that can exist only by ignoring the fates of young men like him.

I also begin with this photograph because it reveals the complexity of the role that local and global book economies play in producing, representing, and engaging with the discourse of Freedom Inc. Many of the pirated books are global bestsellers that write their neoliberal stories of self-fashioning in a universal register while ignoring the divergent local realities within which they are read. Yet these texts reach deeply into disparate locales, partly because they are written in English, which is a pan-Indian vernacular,[4] and partly because they reach their audiences in Indian towns and cities through editions published by local imprints, or through hyper-local pirated book economies. But significantly, the young man's wares also contain equally popular self-help and literary fiction that *begin with* South Asian ground realities to represent and critique the idea of Freedom Inc. For instance, nationally and internationally circulating novels by the likes of Aravind Adiga, Mohsin Hamid, or Arundhati Roy satirize the kind of self-fashioning curated by Freedom Inc. by telling the stories of rural and provincial lives that are enmeshed within difficult social situations and yet strive for more agency. In this way, these texts pose alternative ideas of what a fuller freedom could look like. Significantly, what all these very different kinds of books have in common is their engagement with Freedom Inc. and their simultaneously local and global reach.

These commonalities, which tie together a significant amount of Indian print circulation, testify to the hegemony of Freedom Inc., which persists despite its

---

[3] The fact that these books are pirated testify to the hegemony of Freedom Inc., suggesting that it is books on the theme of absolute autonomy that sell; the sellers of pirated books hawk only the titles that they can rapidly unload. Peddlers cannot afford the infrastructure or the risks involved in storing illegal books for a long duration, thus preferring to minimize the time between when the books are printed and when they are sold.

[4] See Akshya Saxena, *Vernacular English: Reading the Anglophone in Postcolonial India* (Princeton: Princeton University Press, 2022). Saxena argues that to see English as only hegemonic and colonial is to imagine the language too restrictively, for in the new India it functions as a site of anti-caste politics and as a democratic pan-Indian tool for negotiating everyday life.

tenuous relationship to ground truths. While the discourse, through its many actors, claims gender equality for global capitalism, it often reinforces or obscures old and new forms of patriarchy while accounting for very little in the way of real material changes to the lives of women, lower castes, or the poor. Even though the World Bank touts waged work as a route to freedom from patriarchy, the rate of women in the workforce has actually declined since the 1990s when India's economy was liberalized. Similarly, while Freedom Inc. claims to eradicate caste, Dalits in India own just 9.8 percent of enterprises despite constituting 16.4 percent of the population, while testifying that they are often refused loans on account of their caste.[5] And even as government actors claim to eradicate poverty through entrepreneurship, income inequality and unemployment have risen.[6]

This book stresses the contradiction between Freedom Inc.'s claims and ground realities through a reading of post-liberalization Indian literature and culture. Popular and literary storytelling has emerged as a primary vehicle for registering as well as commenting on and critiquing the prevalence of Freedom Inc. As this introduction elaborates, the writing that critiques Freedom Inc. decenters the myth of absolute autonomy that is central to the discourse. Within this myth, individual actors are imagined as having complete power over their circumstances; they are conceptualized as free to mold themselves into revenue streams and as being completely unimpacted by the oft insurmountable social constraints and obstacles they face. I argue that the texts that counter this myth are more likely to be literary and realist and to adapt and modify the bildungsroman form, for it is this kind of storytelling that narrates the individual's actions in terms of their relationship to their social world, throwing into relief the shaping power of context, circumstance, and relationships on individual co-constitution and decision-making, and presenting what Charles Taylor calls a "life in story." The latter is a plot structure that narrates a life by organizing and clarifying which constraints and circumstances bring humans to the particular junctions that they face and that influence their actions. For example, Aravind Adiga's *The White Tiger* (2008) satirically notes the impossibility of simply overcoming crippling poverty or underemployment by becoming an entrepreneur. Adiga

---

[5] Kathryn, Lum, "Why Are There So Few Dalit Entrepreneurs? The Problem of India's Casted Capitalism," *Conversation*, January 18, 2016.
[6] See the recent Oxfam survey on this: "India: Extreme Inequality in Numbers," Oxfam International, https://www.oxfam.org/en/india-extreme-inequality-numbers (accessed January 18, 2021).

captures the horrific reality of what would be required from someone in his protagonist's social position to succeed:

> You are listening to the story of a social entrepreneur ... one who killed his own employer (who is a kind of second father), and also contributed to the probable death of all his family members. A virtual mass murderer ... only a man who is prepared to see his family destroyed—hunted, beaten, and burned alive by the masters—can break out ... That would take no normal human being, but a freak, a pervert of nature. It would, in fact, take a White Tiger.[7]

Similarly, the Pakistani writer Mohsin Hamid's *How to Get Filthy Rich in Rising Asia* (2014), which I include in this study of Indian writing because it is widely read in India as part of a shared regional history,[8] overturns the myth that one's life trajectory is fully in one's own control when its narrative voice asserts: "There are forks in the road to wealth that have nothing to do with choice or desire or effort."[9]

Stories like this perform freedom *in context* and also often posit and perform oppositional, emancipatory ideas of freedom that resist and go beyond Freedom Inc. Hamid undermines the myth of absolute autonomy by telling a story about a protagonist who, during his journey to becoming "filthy rich," realizes that his agency really comes from his personal relationships with those he encounters and loves during his life journey. This story structure provides a compelling framework through which to posit a Sufi idea of individual freedom, achieved when one transcends the self through one's relationships.

To explore the power and workings of Freedom Inc., I also read the texts that, in line with Freedom Inc., conversely emphasize freedom *from context*. In an example of the latter, bestselling author Chetan Bhagat's *One Night at the Call Center* (2014) represents the myth of absolute autonomy through its God character, who saves the life of the disillusioned protagonist on the condition that the boy becomes an entrepreneur. God tells the protagonist, who is stuck in a dead-end, exploitative call center job servicing rich American consumers: "Listen, I will make a deal with you. I will save your life tonight, but

---

[7] Aravind Adiga, *The White Tiger* (New York: Simon and Schuster, 2008), 173.
[8] Hamid is a Pakistani writer who I include in this study of Indian writing because he deliberately sets his fiction in nameless yet identifiably South Asian rather than specifically Pakistani cities and because he is widely read in India as part of a shared regional history rather than as a "Pakistani" writer. This became clear during a recent session of the Jaipur Literary Festival, during which organizers attempted to frame Mohsin Hamid as a "Pakistani" writer in opposition to the category of the "Indian" writer. This move was largely rejected by discussants and participants, who privileged a co-constituted South Asian literary history against a regionally competitive model divided between different nation-states. See Sushil Sivaram, "(Re)Staging the Postcolonial in the World: The Jaipur Literature Festival and the Pakistani Novel," *Comparative Literature*, 71 (4), 2019: 333–56.
[9] Mohsin Hamid, *How to Get Filthy Rich in Rising Asia* (New York: Riverhead Books, 2014), 32.

in return, think about what you really want and what you need to change in your life to get it. Then, once you get out of here, act on those changes."[10] This kind of storytelling willfully overlooks the socioeconomic constraints that trap the protagonist into his job in the first place.

In reading the post-liberalization literary and cultural scene in India through texts like these, but also through regional film, reality shows, and the Dalit memoir, this book asks: How does Freedom Inc. appear in popular and literary texts and how do these texts reinforce or represent and critique it? How does storytelling in the new India posit other more expansive notions of freedom against Freedom Inc.? How do texts capture the collective normative horizons and interdependencies that shape these more expansive kinds of freedom? I point to how various post-1990s novels and cultural texts refashion the idea of freedom to better enable and support a fuller range of opportunities for human flourishing.

The rest of this introduction lays out the stakes of this exploration. I begin by suggesting that other concepts of freedom such as Hamid's Sufi universalism testify to the way that freedom is an idea with many different forms that manifests variously in many contexts, constituting what I call multiple "contextual universalisms." The Indian version of Freedom Inc. is only one such contextual universalism and as a discourse of gendered capitalism it articulates capitalist modes of being through rigid models of masculinity and femininity. Other contextual universalisms of freedom, however, often posit alternative models of gendered action that are less constricting. India remains a fascinating region within which to investigate these more liberating ideas of freedom given the power of Freedom Inc. and the grim reality of globalization in the region. In the next section, I trace Freedom Inc.'s path to power, charting the discourse's historical journey to hegemony out of eighteenth- and nineteenth-century European liberalism and its transformation of the idea of autonomy. I then turn to the way that various literary texts in the new India adapt the bildungsroman form to recover a more expansive idea of autonomous action, which stresses the importance of multiple pathways for self-actualization as well as an awareness of how one's actions are constituted by one's contexts and inter-relationships. I argue that such texts are part of a literary shift that differentiates post-1990s storytelling from colonial and post-independence literature and culture. The latter body of writing defined individual freedom through the political freedom of the nation. The new kind of post-1990s storytelling, meanwhile, engages Freedom Inc.'s linking of an individual's freedom to their nation's participation in the global

---

[10] Chetan Bhagat, *One Night at the Call Center* (New Delhi: Rupa Publications, 2014), 204.

economy. Finally, I explore how both bodies of writing, despite their differences, produce, represent, and interrogate national history through the lens of gender. The gendered focus of post-1990s literature and culture means that it has a unique capacity to examine and represent Freedom Inc.'s limitations and to posit and sustain other ideas of gendered freedom that challenge and transcend it.

## Freedom as a Contextual Universalism

In recuperating more expansive notions of freedom, post-1990s storytelling testifies to the idea that freedom is a "contextual universalism." As I outline in my book, *Literatures of Liberation: Non-European Universalisms and Democratic Progress*, by universalisms I mean discourses that posit normative concepts like "freedom" or "equality" as attributes of "universal" categories such as "humanity" or "Man." I argue that such universalisms are "contextual" because they are born in various contexts in local culturally inflected forms all over the world rather than just, say, in Enlightenment Europe.[11] Take the 2020 film from Kerala, *The Great Indian Kitchen*, which attempts to think through what it means for a woman to be free from patriarchal constraint through the figure of the Hindu Goddess Lakshmi. Lakshmi, this cultural tradition argues, manifests herself in the universalizing category of "every woman" and her splendor is realized in any woman who is able to realize her goals, *lakshya*, for herself.

In investigating such contextual universalisms, I rethink the dismissal of universalisms altogether by critics such as Lisa Lowe or Pheng Cheah, who characterize universalisms like freedom as being inherently exploitative because of the ways they are harnessed within systems like colonialism and neoliberal capitalism.[12] While the pervasive force of Freedom Inc. would seem to support this claim, many concepts of freedom are also expressed for emancipatory democratic purposes within vernacular folkways, in the Dalit memoir, and in realist novelistic or filmic storytelling. These other instantiations of freedom are often anti-hierarchical and focus on liberation for gendered minority groups, including women entrapped in patriarchal structures, Dalit women, and poor or educated yet unemployed men. Thinking about freedom as a contextual

---

[11] See the introduction of my book, *Literatures of Liberation: Non-European Universalisms and Democratic Progress* (Columbus: Ohio State University Press, 2017) for more on the theory of contextual universalisms.

[12] Lisa Lowe, *The Intimacies of Four Continents* (Durham, NC: Duke University Press, 2015), 6. Pheng Cheah, *Inhuman Conditions* (Cambridge, MA: Harvard University Press, 2006), 9.

universalism allows us to recognize multiple manifestations of freedom, as well as the ways that under the current neoliberal dispensation, one particular variant of freedom—which I am calling Freedom Inc.—has become hegemonic, causing other instantiations to be overshadowed and to recede.

My argument that freedom is a contextual universalism relies on identifying various manifestations of a key idea—that of "freedom" or "individual freedom." As readers of *Literatures of Liberation* may remember, I use "freedom" not as a singular linguistic term rooted only in Anglophone origins but as a concept that appears all over the world, in many different languages, in uniquely culturally and historically inflected forms. Moreover, each concept of "freedom" exists within a "conceptual network," by which I mean that it is linked to many other concepts like equality and autonomy, which themselves vary in their nuances according to historical and cultural contexts; each manifestation of these concepts thus has local names that carry the specificity of their situated meaning.

For example, while the concept of "individual freedom" is frequently associated with the Enlightenment philosophical tradition that includes J. S. Mill, my readings of Dalit life-writing like Shilpa Raj's *The Elephant Chaser's Daughter* (2017) in Chapter 2 suggest that in some Dalit activist circles, the concept of freedom refers more frequently to *nirguna bhakti* notions of equality, Buddhist notions of bearing responsibility for one's whole community or *sangha*, and the post-independence Dalit leader B. R. Ambedkar's Pragmatist ideas of "individuality in and for the common interest," with the common interest being designed in a way that is inclusive to all.

Such a rethinking of the concept of "individual freedom" from the ground up restores the importance of social context while shifting away from Freedom Inc.'s simplistic focus on liberation from caste through entrepreneurship. Attending to the contextual specificities of these conceptual networks also revises assumptions about the supposedly one-way direction in which universalisms like freedom traveled from the metropole to the colonies.[13] One of the major assertions in my work continues to be that when we pay attention to universalisms in their specific culturally and historically mediated forms, we change and expand our typically Eurocentric understanding of the concepts themselves.

In order to allow terms like individual freedom, autonomy, and equality to carry their full range of varied uses, I define them in relation to an

---

[13] Priyamvada Gopal makes a similar point of a different context when she argues in her book, *Insurgent Empire,* that colonized non-European subjects were active agents in their own liberation, shaping "British" ideas of freedom and emancipation back in the UK. See Priyamvada Gopal, *Insurgent Empire: Anticolonial Resistance and British Dissent* (London: Verso, 2020).

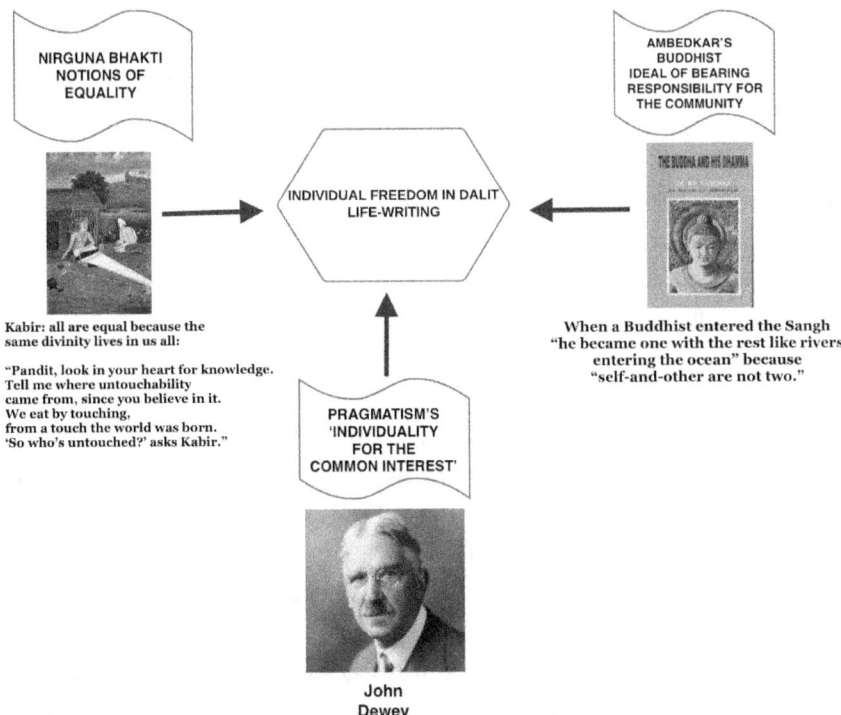

**Figure 1** Individual freedom in Dalit life-writing.[14]

overarching meaning that most of the conceptual networks I examine have in common: a definitional lowest common denominator of sorts. In the rest of this book, "freedom" or "individual freedom" will refer to the possibility of acting in such a way as to take control of one's life and realize one's fundamental purposes in the absence of barriers or constraints.[15] In a collective context, freedom, which is also interchangeably called individual freedom and liberty in many Western contexts, involves the expectation of mutual and active support for maximized self-rule. By "equality," I refer to the right of different groups of people to have equivalent social positions and to receive the same treatment. Equality and

---

[14] "Pandit, look in your heart for knowledge" is a Kabir verse that appears in Gail Omvedt, *Buddhism in India: Challenging Brahmanism and Caste* (New Delhi: Sage, 2013). Kabir Image: Unknown author, http://oldsite.librarv.upenn.edu/etext/sasialalis/mini-paint/company/004.html, Jaipur Central Museum. The "self and other are not two" quote comes from B. R. Ambedkar, *The Buddha and His Dhamma*, annotated and edited by Aakash Singh Rathore and Ajay Verma (New Delhi: Oxford University Press, 2011), 222–3.

[15] This general idea of freedom takes the specific form given to it by philosophers such as Isaiah Berlin, who divide it up into negative (acting in the absence of constraint) and positive (acting in accordance with one's own will) liberty. See Isiah Berlin, "Two Concepts of Liberty," in I. Berlin, *Four Essays on Liberty* (London: Oxford University Press, [1969] 2002).

freedom are linked concepts because equality generally refers to the positive, socially produced conditions that allow an individual to exercise their own will without constraint. Another associated concept in these networks that recurs in this book, "autonomy," is more individualistic, referring to the ability to act according to your own initiative, values, and priorities, without reliance on someone or something else to actualize a given objective. In this sense, autonomy is concerned most with an individual's self-directed thought and action.[16] In the next section, I sketch out the contours of the post-liberalization socioeconomic context within which these concepts are marshalled.

## The Marriage of Economic Liberalization and Freedom Inc. in India

The prevalence and spread of the discourse of Freedom Inc. is a familiar story all over the world but I turn to India to explore its many facets because it is here that Freedom Inc. finds growing resonance at the same time that the number of Indians experiencing economic precarity has also grown. Ironically, growing precarity is why, I suggest, so many Indians are susceptible to the myth of absolute autonomy that Freedom Inc. offers.

India's liberalization process was carried out under intense pressure from international lending agencies such as the International Monetary Fund. Economists collaborated with large Western corporations to claim that liberalization would be a solution to India's economic woes. However, as critics note, liberalization has not reduced poverty across the board. Rather, as economist Amiya Bagchi observes in his description of "corporate feudalism,"

---

[16] Despite its individualistic orientation, the concept of "autonomy" does not ignore the idea that individuals are constituted in and through their contexts. In fact, philosophers have long argued over whether the idea of "autonomy" must take into account the contextual, or "external," factors that enable self-rule. Many ask questions such as: How does one distinguish a self-directed action from one that is a product of other factors that would negate self-directedness? "Internalist" philosophies answer this question by arguing that an action is self-directed if someone's motivation to act coheres with her point of view on the action. "Point of view" may be constituted by her highest-order desires, her evaluative judgments regarding which actions are worth performing, or the outlook that most corresponds with an agent's long-term plans. For versions of this position, see Harry Frankfurt, "Freedom of the Will and the Concept of a Person," *The Importance of What We Care about* (Cambridge: Cambridge University Press, 1988), G. Watson, "Free Agency," *Journal of Philosophy*, 72, 1972: 205–20, and Michael Bratman, *Structures of Agency: Essays* (Oxford: Oxford University Press, 2007). Other philosophers take an "externalist" position, arguing that an agent does not really govern herself unless her motives, or the mental processes that produce them, are responsive to a sufficiently wide range of "external" reasons for and against behaving as she does. See, for example, J. Fischer and M. Ravizza, *Perspectives on Moral Responsibility* (Ithaca: Cornell University Press, 1993).

domestic neoliberal collaborators often pressured their own government to hand out outrageously high profits to transnational corporations by forwarding the false argument that only they had the resources and technology to build needed infrastructure such as power and water supplies or highways.[17] Pranab Bardhan highlights the devastation to fragile economies by billions of dollars of volatile short-term capital stampeding around the globe in herd-like movements.[18] Both economists stress the damage caused to the jobs and incomes of the poor by international trade and foreign investment. They also note the Indian state's unwillingness and inability to compensate for this damage and to invest in the public sector so as to alleviate poverty and inequality. This underinvestment in the public good became morbidly apparent during the Covid-19 crisis, causing a collapse in a severely impoverished and underfunded public health-care system.[19]

The decades since liberalization in 1991 have seen social deterioration, even as liberalization itself has been touted as beneficial. This perception of universal growth and prosperity is partly due to the continued presence and power of the "end of history" narrative within the nation's subconscious. The latter Hegelian narrative, adapted by Francis Fukuyama, refers to the idea that the historical development of humanity culminates in the universal recognition of human freedom, which takes the form of the successful spread of capitalism to all areas of the world. Human freedom, within this discourse, is realized through global capitalism.[20] However, in actuality this discourse exists in concert with negative changes to the freedom of particular groups, including women, Dalits, and lower-class men. While the reasons for this deterioration are complex and manifold, they can at least partly be blamed on three developments: the rise in income inequality, a rise in the number of educated unemployed, and a decline in the number of women in the labor force.

---

[17] Amiya Bagchi, "Neoliberal Imperialism, Corporate Feudalism and the Contemporary Origins of Dirty Money," *Networkideas.org*, networkideas.org/feathm/may2006/Amiya_Bagchi.pdf (accessed January 10, 2020).

[18] Pranab Bardhan, "Globalization, Inequality, and Poverty: An Overview," *Eml.berkeley.edu*, eml.berkeley.edu/~webfac/bardhan/papers/BardhanGlobalOverview.pdf (accessed January 10, 2020).

[19] In 1993, the World Bank released its World Development Report, which focused on health care and directed "third-world governments to reorient public health spending for selective health programs" and to leave the bulk of health care to the private sector by reducing public subsidies and encouraging "social or private insurance" for clinical services. The result: 85.9 percent of people in rural India have no medical insurance and the country has 43,487 private hospitals and a mere 25,778 public hospitals to service the majority of the Indian population. Sanket Jain, "How Neoliberal Austerity Stripped India's Healthcare Infrastructure," https://towardfreedom.org/story/admin/how-neoliberal-austerity-stripped-indias-healthcare-infrastructure/ (accessed April 19, 2021).

[20] Francis Fukuyama, *The End of History and the Last Man* (New York: Free Press, 1992).

The rise in income inequality in India continues despite the much-touted growth of the middle class. India's richest 1 percent acquired 73 percent of the total wealth created in the country in 2017, as per a survey by international rights group Oxfam. The top 10 percent went from having 30 percent of the total wealth in the 1980s to having more than 56 percent in 2019.[21] These figures confirm that the perceived "growth" of the middle class does not take into account the increasing difference between tiers *within* the middle class. Multiple social scientists agree that those included in the top 10 percent, the upper middle classes, benefitted from the liberalization of the Indian economy from the early 1990s onward.[22] However, the economic reforms threatened lower-middle-class access to state subsidies, reduced the supply of government jobs, and undermined state services, such as educational and health facilities. This meant that by the late 1990s a gulf was emerging between an upper middle class in metropolitan India and the lower middle classes elsewhere. This coincided with a rise in media celebrating consumption, leading to a widespread feeling of being left behind for the latter groups. Such a feeling is explicable in terms of the aspirational, teleological force of the end of history narrative, which, in one form or another, has been applied to the Indian context since the colonial era. As Dipesh Chakrabarty argues, through colonial rule, Europe was always saying "not yet" to somebody else. Chakrabarty turns to John Stuart Mill's *On Liberty* and *On Representative Government*, "which proclaimed self-rule as the highest form of government and yet argued against giving Indians or Africans self-rule."[23] According to Mill, Indians or Africans were *not yet* civilized enough to rule themselves. Some historical time of development and civilization through colonial rule had to elapse before they could be considered prepared for such a task. Mill's historicist argument thus consigned Indians, Africans, and other "rude" nations to an imaginary waiting room of history through its discriminatory and false universalism.[24] In the post-1990s moment, the force of the "end of history" narrative updates the "waiting room of history." Discourses about the "developing" versus "developed" world accompany economic liberalization and similarly postpone the non-Western world's relationship to freedom into one of "not yet" and "waiting." Those groups that acquired jobs

---

[21] Professor Himanshu, "India: Extreme Inequality in Numbers," *Oxfam International*, https://www.oxfam.org/en/india-extreme-inequality-numbers.

[22] Jeffrey Craig compiles the analysis of multiple social scientists to this end in *Timepass: Youth, Class and the Politics of Waiting in India* (Stanford: Stanford University Press, 2010), 6.

[23] Dipesh Chakrabarty, *Provincializing Europe: Postcolonial Thought and Historical Difference* (Princeton: Princeton University Press, 2007), 7–8.

[24] Chakrabarty, *Provincializing Europe*, 7–8.

and prosperity have been included within the potency of the nation's forward move toward "development." However, those who have not—a vast proportion of the lower middle classes—have acquired a widespread feeling that they are still "developing," that they have been left behind, that they have not yet achieved freedom.

Such a temporal lag or delay is most felt by the educated unemployed, who have the cultural and intellectual resources to perceive the drive forward toward "development" but not the material resources or the connections to enjoy the economic benefits of globalization. In a second sign of deterioration, the numbers of educated unemployed have risen during the 1990s and early 2000s despite rapid economic growth. There are several reports of young people with master's degrees or even PhDs applying for jobs they are overqualified for[25] and unemployment among the well-educated is thrice the national average. In 2019, there were approximately 55 million people in the labor market with at least a graduate degree—of which 9 million were estimated to be unemployed.[26] Social scientists like Robert Dore have historically blamed such a decrease in well-being on population growth, a lack of expansion in manufacturing and service industries, and increased enrollment in education by lower-middle-class young men who possess the financial backing to obtain education but lack the funds and cultural capital to compete for government jobs.[27] Jeffrey Craig applies these insights to the Indian situation, writing of increasing numbers of young men in small towns who are compelled to wait for years, generations, or whole lifetimes because they are unable to realize their goals. They speak of being lost in time and imagine many of their activities as simply ways to pass the time.[28] Within the end of history's teleological notion of time, these young men see themselves as being stuck and manifestly unfree.

While vast numbers of young men continue to fruitlessly look for work, record numbers of Indian women have dropped out of the labor force altogether. Four out of five women do not work for money in India. Only Yemen, Iraq, Jordan, Syria, Algeria, Iran, and the West Bank and Gaza have a lower female labor force

---

[25] Prashant Srivastava, "Job Crisis Clearly Visible in UP," *The Print*, February 8, 2019, https://theprint.in/india/governance/jobs-crisis-visible-up-3700-phds-applied-messengers-police/189339/ (accessed February 10, 2020).

[26] Sharan Poovana, "In Job Markets, a Higher Education Degree Is Often a Road to Nowhere," *Live Mint*, February 11, 2019, https://www.livemint.com/news/india/in-job-markets-a-higher-education-degree-is-often-a-road-to-nowhere/amp-1549827477203.html?fbclid=IwAR1ANDkpYRgTG30na2q9n_fz3_fgnKoUu- (accessed February 10, 2020).

[27] Robert Dore, *The Diploma Disease: Education, Qualification and Development* (Berkeley: University of California Press, 1976).

[28] Jeffrey Craig, *Timepass: Youth, Class and the Politics of Waiting in India* (Stanford: Stanford University Press, 2010).

participation (FLFP) rate. Moreover, women's labor force participation rate has actually been declining. It was just over 30 percent in 1990 and has since declined to just over 20 percent. Multiple social scientists have argued that this is bad news for India's women because women's wage work is linked to increased autonomy and decision-making power in the household,[29] delays in the age of marriage and first childbirth,[30] and an increase in education for children in the house.

Yet these three negative indicators—the rise in income inequality, a rise in the number of educated unemployed, and a decline in the number of women in the labor force—coexist with Freedom Inc.'s contradictory narrative that the liberalization of the Indian economy has *led* to individual freedom. In *India Unbound*, the writer Gurcharan Das celebrates the post-1991 era, equating it with the actual liberation of the nation, as opposed to the liberation that was achieved from British colonialism. Das substantiates the suggestion that India only truly became free when it embraced a free market economy by stating that "the economic revolution … in the middle of 1991 may well be more important than the political revolution that Nehru initiated in 1947." He further argues that "India's policies after 1947 condemned the nation to a hobbled economy until 1991, when the government instituted sweeping reforms that paved the way for extraordinary growth."[31] In such a vision, the idea of what a free India means has itself changed. A sovereign nation-state is now defined not by political freedom but through its participation within a free market economy. The Indian citizen, meanwhile, is "free" when they are fiscally self-interested in a way that is also patriotic; they are charged with generating an income stream in a manner that moves the nation forward toward economic dominance within a free market. As Ravinder Kaur argues, such an idea is apparent in the Indian government's mega-publicity campaigns—Incredible India, India Shining, Brand India, Lead India—that have been a particular feature of its dramatic makeover from an aid-dependent "developing" nation to a lucrative emerging market in the global economy. The India Shining campaign of 2003–4 inaugurated the emergence of the autonomous figure of the "investor-citizen," "whose belonging to the nation is authenticated primarily through a capacity to invest and grow with the nation." A poem within that campaign declares:

---

[29] Siwan Anderson and Mukesh Eswaran, "What Determines Female Autonomy? Evidence from Bangladesh," *Journal of Development Economics*, 90 (2): 179–91, November 2009.
[30] Robert Jensen, "Do Labor Market Opportunities Affect Young Women's Work and Family Decisions? Experimental Evidence from India," *The Quarterly Journal of Economics*, 127 (2), May 2012: 753–92.
[31] Gurcharan Das, *India Unbound* (New Delhi: Anchor Books, 2002), ix–xi.

So go ahead, make use of this opportunity, and gain from these excellent times.
Spread this proud enthusiasm, and make India stronger and shine even brighter.³²

The poem was part of a campaign to encourage Indians to invest in global financial markets and increase their consumer spending on international luxury items and branded retail goods instead of putting their money in fixed-term bank deposits and gold, thereby stimulating the domestic market. The poem acts as an invitation to collaborate with India itself, a nation that is now presented as an attractive investment proposition. Kaur elaborates that "the bargain is twofold. The citizen is asked to 'invest, build, create,' thereby profiting 'from new possibilities opening up.'" In this way, "the state expects that the entrepreneurial acts of the citizens will … 'make India stronger and shine even brighter.'" As Kaur notes, such an invitation to invest in the nation is indicative of a transformation in the state–citizen relationship. While the earlier idea of India was based on citizens receiving security, rights, and public goods in exchange for accepting the sovereignty of the state, the current contract is "based upon the logic of economic growth, where citizens help grow the nation by diverting their individual capital to the domestic markets. As a consequence, individuals profit from the growing economy and multiply their personal capital."³³

The model of the citizen who helps the nation and themselves by participating in the global economy is a gendered one, using specific ideas of masculinity and femininity as vehicles through which its capitalist logics can be embodied. As I show in Chapter 1 through readings of stories in the *New York Times*, Western journalists and neoliberal economic institutions like the World Bank gender global capitalism in particular ways, characterizing working, wage-earning women as embodiments of freedom and continuing to talk about piece rate work in multinational factories or about development initiatives in India in terms of their potential to free the nation and oppressed Indian women alike.³⁴ These arguments support the contention of feminist scholars such as Christina Scharff that young women in the global south are often constructed as ideal neoliberal subjects who can capably maximize opportunities such as access to the labor market for themselves and for the national economy.³⁵ In other words,

---

³² Ravinder Kaur, "'I Am India Shining': The Investor-Citizen and the Indelible Icon of Good Times," *Journal of Asian Studies*, 75 (3), August 2016: 621.
³³ Ravinder Kaur, "'I Am India Shining': The Investor-Citizen and the Indelible Icon of Good Times," *Journal of Asian Studies*, 75 (3), August 2016: 621, 630.
³⁴ World Bank, "Working for Women in India," March 8, 2019, https://www.worldbank.org/en/news/feature/2019/03/08/working-for-women-in-india (accessed January 1, 2020).
³⁵ See Rosalind Gill and Christina Scharff, eds., *New Femininities: Postfeminism, Neoliberalism and Subjectivity* (Basingstoke: Palgrave, 2011).

women are characterized as being free themselves and as bringing freedom to the nation when they participate in the market regardless of how exploitative that market is or of the persistent patriarchies that sully their gendered lives. And, as I explore in Chapters 3 and 4 through readings of the novels of Aravind Adiga, Mohsin Hamid, and Chetan Bhagat, Freedom Inc.'s "investor citizen," is also gendered through an entrepreneurial alpha-masculinity. The men in these novels are free when they embrace a patriotic entrepreneurial masculinity that elevates their nation's GDP and wins them the girl they hanker for. Within these versions of Freedom Inc., the attainment of a feminized or masculinized version of Freedom Inc. becomes a metric through which to discuss people's success as human beings. A particular kind of Freedom Inc. comes to stand in for and replace more expansive notions of freedom.

To be clear, I am not arguing against the idea that waged work often leads to a qualitative increase in freedom, in people's ability to make decisions for themselves, and to act upon them. I am only protesting (1) the idea within Freedom Inc. that globalized capital necessarily increases the rate of waged work. In fact, given the declining rate of women in the workforce, one could argue that it has done the opposite; (2) the idea that Freedom Inc. is an absolute freedom that eradicates other limitations on agency. Against these assumptions, I show that Freedom Inc. presents access to unlimited consumer choice, entrepreneurship, and working for a wage as the epitome of being free, while ignoring various constraints—whether in the workplace or at home—that hinder the lives of gendered and classed subjects regardless of whether they are wage earners or entrepreneurs. The coexistence of Freedom Inc. with other kinds of unfreedoms is apparent in *India Unbound* when Gurcharan Das narrates his chance meeting with a female factory worker who proudly declares that she makes leather shoes for "Florsheim, Hogarth, Marks and Spencer."

> She said the names in a clear and deliberate manner. She was very proud of her customers. "Yes, we make very good shoes," she added. She told us that her name was Sushila. She was twenty years old, and she earned Rs. 15000 a month. She had been working in the factory since it started three years ago. Ever since then things had changed rapidly in her village. All the girls had jobs now. They could make their own dowries, and they got respect.[36]

Gurcharan Das celebrates Sushila as an embodiment of self-possessed individual freedom because she participates in the global economy, earning Rs. 15,000,

---

[36] Das, *India Unbound*, 233.

or about $200, a month working at a multinational factory. In this narrative, the free market has led to independence, to gender equality. However, such an interpretation would overlook the telling last sentence: "They could make their own dowries, and they got respect."[37] This form of freedom has not eradicated oppressive gendered customs such as dowry, rather it seems to have legitimized them. Dowry-seeking men and their families can look forward to marrying a girl who brings various material possessions with her as well as a monthly wage. This tallies with Uma Narayan's contention that traditions such as dowry have been strengthened by globalization rather than weakened by it.[38]

Yet Das still judges Sushila to be free because such accounts of gendered freedom are, as Wendy Brown puts it, a "governing rationality," which means that the logic of Freedom Inc. has become so pervasive that it appears commonsensical and taken for granted.[39] This rationality switches the meaning of democratic values from a social and political register to an economic register. Equality as a matter of legal standing and participation in shared rule is replaced with the idea of an equal right to compete in a vastly unequal world market.

## The Historical Origins and Development of Freedom Inc.

I have been arguing that, in India, more expansive notions of freedom have been reduced to the discourse of Freedom Inc. as it accompanies the changed allocation of resources in a global economy. Moreover, ironically, this reduction of the meaning of freedom has been part of a purported effort to remove obstacles to autonomy posed by tradition or religion, with various state and corporate actors claiming to free women from patriarchy, Dalits from caste, or the poor from poverty. I use the word "ironic" because Freedom Inc. claims to get rid of all caste, class, and gender related constraints on autonomy but, in doing so, it actually just makes it more difficult to acknowledge the continuing salience of these constraints on individual lives. While the discourse positions itself as signifying an absolute freedom, through an ironic process of inversion, it constricts the idea of freedom to represent only market freedoms tied to the expansion of capitalism. Freedom Inc. thus subsumes the salience of all other forms of freedom—individual, political, social, and economic—within itself. This

---

[37] Das, *India Unbound*, 233.
[38] Uma Narayan, *Dislocating Cultures: Identities, Traditions, and Third World* Feminism (London: Routledge, 1997), 42–81.
[39] Wendy Brown, *Undoing the Demos: Neoliberalism's Stealth Revolution* (New York: Zone Books, 2015).

section investigates the historical trajectory of the constriction and subsuming of freedom, asking: Which particular conceptual network of freedom birthed the discourse of Freedom Inc.? And which other contextual universalisms were forced to recede as a result?

Freedom Inc. emerged out of and is historically related to the notion of the autonomous self in the Enlightenment liberal tradition. One of the key thinkers of this concept was John Stuart Mill, who argued that one's freedom was a private arena within which an individual's freedom to experiment with his or her own lifestyle was absolute, provided that one's choices caused no harm to others.[40] The boundaries between this self and others were clear and distinct and this self's values were independent of the values and priorities of others. The decision-making self of this tradition was "autonomous' because he was not envisioned as an interdependent entity. In contemporary manifestations of this concept of freedom, others still do not form a part of the self, and their values and preferences are not, in significant respects, one's own. If the self is independent, not interdependent, the self is seen as operating independently of the contexts that shape him and the environments within which he acts.

Such an idea of the autonomous self has implications for how we imagine agency—or the decisions and choices people make and the actions through which they realize these decisions and choices. As Saba Mahmood argues, the liberal tradition understands agency only "as the capacity to realize one's own interests against the weight of custom, tradition, transcendental will, or other obstacles (whether individual or collective). Thus the humanist desire for autonomy and self-expression constitute the substrate, the slumbering ember that can spark to flame in the form of an act of resistance when conditions permit."[41] So in order for an individual to be free within this framework, it is required that her choices, and the actions that follow, be the consequence of her "own will" rather than that of tradition or direct coercion. But, as Mahmood points out, this kind of liberal conception of agency is built partly on a myth, because it ignores what Charles Taylor has called "the sources of the self," or the values, "commitments and identifications" through which our wills and intentions are constituted and through which we act on our desires.[42] While the liberal self presents itself as autonomous, our very identity, and therefore our capacity for action, is tied up

---

[40] John Stuart Mill, *On Liberty* (London: J. W. Parker, 1859).
[41] Saba Mahmood, *Politics of Piety: The Islamic Revival and the Feminist Subject* (Princeton, NJ: Princeton University Press, 2012), 206.
[42] Charles Taylor, *Sources of the Self: The Making of the Modern Identity* (Cambridge, MA: Harvard University Press, 1989), 27.

and produced through the social values and contexts that give structure and direction to our lives. The kind of 'individuals' we become, the 'free' choices we make, and the actions we take depend on the cultural and social contexts in which we are born and through which we achieve adulthood. So unless we understand how cultural and material conditions constitute, penetrate, and define the self, we cannot understand why and how we act. This is why, Mahmood argues, agency, or any kind of free action, should be redefined as "a capacity for action that historically specific relations … enable and create (210)."[43] These relations form the conditions of the subject's possibility. Following Foucault and Butler, Mahmood thus points out that the very processes and conditions that secure a subject's subordination are also the means by which she becomes a self-conscious identity and agent.[44]

If all "free" actions are produced through historical and contextual relations, it follows that even Freedom Inc., despite its pretentions of absolute autonomy, is built on and operates within particular constraining contexts. It is partly because we fit everything into a market framework that we expect to have choice and control in all domains of life.[45] But we forget that the market framework is itself a set of constraints that curtail other kinds of choices and freedoms. These invisibilized constraints come into sharp relief when Mill's liberal account of individual freedom gives rise to the idea of homo economicus, which has become a central node within Freedom Inc. in India today.

## The Free Man as Homo Economicus

Homo economicus is a post-Enlightenment characterization of man as a person who freely pursues wealth for his own self-interest through rational judgment. The history of the term dates back to the nineteenth century when Mill first defined the economic actor as possessing a rationality through which he "inevitably does that by which he may obtain the greatest amount of necessities, conveniences, and luxuries, with the smallest quantity of labor and physical self-denial with which they can be obtained."[46] Homo economicus is a rational agent

---

[43] Mahmood, *Politics of Piety*, 210.
[44] Mahmood, *Politics of Piety*, 210.
[45] B. Schwartz, "Self-Determination: The Tyranny of Freedom," *American Psychologist*, 55(1), 79–88, 2000, http://dx.doi.org/10.1037/0003-066X.55.1.79 (accessed March 10, 2021).
[46] John Stuart Mill, "On the Definition of Political Economy, and on the Method of Investigation Proper to It," *London and Westminster Review*, October 1836 reprinted in *Essays on Some Unsettled Questions of Political Economy*, 2nd ed. (London: Longmans, Green, Reader & Dyer, 1874), essay 5, paragraphs 38 and 48.

who acts consistently and without constraint to choose the self-determined best choice of action, which is decided through personal cost-benefit analyses to determine whether the action is worth pursuing for the best possible outcome.[47] Homo economicus's relentless individualism proclaims that each person knows his own interest better than the government and that the interest of the individual is the interest of all. Thus homo economicus expects the individual's quest for freedom through unrestrained, competitive struggle to tally with the quests for freedom of all others. As the economist Heinrich Pesch noted, the problem with this formulation is that it pretends that universal dictates of right and wrong exist within nature, and that homo economicus displays the "natural" goodness of man through his actions.[48]

Building on the post-Enlightenment idea of homo economicus, Foucault defined the latter as not just someone who sells his labor for his wage, but who styles himself as entrepreneur of himself, a notion that gained ascendancy after the Second World War when some economists used it to attack the social policies of the welfare state. Previously, the citizen of the welfare state was conceptualized as exchanging his labor or the product of his labor in the market and receiving a wage or payment for it. The citizen's income was in turn supported by state welfare programs, kinship networks, and government interventions in the market economy. But the neoliberal bid to dismantle the welfare state meant that the individual could no longer be conceived as the responsibility of the state. The individual needed to be responsible for himself alone, the sum total of his identity reduced to his success on the market. The individual would have to become the locus of competition, and the market would change from being a place of exchange to becoming a site of competition.

Seeing an individual as the locus of competition meant that labor was not the only element of the worker commodified for exchange. Rather, as Foucault explained, the worker's capital—that which can be exchanged for an income— is the full range of diverse motivations and interests linked to who the worker is: "This is not a conception of labor power; it is a conception of capital-ability which, according to diverse variables, receives a certain income that is a wage, an income-wage, so that the worker himself appears as a sort of enterprise for himself."[49] This is another way of saying that the worker's capital, for which

---

[47] Scott, John, Gary Browning, Abigail Halcli, and F. Webster, "Understanding Contemporary Society: Theories of the Present," *Rational Choice Theory* (2000): 126–32.

[48] Heinrich Pesch, Lehrbuch der Nationalökonomie/*Teaching Guide to Economics*. Vol. 3. Bk. 1. Translated by Rupert J. Ederer (Lewiston, NY: Edwin Mellen, 2002), 29.

[49] Michel Foucault, *The Birth of Biopolitics, Lectures at the Collège de France, 1978-1979* (London: Palgrave Macmillan, 2008), 225.

he earns an income, is all those physical and psychological factors that make someone most competitive in terms of being able to earn this or that wage. This could include his or her race, sex/gender, physical attractiveness, manners, or cheerfulness, just as, controversially, an air hostess's sex/gender, physical attractiveness, and capacity to charm has historically been considered integral to her wage-earning ability, thereby amounting to her capital. In this case, capital is inseparable from the person who possesses it. The ability to work, the ability to act on a particular skill, cannot be severed from the person who works to produce an income stream.

If the individual is capital, it means that market principles can be applied to all of her, even to those behavioral characteristics traditionally considered external to the market. The individual as capital considers the "profitability" of decisions about who to fall in love with, or who to make friends with, or even about what food to eat. The model demands the absolute submission of all areas of life to the market, in that any interests that are not competitive or marketable are illegitimate, and interests that are not mediated through the market are necessarily "unreasonable," because reason itself is defined through the market. Everything is submitted to the test of success or failure on the market.

This history of homo economicus explains how the once capacious notion of freedom constricts when one facet of the liberal account of individual freedom is magnified by the expansion of capitalism. Mill's free autonomous individual turns into someone whose autonomy is realized through rational decision-making, and what counts as "rational" is itself defined through the metric of competitiveness and profitability. The result, homo economicus, is the "individual as capital," rather than the human more expansively conceived. Freedom has mutated to mean an individual acting alone by making competitive, "rational" choices at nodal points along their life-course trajectory toward the end of generating an income stream. Since the constraints of the market are not recognized as constraints within this model of homo economicus, these choices are seen as the result of "absolute autonomy." And because the individual is seen as acting alone, he is required to take sole responsibility for the consequences of the choices he makes, even though these "autonomous choices" are too often the product of a competitive and harsh environment. The myth of absolute autonomy that produces homo economicus is why I use the abbreviation "Inc." to describe this discourse of freedom and its governing logics. To be an incorporated business means to exist as an entity within which the abstract idea of absolute autonomy has been made concrete. This is because, by law, the corporation exists as a separate entity from the human beings that constitute it. The corporation is individualized to the extent that it claims the legal rights of personhood. Yet, because legally it exists separately from the people who constitute it, the corporation also bears little legal responsibility for the effects of its practices. Conversely, the person under Freedom Inc. is corporatized. They are imagined as operating independently from their contextual limitations and relationships, even though in actuality they are a product of their environments. This means that when things go wrong, the individual is held wholly liable for their losses.

## The Task of Recovering Autonomy

If constraining contexts are the grounds that make freedom and agency possible, thereby rendering absolute autonomy impossible, should the notion of autonomy itself be discarded? Philosophers such as Mahmood argue that it should. Yet, this book contends that getting rid of the idea of autonomy altogether is not viable because a nuanced version of the concept has the potential to do valuable work toward the human potential for the good, for flourishing, for happiness. The jettisoning of the concept of autonomy altogether would make it more difficult to change the conditions that do not satisfy context-specific markers of a good life. This is a central reason why this book suggests that while all actions are indeed the products of context and therefore not purely "autonomous," "autonomy" may be defined, more usefully, as pertaining to the actions that the subject *perceives* as autonomous and also to those actions that have been carried out as the result of an active process of deciding between the widest possible array of life choices. "Choice" here does not refer to Freedom Inc.'s consumer model of choice. Rather, my rethinking of autonomy expands on the idea of choice through various post-1990s texts that define autonomy as the ability, born of opportunity, to decide between multiple modes of well-being, life paths, and possibilities for self-actualization.

Such a rethinking of autonomy produces a fuller account of freedom via the recognition that simply feeling free does not account for whether the desires and choices that one makes are, in fact, qualitatively free. Take rural Indian women like Gurcharan Das's Sushila or the *New York Times's* factory workers whom I write about in Chapter 1. These girls "choose" to work and earn money rather than carry out domestic chores, but how free is this "choice" if they have not had opportunities to live and think outside the gendered binary of waged versus domestic work or outside of patriarchal systems like dowry?

And, how free is their choice if a lack of opportunity beyond this binary has led to an inability to evaluate their actions so as to discern what their "wills" truly are? Similarly, if an educated underemployed man—say the small-town protagonist of one of Chetan Bhagat's bestselling popular novels that I read in Chapter 4—turns to "entrepreneurship" because there are no good jobs or social security nets available, how far is this choice or desire one he would identify as liberating if circumstances had been different? The texts I read suggest, either explicitly, implicitly, or inadvertently, that a nuanced concept of freedom and autonomy should emphasize the contexts that offer opportunities and resources for multiple modes of self-transformation, alongside a concomitant ability to evaluate what would be best to choose or become. Discerning the sources of one's "will," and therefore being able to understand one's will itself, is only possible and meaningful in a society that offers multiple modes of being and living.[50] By these metrics, Sushila the factory worker or the small-town entrepreneur in Bhagat's popular novels cannot be regarded as free because their life choices remain wholly circumscribed by their gendered and classed life situations.

Such a rethinking does not redefine autonomy only as actions carried out through the availability of multiple opportunities for self-fulfillment and self-actualization but also as those born of the recognition that one is enmeshed within communities and produced by one's relationships within those communities. This book illustrates this rethinking of autonomy through the contextual universalisms of individual freedom offered by the various post-1990s texts I read. Shilpa Raj's *The Elephant Chaser's Daughter* (2017), Mohsin Hamid's *How to Get Filthy Rich in Rising Asia* (2014), and Manju Kapur's *Custody* (2011), for instance, each rethink autonomy in terms of the self's constitution within one's social contexts and interrelationships, so that free actions are formed in and through them.

---

[50] John Christman argues something similar when he defines liberty/individual freedom according to the *ways* in which desires are formed. An action is free if it is the result of rational reflection on all the options available, not if it is a result of pressure, manipulation, or ignorance. The *content* of an individual's desires does not matter. There is not only one right answer to the question of how a person should live. Take the example of a woman who claims to espouse the fundamentalist doctrines generally followed by her family and community. On Christman's account, this person is unfree only if her desire to conform is the result of manipulation or indoctrination. However, she is free if her desire to conform comes out of a process of being aware of other reasonable options and of weighing and assessing these other options. To promote freedom, a society would need to encourage a plurality of opinions and options for living and being. See John Christman, "Liberalism and Individual Positive Freedom," *Ethics* 101: 343–59, 1991. John Christman, "Saving Positive Freedom," *Political Theory*, 33: 79–88, and John Christman, *The Politics of Persons. Individual Autonomy and Socio-historical Selves* (Cambridge: Cambridge University Press, 2009).

## The Role of Storytelling within the Quest for Freedom

Such novels testify to how stories are powerful structures through which to posit the expanded, contextually constituted rethinking of autonomy that I lay out above. This is because one of the most fundamental things that stories—and especially the richly textured worlds of the realist novel—do, is to construct agency as the product of a dialectic between the individual subject and sociohistorical forces that precede and transcend the individual. This means that the discourse of Freedom Inc., obsessed as it is with an isolated, fully autonomous individual, may be fundamentally at odds with storytelling's weaving of an individual into a social fabric, and with that fabric's multiple interwoven threads of connections, interrelationships, and ties.

For Charles Taylor, storytelling's quality of interweaving individual lives with larger contexts is what makes it central to the way humans live and act. In his philosophical treatise, *Sources of the Self,* Taylor argues that humans decide how to act by situating their actions within a story they tell about their lives:

> Because we cannot but orient ourselves to the good, and thus determine our place relative to it and hence determine the direction of our lives, we must inescapably understand our lives in narrative form, as a "quest." But one could perhaps start from another point: because we have to determine our place in relation to the good, therefore we cannot be without an orientation to it, and hence must see our life in story. From whichever direction, I see these conditions as connected facets of the same reality, inescapable structural requirements of human agency.[51]

Taylor is arguing here that the very ability to act, to be free, and to have agency involves situating choices within a larger story pertaining to what we define as the "good" of our lives and of those around us. This story is the frame through which we understand our own choices, and our vehicle for determining the actions these choices produce. In other words, understanding our lives in the context of a "story structure" is what enables us to act because it enables us to best understand the causes, stakes, and possible consequences of our decisions. A "story structure" refers to the order in which elements of a narrative are presented to the reader, including the chain of events as well as the underlying factors—the circumstances and setting—that set off that chain of events and give them their meaning. In other words, "story structure" places an understanding

---

[51] Taylor, *Sources of the Self,* 51–2.

of one's actions as a product of self-directed will *alongside* an understanding of the external constraints, circumstances, and relationships that shape that will and therefore that action. It is not surprising, then, that the stories we tell ourselves about our lives are the sources within which our freedom to act, and obstacles to that freedom, can best be discerned and investigated.

Let's flesh out Taylor's assertion that humans decide how to act for their own and greater "good" by narrating their lives as a story, and that there is something about this story structure that enables a more nuanced understanding of autonomy. Take Das's narrative about Sushila's journey toward becoming autonomous. If we add a story structure to Das's framing narrative, Sushila's journey sounds something like this: "When I finished school, my parents were very worried. They didn't know how they would find a husband for me. They didn't have money for my dowry. I spent all my time helping my mother with domestic chores at home and still felt like a burden to them. I could wait for them to find me a match, and to go into debt to marry me off, and then I could wait to be disparaged and dominated by my in-laws. Or I could take control of my own life so that I could help my parents and get respect. I decided to get a job, and now I am truly free. I can make my own money for dowry and my husband and in-laws value me." Even though I have made up this story structure from the little that Das tells us about Sushila, it feels more nuanced than his account solely by virtue of its form. This is because even as my story structure foregrounds Sushila's understanding of her own actions as a product of her self-directed will, it also includes the various constraints, circumstances, and relationships that shape her decision to work in the factory. Das's quote, on the other hand, in privileging his ideological position as a proponent of India's economic liberalization, simply glosses over Sushila's motivations for working in the first place, mentioning the dowry as an aside rather than as a shaping constraint that Freedom Inc. does not eradicate.

As the literary analyses in this book will attempt to show, story structures that frame individual agency within its shaping contexts are fitting vehicles for more nuanced conceptions of autonomy. In particular, this book explores the realist novel as a form in which, as Terry Eagleton notes, "characters ... are caught up in a web of complex mutual dependencies. They are formed by social and historical forces greater than themselves and shaped by processes of which they may only be fitfully conscious .... The realist novel tends to grasp individual lives in terms of histories, communities, kinship, and institutions. It is in these frameworks that the self is seen as embedded." Significantly, Eagleton adds: "This is not to say that they are not free. On the contrary, they play an active part in shaping their own destinies."⁵² Elaborating on this point, I argue that the realist bildungsroman offers a way to reimagine autonomy as the product of "histories, communities, kinship and institutions," for the bildungsroman is a form devoted to telling coming-of-age tales in terms of the various social structures and constraints that an individual must navigate to act within her immediate contexts.

Yet, this claim about a large swathe of post-1990s Indian bildungsromane does not mean that the bildungsroman *tout court* is inherently more suited to countering Freedom Inc's myth of absolute autonomy. Rather, as Joseph Slaughter has argued, and as Chapter 1's analysis of journalistic storytelling about Indian women's lives will testify, the bildungsroman form too often legitimizes and naturalizes dominant definitions of the "human person" by making its "common sense legible and compelling."⁵³ Slaughter calls this type of story an "affirmative bildungsroman," which narrates the normative story of how ... the individual might become civil and social."⁵⁴ The subject of many of these affirmative bildungsromane, as Marc Redfield elaborates, is "possessed of a coherent identity that unfolds over the course of an organically unified narrative oriented toward an ending in which ... 'maturity' functions as a metaphor for the protagonist's accommodation to social norms."⁵⁵ Rather than being produced in and through social contexts, the individual begins her life opposed to the social order and ends up uncritically personifying it.

Moreover, historically the bildungsroman's representation of a character's accommodation to the dominant social order has very often been an accommodation to capitalism. As Franco Moretti points out, during the late eighteenth and nineteenth centuries, the genre was preoccupied with the individual's integration into a transitioning society shaken by the "new and destabilizing forces of capitalism."⁵⁶ The story arc often represented the protagonist's integration into this new social order as a journey toward autonomy because, as Ian Watt argues, at the time capitalism significantly increased economic specialization, which, combined with a less rigid social structure and more democratic political system, enormously increased individual freedom. By this Watt means that social arrangements were not compelled anymore by the hierarchical family or church; rather, the individual was primarily responsible for

---

[52] Terry Eagleton, *How to Read Literature* (New Haven: Yale University Press, 2013), 64.
[53] Joseph Slaughter, *Human Rights Inc.* (Fordham: Fordham University Press, 2009), 3.
[54] Slaughter, *Human Rights Inc.*, 26.
[55] Marc Redfield, *Phantom Formations: Aesthetic Ideology and the Bildungsroman* (Ithaca, NY: Cornell University Press, 2018), 191.
[56] Franco Moretti, *The Way of the World: The Bildungsroman in European Culture* (New York: Verso, 2000), 4.

determining his own economic, social, political, and religious roles. The realism of the novel developed as a way of representing this new "discrete particular, the directly apprehended sensum, and the autonomous individual." The European individual of the eighteenth and nineteenth centuries, in other words, emerged in opposition to collective units and normative horizons because in the past these had been defined by oppressive feudal structures and were more of a threat to autonomy than capitalism itself.[57]

I bring up this history to note that the post-1990s Indian bildungsroman is a result of a different history within which individual freedom was not linked to capitalism in the same way as it was in the European novel. This may be because global capitalism in India was always tied to colonial expansion in the form of primitive accumulation and exploitation carried out in the name of the "free market." It hence did not hold emancipatory promise for the majority until it was repackaged and marketed for the age of postcolonial globalization in the process I describe earlier. The non-affirmative Indian bildungsroman bears witness to this uneasy transition in the way global capitalism is represented because the genre does not simply convey social accommodation in its bid to understand and expand individual freedom. Rather, it interrogates global capitalism in two ways: first, by representing the collapse of its briefly held emancipatory promise through a protagonist who refuses to reconcile with an exclusionary social order and who seeks instead to reform it; second, by pointing to other more expansive contextual universalisms of individual freedom through which such reform may be possible.

To flesh out the first, consider Dalit life-writing like Yashica Dutt's *Coming Out as Dalit* (2019), which I explore in Chapter 2. The text adapts the bildungsroman form to capture the precarity of the low-caste individual, emphasizing the ways that she is at the mercy of a social context that should *not* be assimilated into. Many other novels achieve such a critical end through formal innovations, representational techniques, and innovative modes of realism. For instance, Aravind Adiga's epistolary *The White Tiger* (2008), explored in Chapter 3, caricatures, satirizes, and exaggerates reality in an effort to capture the extreme social effects of economic liberalization on the poor. As Ulka Anjaria argues in her rethinking of the project of Indian realism, certain features, including "communicative gaps, aesthetic discontinuities, and formal ruptures" are less a departure from realism than realist choices within a "complex and self-conscious

---

[57] Ian Watt, *The Rise of the Novel, Studies in Defoe, Richardson and Fielding* (Berkeley: University of California Press, 2001), 62.

literary mode" because they continue to represent "something irreducibly true" about a place and historical period.

The second way that the non-affirmative bildungsroman form interrogates capitalism is by pointing to other more expansive contextual universalisms of individual freedom. For Anjaria, texts that offer up such liberating potentialities are "realist" in containing a utopian urge for the actualization of future realities that do not yet exist but that are brought into closer fruition through storytelling.[58] This formal and generic potential for utopian transformation is partly why the novel remains such a rich vehicle for representing and interrogating the changing contours of "the Idea of India" and its linked conceptions of individual freedom.

## Individual Freedom, Gender, and the Changing "Idea of India" in Indian Literature

Scholars of Indian literature are increasingly recognizing the ways that Indian and South Asian writing has entered a new phase of postcoloniality very different from what came before. Alex Tickell characterizes this shift as being "born out of South Asia's accelerated economic and demographic growth, its global reach and its complex internal and regional politics."[59] Anita Desai notes that "one could not really continue to write, or read about, the slow seasonal changes, the rural backwaters, gossipy courtyards, and traditional families in a world taken over by ... large-scale industrialism, commercial entrepreneurship, tourism, new money."[60] Such changes in theme, this book argues, are partly the result of the transformation in the post-1990s era of what Sunil Khilnani has called the Nehruvian "idea of India." The latter arose in the years surrounding independence as a preoccupation with how India could best achieve and retain its freedom as a nation, and with what shapes that freedom would take in the lives of individual citizens. For Nehru, the successful realization of freedom from British rule would "coordinate within the form of a modern state a variety of values: democracy, religious tolerance, economic development and cultural pluralism."[61] However, as this introduction has shown, the idea of India itself

---

[58] Ulka Anjaria, *Realism and the Twentieth-Century Indian Novel: Colonial Difference and Literary Form* (Cambridge: Cambridge University Press, 2012), 30.
[59] Alex Tickell, *South-Asian Fiction in English: Contemporary Transformations* (New York: Springer, 2016), 2.
[60] Anita Desai, "Passion in Lahore" (December 21, 2000), https://www.nybooks.com/articles/2000/12/21/passion-in-lahore/ (accessed February 18, 2020).
[61] Sunil Khilnani, *The Idea of India* (New York: Farrar, Straus and Giroux, 1999), 12–13.

has changed to emphasize a nation that participates in a global economy, bringing with it a transformation in how the freedom of individual Indians is conceptualized. Such a transition is most apparent when one turns to the history of the Indian novel before the 1990s.

As many scholars have argued, the Indian novel before the 1990s largely tied its definition of individual freedom to the political independence of the nation from colonialism. For Priyamvada Gopal, the narration of nation, of what a free India would look like, gave the novel in India "its earliest and most persistent thematic preoccupation, indeed, its raison d'etre as it attempted to carve out a legitimate space for itself."[62] Against colonial discourse that claimed Indians lacked "the essential self-consciousness of the concept of freedom"[63] because they existed outside world history, in "prehistory," India's first novelists used prose to prove that they did, in fact, possess a world history, and therefore did deserve individual freedom. The novel claimed this freedom for Indian citizens by narrating private stories in relation to public national histories, thereby connecting the individual freedom of Indians to the national struggle for independence.[64]

In linking individual freedom to national sovereignty, novelists in the immediate lead-up to independence were not only taking their cue from colonial discourse but also from their own nationalist leaders. Gandhi's most significant contribution to the discourse of Indian independence lay in his insistence that national sovereignty—swaraj or "self-rule"—would be meaningless without achieving freedom of the self, which he expressed as a supreme sort of self-control that would lead to a fundamental transformation of individual character. Only once Indians had learned how to reform their own characters through a program of nonviolence, prayer, the elimination of caste discrimination, and economic self-sufficiency, would the nation be worthy of freedom from the British. A number of novels in the decades leading up to independence, including Mulk Raj Anand's *Untouchable*, and R. K. Narayan's *Waiting for the Mahatma* and *Guide*, contested the Gandhian connection between individual freedom and national freedom by representing and interrogating the blind spots

---

[62] Priyamvada Gopal, *The Indian English Novel: Nation, History, and Narration* (Oxford: Oxford University Press, 2009), 6.
[63] Ranajit Guha, *History at the Limit of World History* (Delhi: Oxford University Press, 2003), 23.
[64] Shoshee Chunder Dutt (1824–85). "The Republic of Orissá; A Page from the Annals of the Twentieth Century." *The Bengal Hurkaru and India Gazette* (May 25, 1845). Rpt. in *Bengaliana: A Dish of Rice and Curry, and Other Indigestible Ingredients* (Calcutta, India: Thacker, Spink, and Co., [1878]), 347–56. https://archive.org/details/in.ernet.dli.2015.91713/mode/2up, accessed January 14, 2023 and Kylas Chunder Dutt, *A Journal of Forty-Eight Hours of the Year 1945, Wasafiri*, 21:3 (2006), 15–20.

in his ideas of self-fashioning. These authors critiqued the toll that embodying the project of independent nation building had on individuals from the lower castes, on women, and even on the upper-caste Hindu men who were the prime subjects of Gandhian self-fashioning.

Even decades later, all the way up to the 1990s, the Indian novel was still echoing, interrogating, or reinforcing the connection between individual freedom and national political sovereignty. Most famously emblematic is Salman Rushdie's *Midnight's Children* (1981), an explicitly allegorical text where the life of the protagonist is both inextricably linked to and represents the life of the Indian nation, which is born at the same time as he is. At its outset, the narrative announces:

> There is no getting away from the date. I was born in Doctor Narlikar's Nursing Home on August 15th, 1947. And the time? The time matters, too. Well then: at night. No. It's important to be more … On the stroke of midnight, as a matter of fact. Clock-hands joined palms in respectful greeting as I came. Oh, spell it out, spell it out: at the precise instant of India's arrival at independence, I tumbled forth into the world.[65]

Yet, *Midnight's Children* becomes increasingly disillusioned by the betrayal of the "idea of India" as the story progresses and Indira Gandhi's Emergency takes hold.

The later novels of this era would retain an obsession with the concordance—or lack of it—between individual freedom and the Nehruvian national idea by pointing to how individual freedom was repeatedly sacrificed by the postcolonial state. Rohinton Mistry's *Such a Long Journey* (1991) and *A Fine Balance* (1997), are preoccupied with the betrayals of independence. Mistry's protagonists grapple with their inability to partake of the grand narratives of national freedom, as their social and economic difficulties are compounded by Indira Gandhi's increasingly draconian rule and its effects on the poor and lower castes. Amitav Ghosh's *The Shadow Lines* (1988) explores the betrayal of the "idea of India" in another way, representing the ways that national boundaries are random and yet lethal ways in which identities are created and maintained, fomenting communal and sectarian religious tensions to which countless individuals have lost their lives. Other novels, like Arundhati Roy's *The God of Small Things* (1997), focus on the sorry lives of women and lower castes in a "free" India.[66] These novels

---

[65] Salman Rushdie, *Midnight's Children* (New York: Random House Trade Paperbacks, 2006), 3.
[66] These novels' preoccupation with the classed and caste exclusions within the national idea is ironic given their upper-middle-class authors; as Sisir Kumar Das points out, the making of the idea of India through literature was itself a classed project. From the very start, "literary activities were dominated

capture the exclusions within the national idea, which sacrificed the individual freedoms of classed and gendered minorities instead of safeguarding them.

In its concern with the democratic fate of minorities as well as the degradations brought about to local cultures and economies by globalization, *The God of Small Things* signals its status as a text that straddles the older body of Indian writing concerned with the Nehruvian idea of India and the newer one concerned with the effects of economic liberalization. What ties both bodies of writing together, however, is a concern with interrogating national history through the lens of gender. In the nineteenth century, writers across the nation explored "the woman question," thinking the trials of the nation through the condition of its women. Unlike Roy, though, many novels did not make their female protagonists the subjects of their stories but allegorical representations of conflicting ideas of India. Domestic fictions like Krupabai Satthianadhan's *Kamala*, the first novel in English written by an Indian woman, presented women as carriers of "authentic" cultural and religious traditions that, within nationalism, represented civilizational and national essences. In Satthianadhan's proselytizing narrative, the Hindu protagonist, Kamala, denies herself the possibility of remarriage after she is widowed because of "the trammels of custom and tradition, the weight of ignorance and the bewildering, terrifying grasp of superstition." Christianity, on the other hand, represents, for Satthianadhan, a "land of freedom."[67] Rabindranath Tagore's *Home and the World*, like Satthianadhan's *Kamala*, uses gender to signify different cultural ideals, with two different kinds of masculinity representing different national paths forward. The female protagonist, Bimala, emerges as the site for a contest between these two ideals.[68]

In many such texts of the era, then, women were simply the terrain on which contests over the shape of national freedom were fought.[69] This is why in their classic work, *Women Writing in India*, Susie Tharu and K. Lalita note that mainstream writing that was steeped in nationalist discourses, or even

---

by a class of professionals, coming from the middle class. The unity of Indian literature comes mainly from the commonality of values and attitudes of this class, their various sub-groupings and differences in respect of religion, language, caste, political ideology and gender notwithstanding." Sisir Kumar Das, *A History of Indian Literature 1911–1956 Struggle for Freedom: Triumph and Tragedy* (New Delhi: Sahitya Akademi, 1995), 8.

[67] Krupabai Satthianadhan and Chandani Lokuje (ed.), *Kamala: The Story of a Hindu Child Wife* (New Delhi: Oxford University Press, 2002), 13.

[68] Rabindranath Tagore, *The Home and the World*. Edited by William Radice. Translated by Surendranath Tagore (London: Penguin Classics, 2005).

[69] These texts reflect how, as Partha Chatterjee has documented, Indian nationalism tied freedom for women to their embrace of an "authentic" cultural essence connected to their embodiment of spiritual gender roles within Hindu marriage and the home. Partha Chatterjee, "Nationalist Resolution of the Woman Question," in Kumkum Sangria and Sudhesh Said (eds.), *Recasting Women: Essays in Indian Colonial History* (New Brunswick, NJ: Rutgers University Press, 1990).

writing like Tagore's that critiqued the violent effects of these discourses, still reduced women to an "Other" whose freedom was cast in terms of the forging of a national identity. In response, Tharu and Lalita note a need to read women's writing of the period, asking: "What forms did their dreams of integrity or selfhood take? What modes of resistance did they fashion? How did they avoid, question, play off, rewrite, transform, or even undermine the projects set out for them?"[70]

This book builds on these questions in relation to the newer era of economic liberalization. The authors I read show that, in the post-liberalization moment, women's bodies are still the grounds on which the meaning of the nation is worked out. In the works of Hamid, Adiga, and Bhagat, Freedom Inc. constructs entrepreneurial masculinities in relation to prescriptive femininities that register female bodies only as prizes to be won by men who successfully embody the investor-citizen. Despite its critique of Freedom Inc., *How to Get Filthy Rich in Rising Asia* reproduces some of its discursive logic in conceptualizing female characters as sexual capital. The female love-interest is known to the reader only as "the pretty girl" in terms of her sexual attractiveness, and pops in and out of the narrative to move the male protagonist's own life journey forward.

Much of the women's writing I look at, on the other hand, is uniquely illuminating for its insights into how Freedom Inc. affects the quests for happiness, integrity, and self-definition of new Indian women. Thrity Umrigar's *The Space between Us* (2008) takes on the idea that working for a wage is an uncomplicated route to freedom by demonstrating that the workplace can also be a patriarchal space of oppression, particularly for domestic servants and other women in the lower classes who work in the informal economy. Manju Kapur's *Custody* (2011), meanwhile, depicts the deleterious consequences of treating women as commoditized conquests of entrepreneurial masculinity. The novel tells the story of the breakdown of a family following the seduction of a young mother by the corporate head of a multinational beverage corporation who sees her and "the world as a marketplace with all its wares for sale."[71] And Nayantara Sahgal's *The Fate of Butterflies* (2019) is concerned with how right-wing governments preserve the balance of power in a global economy by using rape as a weapon of religious warfare. It is women's writing, too, that is concerned with working out what more expansive freedoms can look like. The Dalit writer,

---

[70] Susie Tharu and K. Lalita, eds., *Women Writing in India: 600 BC to the Present. Volume 1: 600 BC to the Early Twentieth Century* (New York: Feminist Press, 1991), *Volume 2: The Twentieth Century* (New York: Feminist Press, 1993), 40.
[71] Manju Kapur, *Custody* (London: Random House, 2011), 354.

Shilpa Raj, builds on B. R. Ambedkar's vision of freedom to show that women's liberation cannot happen independently of liberation from caste, depicting the education of low-caste girls as a way to reform the entire social structure and not just the lives of the girls themselves. Raj, like other writers I consider, taps into alternative conceptions of individual freedom, drawing attention to contextual universalisms that precede economic liberalization, that continue to have a rich life in the subcontinent, and that therefore contain potential tools through which to counter Freedom Inc.

The promise of potential transformation contained in the form of these feminist story structures also works at a metatextual level through the reader. When we read them, we emerge transformed ourselves. We are drawn to the representation of a human life within a narrative structure because it enables us to reflect on our own constitution through our social contexts, and thereby on the actions that can lead us to greater freedoms. Telling ourselves stories about our own lives and reading and thinking about stories about other lives may be a way that we negotiate, understand, and quest for our freedom.

This penchant for understanding oneself through narrative is true of my own quest for freedom. I begin each chapter with personal stories, each of which testifies to how I became aware of the power of different constructs of individual freedom on my own self-constitution as a gendered upper-middle-class and upper-caste subject who, despite my obvious privileges, often felt constrained by the life paths available to me. The inadequacy of Freedom Inc. to lead me to what *I* considered a personal liberation led me to seek out other story structures, and to construct other tales of transformative possibility in relation to the most prominent women in my life—my mother, and my mother-in-law. I often first encountered these alternative story structures within the texts I read in each of the chapters. These narratives became the counter stories that helped me overcome Freedom Inc.'s strange magnetic pull as well as its limiting constraints. Many of these novels, films, and memoirs became for me what Foucault calls "technologies of the self," vehicles that permitted me to understand my own self-constitution as a heterosexual Non-Resident Indian woman in a conservative upper-class/caste family, and to transform myself and my circumstances in ways that would allow me to attain a certain state of happiness. I tell these personal stories of self-constitution in relation to the texts I read partially as an exercise in "autotheory," a genre that fuses memoir and autobiography with theory and philosophy. I write in this tradition to partake of a feminist praxis that has long insisted on the hierarchical artifice of separations between art and life, and theory and practice. This means that I offer this book not just as a study of an important moment in the subcontinent's cultural history of freedom, of the continuing relevance of gendered ideologies on the pursuit of autonomy in India, of the subversive possibilities of literary form, or as a local account of the latest stage in the expansion of capitalism, although it is all of these. I also offer this book in the hope that its simultaneously personal and academic lens will provide countercultures of freedom for others who find themselves similarly curtailed by the gendered possibilities offered to them.

## The Chapters

Chapter 1, "Working Women and the Quest for Freedom in Bildung Narratives," explores the idea, prevalent within the discourse of Freedom Inc., that waged work, no matter how exploitative, is the route to freedom for Indian women. This is a discourse that I myself internalized in relation to my mother who is a housewife and was oppressively bound, in my estimation at the time, to domestic work and child-rearing. While popular newspapers, including the *New York Times*, propagate a similar idea of freedom as waged work for women, other Indian novels, including Thrity Umrigar's *The Space between Us* (2008) and the film from Kerala, *The Great Indian Kitchen* (2021), complicate it by stressing the importance of the circumstances within which women do waged work. Work does not automatically increase women's autonomy if they remain bound by exploitative working conditions, patriarchal codes, and class and caste inequalities. Waged work offers a relative autonomy only when it is carried out in a context that offers multiple ways for women to be free and removes obstacles to that freedom. In this vein, *The Great Indian Kitchen* posits another contextual universalism of individual freedom through the figure of the Goddess Lakshmi, who symbolizes autonomy as the right to choose between multiple modes of self-actualization against Freedom Inc.'s binary choices for women between domestic and waged work.

Chapter 2, "Dalit Women and the Quest for Freedom in Ambedkarite Life-Writing," builds on my analysis of how texts by and about women challenge Freedom Inc. I consider how Dalit memoirs contest the belief, predominant in the discourse of Freedom Inc., that disadvantaged groups such as lower-caste women can attain freedom from gender and caste constraints through entrepreneurship. While government bodies, NGOs, and identarian community organizations in the neoliberal state promote such a notion, various

Dalit texts and memoirs interrogate this link by posing an older intersectional notion of freedom grounded in B. R. Ambedkar's legacy of struggle on behalf of Dalits. For Ambedkar, individual actions could never be truly free within a hierarchical society defined by separate spheres for different castes and genders. He therefore stressed the importance of working toward a society within which a common good that included the bottom of that hierarchy—Dalit women—could be achieved. To that end, he harnessed the Pragmatist redefinition of individual freedom as "individuality operating in and for the common interest," where "common interest" signified a society that included the interests of Dalit women in its development toward freedom. Feminist Dalit life-writing, including Shilpa Raj's *The Elephant Chaser's Daughter* (2017) and Yashica Dutt's *Coming Out as Dalit* (2019), takes up Ambedkar's contextual universalism of "individuality in and for the common interest," positing the idea that education rather than entrepreneurship is the vehicle through which such a freedom can be realized for women. Through education, individual Dalit women can not only exercise their own will toward freedom but also work to remove the social constraints that mar the potential for freedom of their community members.

Chapter 3, "Underemployed Young Men and the Quest for Freedom in the Self-Help Novel," returns to Freedom Inc.'s discourse of entrepreneurship as empowerment, examining how it is absorbed and harnessed by underemployed young men, and by women of various classes, through the self-help genre. I first encountered the popularity of this genre in India through my mother-in-law, who enthusiastically imbibed this gendered discourse of entrepreneurial agency. Through her experiences, I was able to discern how such a discourse earns its popularity through a masculinity that is unembedded from any social processes and institutional frameworks, sexually dominant, fully in control, and remodeled as a revenue stream. But ironically, as my mother-in-law's journey within the realm of self-help testifies, this discourse is also adopted as a tool of empowerment by women who have the privilege to do so. The chapter then turns to how self-help books in India are wielded in diverse, often counter-intuitive ways not just by readers like my mother-in-law, but also by literary fiction. Adiga's *The White Tiger* (2008) uses the self-help genre's form to critique the kind of Freedom Inc. that the post-1990s self-help genre propagates for the underemployed young men who try and embody it as a way out of poverty. Hamid's *How to Get Filthy Rich in Rising Asia* (2014) builds on this critique of Freedom Inc. by positing another contextual universalism, derived from Sufi mysticism, of freedom as self-transcendence through love. Hamid describes Sufi love poetry as the "first form of self-help" and harnesses that form within his bildungsroman. Hamid's novel, like self-help books and like Sufi love poetry, addresses a "you" that transcends the narcissistic "me"-centered self of Freedom Inc. This mutual rewriting of contemporary self-help and Sufi universalism suggests that the ground of any action, and therefore one's freedom, is constituted through one's relationships with others.

The first three chapters explore the construction of particular femininities and masculinities within the discourse of Freedom Inc., as well as counter discourses that posit other contextual universalisms of individual freedom and gendered being. Chapter 4, "Chasing Freedom through Romantic Love in Popular and Literary Fiction," turns more explicitly to the ways that Freedom Inc. positions men and women in relation to one another, particularly in the domain of romantic love. I came to realize the presence and power of multiple, contrasting Indian discourses of romantic love during my own courtship, in which I struggled with my parents' process of formalizing my choice of spouse into a marriage. I eventually realized that while I was working with an idea of romantic love as an autonomous decision that had to do with my compatibility with my spouse, my parents did not understand love in this way. For them, my freedom lay in an older understanding of love as the capacity to mold oneself to a moral purpose that transcends individual desires and interests, confirming one's obligations to others. The latter is a notion of love and freedom that is reflected in post-independence texts such as Vikram Seth's *A Suitable Boy* (1993) and Manju Kapur's *Difficult Daughters* (1998). I read these texts to consider how both these older notions of love have been pushed aside by Freedom Inc. Thus in the popular fiction of Chetan Bhagat, romantic love is a metric for success that relies on a dominant entrepreneurial patriotic masculinity against a submissive femininity that has to be won and subdued by a successful man. Manju Kapur's *Custody* (2011) takes stock of Freedom Inc.'s version of romantic love through a representation of its debilitating effects on female autonomy.

The coda considers how in recent decades, the new "idea of India," marked as it is by Freedom Inc., works hand in hand with a heavily gendered militant Hindu nationalism, whose ideological ancestor is so well represented in Tagore's *Home and the World*. This creed defines the freedom of Indians as a compulsion to be Hindu and to embody narrowly defined gender roles. Nayantara Sahgal's *The Fate of Butterflies* (2019) and Githa Hariharan's *In Times of Siege* (2003) represent the ways that neoliberal globalization encourages racial and religious hierarchies to maintain the economic balance of power within and between nations while reducing women and sexual minorities who do not comply to collateral damage. These novels testify to how literature in the new India has the potential to critique the toxic set of equations between national sovereignty, a free market economy, and a gendered and politicized exclusionary religiosity.[72]

Together, these chapters seek to excavate the ways in which—through social struggle—an individual's contexts, situations, circumstances, and interrelationships become the grounds through which a more expansive notion of freedom can be achieved against various discursive and material constraints. Literary form, through story structures that center an individual constituted through society, becomes central to the representation of this struggle toward freedom. The bildungsroman, the realist novel, and other associated cultural media such as film and reality shows, regardless of their use of English and/or the bhashas,[73] all plot various "lives in story" through which multiple freedoms can be thought through, revealed, interrogated, and won.

---

[72] The texts I choose in these chapters are united by their engagement with the idea of individual freedom and by references to the way that individual agency is enacted within social contexts and shaped by gendered ideals. This means that I am interested in texts that deal with life in India, or that are written for an Indian audience, rather than texts about life in the South Asian diaspora, or those that are written primarily with a global audience in mind. The book's thematic preoccupation also means that I do not discriminate against certain genres, referencing novels, film, advertisements, journalism, and reality television. All these are diverse cultural products that are nevertheless preoccupied with what individual freedom looks like in contemporary Indian life and in relation to Freedom Inc., and that are in intertextual conversation with one another.

[73] A note about language—the texts I examine are composed in regional languages, the bhashas, or in an English that is intertwined with the bhashas. In his *History of Indian literature in English* Arvind Krishna Mehrotra explains this multilingualism in terms of class, noting that many who write at all belong to a privileged stratum who are well versed in English but also in the Indian mother tongues of their homes. Mehrotra's examples include the Mysore born A. K. Ramanujan, whose mother tongue was Tamil and who published his first collection of English poems and three years later followed it with his first collection in Kannada. Similarly, Aravind Adiga writes his novels in English but celebrates regional writing and is an avid reader of the Kannada press. For Mehrotra, this kind of "instinctive" multilingualism is "what umbilically ties the writing done in English to the other Indian literatures." See Arvind Krishna Mehrotra, *History of Indian Literature in English* (New York: Columbia University Press, 2003), 23. The style of the authorial use of English also reflects this multilingual heritage, so that Chetan Bhagat's English is mixed with Hindi colloquialisms, producing a uniquely Indian version of English that has developed in opposition to what he considers elitist literary culture. His books are written for provincial Indians who are looking to improve their English through their reading of popular fiction. It is this mix—this Hinglish—that lends Bhagat's books to translation into the bhashas, with many being made into Bollywood films. This multilingualism is true of literary fiction too, so that Manju Kapur's *Custody* was adapted into a Hindi television serial. Because of this intertwined multilingual history and the oft interchangeable use of English and bhashas by writers, I consider sources that are written in English, that are a mix of English and the bhashas, or that are composed solely in particular bhashas. The texts that are in English often reflect their address to a local audience and the status of English as an "Indian vernacular," for they do not include glossaries of bhasha words or italicized colloquialisms buttressed with explanatory clauses, as do many books written primarily for Western audiences.

# 1

# Working Women and the Quest for Freedom in Bildung Narratives

When I was a teenager, I promised myself that I would never be a financially dependent housewife like my mother.[1] Every week my father would give her cash to pay for household expenses. Her sense of self-respect meant that she hated to ask him for more when she needed it. Instead, she was careful to save any money left over from daily expenses in a small pouch in her locked almirah. Being around her convinced me that when I grew up, I would never need to ask someone else for money to fulfill my own basic needs. My equating of waged work with financial independence, with freedom itself, rang true to me despite my mother's stories about her own life before marriage.

Before my mother met my father, she was a Math teacher in a government school in Jaipur. It was a difficult job. She worked for very little pay in very poor conditions in an environment full of corruption. She did it out of necessity. Her father had died when she was a little girl and she and her sister found themselves forced into an early adulthood. They were the only sources of financial support for their mother. Waged work in this situation was compulsion not freedom. When she met my father for an arranged marriage, she regarded him as an opportunity to fulfill her real dream—that of being a mother. Like many women of her time, she married because she wanted children and a family. Falling in love with my father was a bonus.

I recount the story of my mother's relationship with paid work here to contextualize the complex ways in which Indian women have defined and experienced freedom. Because I was born into an upper-middle-class situation, I had the luxury of defining freedom as financial independence through waged

---

[1] I use the pejorative term "housewife" here instead of the more neutral "homemaker" to convey how much I had internalized patriarchal-capitalist attitudes toward women like her. My mother was a busy woman whose contributions to the household rivaled and even exceeded my father's. Yet her lack of monetary income rendered that labor invisible in my eyes.

work. But for my own working-class mother, waged work had been compulsion. Domestic life, even though it came with its own pressures, had felt more like freedom to her. When I became a grown woman myself, I could look back at my mother's choices with more understanding. Motherhood and domesticity were relatively liberating to her because freedom was complex. Freedom was classed.

Despite the complexity of how women of different backgrounds define freedom, waged work for women has almost universally been linked with increased autonomy. Multiple social scientists have argued that women's wage work is connected to increased decision-making power in the household, delays in the age of marriage and first childbirth, and an increase in education for their children.[2] In other words, they have tied waged work to freedom for women. This is why researchers worry about the fact that four out of five women do not work for money in India; that only Yemen, Iraq, Jordan, Syria, Algeria, Iran, and the West Bank and Gaza have a lower female labor force participation (FLFP) rate; that the FLFP rate has actually been declining; it was just over 30 percent in 1990 and has since declined to just over 20 percent. A larger proportion of women worked for a wage in India when my mother was young in the 1970s than do now.[3]

Neoliberal global institutions like the World Bank have also linked waged work to women's freedom. The World Bank notes on its website that women not working is associated with submission and oppression, with a drop in gender equality, and celebrates its own efforts to reverse India's negative trend: "the World Bank promotes gender equality across the country, encourages more girls and women to join the workforce, and gives them the education and skills they need to compete in the marketplace."[4] This is a nationalist discourse too, stressing that Indian women should work not just to help themselves but to help the nation as a whole. "As India poises itself to increase economic growth and foster development, it is necessary to ensure that its labor force becomes fully inclusive of women," proclaims the World Bank study.[5]

It is ironic that an agent of neoliberalism laments the decline of women in the workforce given that the drop in working women has coincided with

---

[2] Robert Jensen, "Do Labor Market Opportunities Affect Young Women's Work and Family Decisions? Experimental Evidence from India," *The Quarterly Journal of Economics*, 127 (2), May 2012: 753–92.
[3] Soutik Biswas, "Why Are Millions of Indian Women Dropping Out of Work?" *bbc.com*, May 18, 2017, https://www.bbc.com/news/world-asia-india-39945473.
[4] World Bank, "Working for Women in India," https://www.worldbank.org/en/news/feature/2019/03/08/working-for-women-in-india.
[5] World Bank, "Working for Women in India," https://www.worldbank.org/en/news/feature/2019/03/08/working-for-women-in-india.

the liberalization of the Indian economy. If we accept the easy link between freedom and waged work, it seems that neoliberalism has been bad for women. This contention is supported by research showing that women are not at work because of a lack of opportunities caused by failures of the market, turning India into a place where only the poorest and wealthiest women work for a wage. The poorest work because they have to, and mostly do so in the informal subsistence economies comprising activities that fall outside of government protection and regulation. The type of work found in this sector is vast; domestic servitude, street hawkers, shoe shiners, garment workers, street children, home businesses, and garbage collectors are all part of it. Government figures show that the informal sector accounts for 90 percent of non-agricultural employment, and at least half of total GDP.[6] The wealthiest women, meanwhile, work because they have access to the formal economy and to the protection of government regulations, while also being able to afford to hire other women to perform their domestic chores.[7]

The pressures of domestic work are another factor that explain why the majority of Indian women remain unwaged. Indian women are often required to prioritize domestic work, particularly if they are married, due to cultural expectations of women as caregivers. In the Indian National Sample Survey (NSS) for 2011–12, over 90 percent of women who did not work for a wage were primarily engaged in domestic duties. Around 92 percent of these women stated that their principal activity was domestic work in the previous year because they were "required (needed) to do so," with 60 percent of women in rural areas and 64 percent in urban areas adding that their primary reason for not working for a wage was that there was "no other member to carry out the domestic duties."[8] This research is backed by other surveys which show that women continue to do a majority of housework in India. On average, Indian women perform nearly six hours of unpaid work each day, while men spend a paltry 52 minutes, according to the Organization of Economic Cooperation and Development (OECD).[9]

---

[6] Government of India Ministry of Labour and Employment, "Employment in Informal Sector and Conditions of Informal Employment Vol. IV," 2013–2014, https://labour.gov.in/sites/default/files/Report%20vol%204%20final.pdf.

[7] Sher Verick and the International Labor Organization, "The Paradox of Low Female Labour Force Participation," ilo.org, March 9, 2017, https://www.ilo.org/newdelhi/info/public/fs/WCMS_546764/lang--en/index.htm.

[8] National Sample Survey Office, Ministry of Statistics and Programme Implementation, Government of India, "Participation of Women in Specified Activities along with Domestic Duties," July 2011–June 2012, http://mospi.nic.in/sites/default/files/publication_reports/nss_report_559_10oct14.pdf.

[9] Organization for Economic Co-operation and Development, "Employment: Time Spent in Paid and Unpaid Work, by Sex," https://stats.oecd.org/index.aspx?queryid=54757, July 2020.

In this chapter, I examine the state of gendered work in India through an exploration of how women's freedom is represented in literature and media. Do novels, films, and reporting on Indian women tie freedom to waged work? How does it benefit our understanding of the quality of women's lives if freedom is equated to waged employment? What does this simple linking miss? I approach these questions through Ellen Barry's *New York Times* story on rural female factory workers "Young Rural Women in India Chase Big-City Dreams" (2016), Thrity Umrigar's novel *The Space between Us* (2017), and Jeo Baby's film, *The Great Indian Kitchen* (2021). While "Big-City Dreams" ties women's autonomy to waged work regardless of the exploitative nature of that work, *The Space between Us* critiques such an easy link between waged work and freedom. Instead, the novel represents how women of lower classes experience waged labor differently from women of other classes. For the protagonist of Umrigar's novel, working as a domestic servant in the home of her employer is a matter of compulsion, while for her high-class employer working outside the home is a mode of autonomy. The novel suggests that it is not waged work alone that leads to freedom but the absence of patriarchal exploitation and class hierarchies, for the latter are institutionalized in waged labor as well as in domestic work. The continuing salience of a Hindu form of patriarchy is also illuminated by *The Great Indian Kitchen,* which critiques the burden of domestic work placed on married women while complicating an easy link between waged work and freedom. The film suggests that waged work is a form of freedom from patriarchy only insofar as it represents a realization of a woman's hopes and dreams for herself. In the film, the goddess of wealth, Lakshmi, embodies a freedom defined as a wealth of choices made toward material, sensual, moral, and spiritual forms of self-fulfillment. As my mother's story of being unfree as a waged worker and also constrained as a financially dependent homemaker suggests, true wealth is not just a wage; it is self-realization through the availability of a whole range of achievable goals and opportunities.

## Freedom as Waged Employment in the *NY Times*: "Young Rural Women in India Chase Big-City Dreams"

On a summer's day in late May 2016, two "pretty sisters" from a far-off village, "fizzing with laughter," walked down a lane that led to the Bangalore factory in which they would work. Prabhati was twenty-one and Shashi, eighteen. When

**Figure 2** The *New York Times* page for "Young Rural Women in India Chase Big-City Dreams."

they got to the factory, the laughter was replaced with a language they did not understand—with words like "work" and "faster." Ellen Barry, who tells us the story of these girls, proclaims that these were words "of capitalism, of men and of a bit of freedom" (Barry 2016).[10] Barry's fairytale of freedom, published in September 2016 in the *New York Times*, covers the journey of the sisters from Ishwarpur, Orissa, to the urban environment of Bangalore. There, they serve as piece-rate garment workers in a factory that makes clothes sold in European and American department retail chain stores such as Marks and Spencer and H&M. The article uses a seemingly objective, fact based, third person journalistic voice to narrate the journey of these two exotic rural Indians, with Shashi serving as the protagonist, and Prabhati as her foil. Within the article's story arc, as the quote given earlier suggests, the introduction of Shashi to globalized capitalism ends in freedom.

Barry's journalism is essayistic, investigative, offers cultural critique, and also contains an element of advocacy for the women she covers.[11] Nevertheless, despite her advocacy, Barry registers capitalist violence only to accept it for the "bit of freedom" it offers. Her equation of waged work with freedom is marked by two pervasive liberal discourses—that of laissez-faire capitalism, and that

---

[10] Ellen Barry, "Young Rural Women in India Chase Big-City Dreams," *New York Times*, September 24, 2016, https://www.nytimes.com/2016/09/25/world/asia/bangalore-india-women-factories.html.

[11] Ellen Barry is the South Asia Bureau Chief for the *NY Times* and wrote several articles in 2016 and 2017 that focused on women in rural India.

of the "end of history" narrative. The first, the concept of laissez-faire, arose in eighteenth-century France and expressed a belief in a natural order under which individuals followed their selfish interests within a marketplace and in doing so contributed to the general good.[12] Philosophers like Adam Smith thus characterized it as a moral program that used the market as its instrument to ensure men true freedom.[13] In this sense, laissez-faire was a universalism that defined freedom narrowly in line with free market capitalism. It was an extension of the idea of natural law, asserting that certain rights are endowed by nature, and that these can be understood universally through human reason. Since this natural order functioned successfully without the aid of government, the state needed to restrict itself to upholding the rights of private property and individual liberty, to removing all artificial barriers to trade, and to abolishing all seemingly useless laws.[14] The second discourse that underlies Barry's story is the "end of history" narrative, derived from Hegel, in which the historical development of humanity in the West culminates in the universal recognition of human freedom, which, according to Francis Fukuyama, is in turn associated with the successful spread of capitalism to all areas of the world.[15]

Barry embeds these two discourses into her story using a literary form indebted to the bildungsroman, lending strength to Joseph Slaughter's argument that the form often naturalizes and legitimizes the human person's embodiment of the dominant social premises of the era.[16] Barry's bildungsromanian embedding of the "human person" within the dominant social orders of liberal capitalism, I show, depends on constructing a very narrow idea of freedom through competing notions of Indian femininity. Barry defines freedom by contrasting "idle," "unmonetized," and supposedly vulnerable, powerless, passive, and dependent Indian women with superior self-managing autonomous subjects who sell their labor for a wage within the globalized marketplace.

---

[12] Adam Smith, "The Wealth of Nations," in Isaac Kramnick (ed.), *The Portable Enlightenment Reader* (London: Penguin Books, 1995), 509–11.
[13] Smith, "The Wealth of Nations," 507.
[14] Smith, "The Wealth of Nations," 510.
[15] Francis Fukuyama, *The End of History and the Last Man* (New York: Free Press, 1992).
[16] Joseph Slaughter, *Human Rights Inc.* (Fordham: Fordham University Press, 2009).

## Competing Femininities: The Working Woman versus the Grha Lakshmi

Barry's story participates in a discourse of femininity that ties working women to freedom and equality, which she defines as freedom from domestic chores. Describing rural Indian girls like Shashi and Prabhati, she notes that:

> A government program has drawn the trainees from the vast population of rural Indian women who spend their lives doing chores. In 2012, the last time the government surveyed its citizens about their occupation, an astonishing 205 million women between the ages of 15 and 60 responded "attending to domestic duties." Economists, with increasing urgency, say India will not fulfill its potential if it cannot put them to work in the economy. They say that if female employment were brought on par with male employment in India, the nation's gross domestic product would expand by as much as 27 percent.[17]

Barry posits a laissez-faire narrative of the good of an individual woman coinciding with the greater good. If women are free of oppressive "chores," India will be able to "fulfill its potential," expanding its GDP considerably and thereby advancing the nation as a whole.

The second discourse on femininity that the article makes a note of, only to associate it with backwardness, is an older nationalist discourse that ties respectable femininity to the home. Barry describes villagers who react to the possibility of their daughters going away to work with incredulity: "No. Letting go of female children is dishonorable, in itself ... Not everyone wants a daughter-in-law who is a working woman ... they think she has lost her chastity." Such a discourse of respectable feminine domesticity can be traced back to the colonial period, which saw the formation and rise of the British middle class in the nineteenth century. The latter idealized the position of women in the home and family, where stability and order prevailed, and tied masculinity to an occupation outside the home. Indian nationalist discourse picked up on this by creating a set of binaries that were inevitably gendered: home/inner/spiritual/feminine versus world/outer/material/masculine. Men bore responsibility for accommodating changes happening in the outside world. The essential inner world, the realm of the "spiritual," however, in which the East was superior and undominated by the West, had to remain free of contamination and be associated with the feminine.[18]

---

[17] Barry, "Young Rural Women in India Chase Big-City Dreams."
[18] Partha Chatterjee, "Nationalist Resolution of the Women's Question," in Kumkum Sangari and Sudhesh Vaid (eds.), *Recasting Women: Essays in Indian Colonial History* (New Brunswick, NJ: Rutgers University Press, 1990), 233–53.

Contemporary constructions of good womanhood build on these binaries by tying domesticity to devotion to the Indian (implicitly Hindu) family. This ideal femininity is often expressed through the figure of the Goddess Lakshmi as Grha Lakshmi—or goddess of the household—who is associated with God Vishnu, Preserver of the Universe, as the ideal wife and consort, obediently serving her husband and household. Drawing upon Vishnu and Lakshmi as the source of all prosperity and well-being, the Hindu wedding ceremony casts the bride and groom as living representatives of the divine couple, roles that are to continue onward into married life. A married woman becomes a Lakshmi in her household in fulfillment of a woman's *stri dharma*, or the inherent powers and responsibilities entailed in living a woman's life. Many of these responsibilities involve integrity in relationships—with her spouse, children, extended family, and with the gods—as well as attention to overseeing the acquisition, storage, and preparation of food, the upkeep of the home-space, and, in rare cases, the management of finances.[19] As Barry's article demonstrates in its coverage of women who are constituted by these discourses, in line with this ideal, the girls can only embody a respectable Indian femininity through marriage and by serving the families of their husbands and in-laws.

In what follows, I argue that Barry stages a conflict between these two competing discourses of femininity and grants victory to the first, tying working women to individual freedom, equality, and the progress of the nation as a whole. Shashi and Prabhati must, according to the genre of the bildungsroman, master processes of bildung—or self-cultivation and self-transformation. They must embody a discourse of modern wage-earning femininity by becoming subjects who can lead autonomous lives through self-transformation.[20] Yet such iterations of femininity risk limiting the idea of individual freedom to the kinds of agency that can be reconciled with the dominant social order of capitalism. If we think back to this book's introductory redefining of freedom as agency that is constituted through the ability to choose between a wide array of life choices, Barry's schema of competing femininities would fall short. For the girls are faced only with binary choices; they can only choose between factory work or domestic chores. Within Barry's binaries, factory work is freedom, which itself

---

[19] Constantina Rhodes, *Invoking Lakshmi: The Goddess of Wealth in Song and Ceremony* (Buffalo: SUNY Press, 2010).

[20] This interpretation fits the analysis of feminist scholars such as Christina Scharff who have argued that young women in the Global South are often constructed as ideal neoliberal subjects who can capably maximize opportunities such as access to the labor market. Christina Scharff, "Gender and Neoliberalism: Young Women as Ideal Neoliberal Subjects," in Simon Springer, Kean Birch, and Julie MacLeavy (eds.), *Handbook of Neoliberalism* (New York: Routledge, 2016), 217–26.

overlooks her production of these girls' wills through discourses like laissez-faire and the "end of history" narrative.

Let's take a closer look at the way these discourses underpin Barry's idea of freedom as waged labor. Barry relies on the laissez-faire characterization of the waged laboring individual as the main unit of society and an embodiment of freedom. The piece begins with the subtitle: "Experiments like one in Bangalore, luring migrants to fill factory jobs, collide with an old way of life that keeps women and girls in seclusion until an arranged marriage." Right at the beginning of the piece, then, the "end of history" narrative and laissez-faire discourses result in old Orientalist binaries between unfree non-Western women subjected to seclusion and arranged marriages, and the forces of capitalist modernization that offer the only way out to freedom. These binaries overdetermine the characterization and plot of the article so that Barry does not spend much time on the complex interiorities of women like Shashi and Prabhati. In the countryside, because they are not yet individuals—synonymous here with waged laborers—the two sisters are presented as personifications of an abstracted collective rural sensibility. They are not yet monetized individuals working to pursue their selfish interests for the good of their wider society so they are not yet modern subjects possessed of individual freedom. Therefore, they can only embody backward, rural tradition:

> The new girls smell of the village. They have sprinklings of pimples ... Their braids bounce to their hips, tight and glossy ... On their ankles are silver chains hung with bells, so when they walk in a group, they jingle.[21]

The imagery of the ankles hung with silver chains not only suggests imprisonment but collective entrapment, for it is when they "walk in a group" that they jingle. Their reaction to the urban environment of Bangalore furthers the impression of backward oppression and entrapment being obliterated by modern, capitalist urban space:

> Bangalore is the first city the 37 trainee tailors have seen. They are dazzled by the different kinds of light. Picking their way through the alleys around the factory, a column of virgins from the countryside, they stare up at an apartment building that towers over the neighborhood and wish their mothers could see it.[22]

When they first arrive to work in the city, the girls are a monolithic group, "a column," that stands in juxtaposition to the other columns of factories and

---

[21] Barry, "Young Rural Women in India Chase Big-City Dreams."
[22] Barry, "Young Rural Women in India Chase Big-City Dreams."

skyscrapers. Significantly, this "column" from the village is constituted by "virgins from the countryside," an Orientalist characterization that highlights their lack of sexual freedom over any other characteristic. The article continues to reinforce this idea of conservative, oppressed female collectivities being central to relatively un-monetized environments such as Ishwarpur: "They have come from a village at the end of a road, a place so conservative that the single time they went to a movie theater, their male cousins and uncles created a human chain around them, their big hands linked, to protect them from any contact with outside men."

The characterization of these girls as precapitalist collective blank slates on which urban capitalism can realize its freedoms ends up meaning that the village girls have no inner desires or agency in and of themselves, either before or after they enter the workforce. Beforehand, they are portrayed as simply "waiting to see what will happen to them," continually shielded from any process of self-discovery by "big hands" and "human chains." The article authoritatively confirms their fate if they had stayed in the village:

> Upon reaching adulthood, they would be transferred to the guardianship of another family, along with a huge dowry that serves as an incentive to treat them well. The transfer is final. Once married, the new bride cannot return to visit her parents without permission, which is given sparingly, so that the bonds to her old home will weaken. She must show her submission to the new family: She is not allowed to speak the names of her in-laws, because it is seen as too familiar, and in some places she is not allowed to use words that begin with the same letters as her in-laws' names, requiring the invention of a large parallel vocabulary. Each morning, before she is allowed to eat, the daughter-in-law must wash the feet of her husband's parents and then drink the water she has used to wash them.[23]

The passage begins in an ambiguous future voice in the conditional tense, in subordinate clauses, and refers to times and places that are not represented within the article. Then it shifts to the simple present tense as if to confirm its described reality as an objective and transcendent state of horror that habitually and definitively affects such women. In contrast are the wage-laboring women in Bangalore, well on their way to becoming individuals, whose prospects for oppressive marriages are replaced with love and romance. Once they become waged laborers in the city, these girls

---

[23] Barry, "Young Rural Women in India Chase Big-City Dreams."

spend their evenings in quiet conversation with boyfriends, whose existence is unknown to their parents. They examine each other's palms for creases that indicate they will be among the small number of Indians—as low as 5 percent, according to one survey—who marry for love. At the factory, they stitch their boyfriends' names on scrap fabric. Male tailors stroll by as they work, dropping love letters folded into fat wads, and the girls read them aloud, to comic effect, at the hostel. "My dear, my lever," someone writes to Shashi in broken English. "I have tied you up in my heart."[24]

Barry's story, here, continues to confirm that the terrible jingling entrapment these girls endure can only be drowned out, symbolically and literally, through incorporation into the globalized labor force. In other words, while the evils of dowry and arranged marriage represent the oppressive past, the empowered, enlightened end of history is represented by the work of the factory. The girls' determination to make that journey is epitomized through an "anthem about self-sufficiency," sung with such reverence that it is given the sanctity of a spiritual experience.

> This job is the story of our lives
> The job is as important as prayer
> We won't fear, and we will go ahead.[25]

Once these women begin to work, Barry's article calculates their value solely in monetary terms as the fulfilling of a function, as commodified labor that can produce profit. If these objects remain unmonetized, they are regarded as "idle," no matter the work they are actually doing. This is why when Shashi's sister Prabhati is sent back to the village too sick to work, her vacant sewing machine comes to represent all of her being:

> On the assembly line, someone covers Prabhati's sewing machine with plastic sheeting. Three weeks later, two burly men come to push it to an area marked "idle machines." Just like that, Prabhati is back in her mother's thatch hut, feeding kindling into a clay oven ... The neighbors stop by, seeking an outcome to the family's experiment. "So, are your daughters back from their jobs?" asks one, in a voice thick with self-satisfaction.[26]

With Prabhati gone, her sewing machine becomes a metonym for her whole selfhood. The syntax of the sentence suggests that she herself is now rendered an

---

[24] Barry, "Young Rural Women in India Chase Big-City Dreams."
[25] Barry, "Young Rural Women in India Chase Big-City Dreams."
[26] Barry, "Young Rural Women in India Chase Big-City Dreams."

"idle machine" pushed into a corner of the globe—the village—to face the scorn of her neighbors and traditional domestic unfreedom.

## Global Capitalism as Plot Obstacle in Barry's Bildungsroman

One consequence of equating waged work with freedom is that other systematic structures of inequality than those tied to domestic life are overlooked. The conflation of waged labor under global capitalism with individual freedom means that capitalist structures of inequality are presented simply as obstacles that main characters need to overcome to achieve happiness. Systematic forms of oppression tied to global capital are just plot conflicts in the style of the affirmative bildungsroman—existing only to be overcome and reconciled with, thereby achieving a predetermined narrative conclusion. Barry's article unwittingly adopts the narrative assumptions and plot structure of this kind of bildungsroman to both individualize the capitalist worker and objectify her in line with the dominant social order—that of liberal capitalism. In accordance with the bildungsromanian form of the narrative, with its potential end in the realization of individual freedom, the girls' journey to Bangalore to work in the factories is celebrated as a trial that only the strongest will survive. The article's focus on two sisters as its main protagonists affirms this plot structure, for Prabhati is sent back to the village after she is unable to overcome an illness caused by overwork, fatigue, and the lack of health care. Shashi, on the other hand, survives and stays on.

To affirm Shashi's victory over the backward forces in the village that await her should she "fail," as her foil Prabhati does, Barry represents the hardships the girls are subjected to as character-building obstacles that only Shashi has the strength to overcome. Yet Barry does note the toll the work takes on the girls, for they are not paid on time, have to go without food for days, and then when eventually paid, only receive the equivalent of $28 for two weeks of work "after withholdings for pension, health insurance, lodging, food and kitchen furnishings." In a style befitting journalistic objectivity, Barry does not hold back from commenting on the exploitative elements of this labor:

> Incredibly, garments worn in the West are still made by humans—nearly all of them women, working exhausting hours, with few legal protections and little chance of advancement, for some of the lowest wages in the global supply chain.

> Cuddles is among the first in the group to be integrated into an assembly line, bent over, eyes straining. Her task is to stitch together three small tags for the Marks & Spencer stretch corduroy skirt: one that identifies the brand, one that

gives washing instructions and one a scrap so tiny that it is nearly impossible to hold straight between finger and thumb. If she allows a tag to slip to the floor, or fly away in the gusts from the ceiling fan, her salary will be docked. She will be under pressure to complete this task 100 times per hour for eight hours, with one half-hour break for lunch, for a base daily wage of around $2."[27]

Barry notes the painstaking, exhausting nature of this work as well as the draconian ways in which it is enforced. The girls are forced to be efficient because profits depend on how much labor can be squeezed out of workers in the least amount of time and for the least amount of money. The lunch break is thus only "one half hour" and the labor is remunerated for a shameful sum. However, Barry's response to these appalling numbers, amounting to less than $2 a day, and leading Prabhati to seek medical care from a roadside quack, is only to stress that this is still "more than most of their fathers make."

In fact, Barry notes that ultimately "the amount of the paycheck is not relevant" because it represents a culmination of individual freedom. "They have never earned money before, only asked their fathers for it. A wave of happiness washes over all of them. They do not feel like girls, they say: They feel like boys." In other words, the structural violence of global capital, which uses these women as nothing more than automatons and exploits their labor in order to realize a profit for the 1 percent on the other side of the globe, is simply excused, skipped over. The low paycheck is no longer exploitation but simply the result of capitalism's deduction of the price of freedom from their paycheck. Barry's characterization of Shashi after she receives her paycheck is indicative of this equation between freedom and the exploitations of multinational waged labor:

> Shashi dances down the stairs and most of the way home. The money sends a wild thrill through her, so that she wishes she could fast-forward through the next month, and the month after that, and after that. So that life is a long string of paydays.[28]

Shashi's joy is characterized as the opposite of exploitation; the "wild thrill" of $2 a day makes her wish for life to be nothing more than paydays. In effect, it is a life narratively reduced to no more than the freedom of waged labor, a product of the "historically specific relations of subordination" enabled and created by liberal capitalism.[29]

---

[27] Barry, "Young Rural Women in India Chase Big-City Dreams."
[28] Barry, "Young Rural Women in India Chase Big-City Dreams."
[29] Saba Mahmood, "Feminist Theory, Embodiment, and the Docile Agent: Some Reflections on the Egyptian Islamic Revival," *Cultural Anthropology* 16 (2): 210.

Because capitalist freedom amounts to all other kinds of individual freedom in this narrative framework, the story of Shashi's incorporation into global capitalism is increasingly padded with information that characterizes her as a person, in opposition to Prabhati who largely remains a type. We are told that Shashi likes dirty jokes, calls herself 45 kilograms of hotness, and had a secret boyfriend whose existence Prabhati revealed to their parents in an act of betrayal. In Bangalore, Shashi continues to communicate with this boyfriend by spending most of her factory salary on a new smartphone. Barry notes that "Shashi finds it interesting that she, the screw-up in the family, is the one becoming a city person. She examines her face in the mirror for signs that she is becoming paler. She tells the family that Prabhati should not return, and that she cannot send money home this month. Instead, Shashi arranges for a meeting with Sunil, a boy from a neighboring village whom she wants to marry." The message is clear: Shashi deserves to be rescued by capitalism for embodying liberal ideals of freedom, while Prabhati does not. Within Barry's article-bildungsroman, Shashi the individual has overcome enough plot obstacles to achieve a freedom in line with the dominant social order of liberal capitalism. Prabhati, meanwhile, has failed and therefore cannot be free.

Thinking beyond these binaries toward a more expansive notion of freedom reveals the ways that the liberal autonomous will legitimates certain forms of oppression—such as poorly paid exploitative piece-meal factory work—while decrying others—such as farming and domestic chores including marital duties such as cooking and cleaning for the family—as markers of tradition. Reading between the lines of Barry's article suggests that waged work is linked to certain forms of oppression and domestic work to others. If we think back to our two metrics in the introduction, which theorize freedom as (1) access to what feels as free (2) alongside a substantive quantity and quality of choices available to the chooser, we are left asking: How free is Shashi's choice to work in the factory when other choices, beyond marriage and domestic work, are not available to her? How free is Barry's vision of freedom after all?

## *The Space between Us*: Complicating the Idea of Waged Work as Freedom

If Barry's equation of waged work with freedom overlooks multiple other ways of being free by presenting a life-in-story that obscures a wider range of life choices, Umrigar's novel *The Space between Us* (2007) builds on this analysis by representing the ways that waged work means different things for women of different classes. The novel follows the life of Bhima, who works as a domestic servant for Sera. For Bhima, her job is a matter of compulsion, while for her high-class employer waged work is a mode of autonomy. The novel suggests that it is not waged work itself that is oppressive but the structural conditions that confine Bhima to poverty and subjugation combined with ideologies of patriarchy, which are institutionalized in certain forms of work differently for women of different classes.

In telling Bhima and Sera's stories, the novel illuminates how globalization has exacerbated the differences in how women of dissimilar classes experience waged work. The liberalization of the economy has increased the number of lower-class women forced to work in the informal subsistence economy defined by exploitative forms of labor such as domestic servitude. Economists have noted that since 1991, most employment opportunities have been generated in the informal economy, which now contains about 92 percent of all workers. Poor women have suffered disproportionately under this shift, working for low earnings with limited or no social protection. The researchers conclude that these "changes in employment pattern may reflect the intense competition, risk and uncertainty, which both the employers and employees face due to globalisation."[30] Indeed, the globalized economy, as Pierette Hondagneu-Sotelo writes, has created a whole new subaltern class of peoples in the Global South, forced into menial forms of "unskilled" labor in their own countries and abroad.[31] Robert Young describes this reality as "almost more brutal" than the colonial societies that served as its antecedents. He writes of "those countless individuals in so many societies, who are surplus to economic requirements, redundant, remaindered, condemned to the surplasage of lives full of holes, waiting for a future that may never come."[32]

Set in postcolonial Mumbai and written for an audience of educated Indians and non-Indians, the novel can be read as a reaction to the rise of domestic service worldwide in the wake of globalization. The domestic servant figure represents the coming together of neoliberal inequalities tied to "development" with the sustained exacerbation of feudal and semi-feudal forms of discrimination such as caste-based notions of bodily purity and pollution.

---

[30] Government of India Ministry of Labour and Employment, "Employment in Informal Sector and Conditions of Informal Employment Vol. IV," 2013–2014, https://labour.gov.in/sites/default/files/Report%20vol%204%20final.pdf.
[31] Pierette Hondagneu-Sotelo, *Domestica: Immigrant Workers Cleaning and Caring in the Shadows of Affluence* (Berkeley: University of California Press, 2007), x.
[32] Robert J. C. Young, "Postcolonial Remains," *New Literary History*, 43(1), Winter 2012: 19–42.

Indeed, texts like Umrigar's capture the way that the global economy does not eradicate but rather benefits from, and aggravates, these older cultural divisions and feudal forms of segregation. Raka Ray and Seemin Qayum flesh out some of these supposedly precapitalist attitudes in their identification of particular "cultures of servitude," or "a culture in which social relations of domination/subordination, dependency and inequality are normalized and permeate both the domestic and public spheres."[33] The servant typically receives a nominal payment in exchange for labor that comes with an expectation of internalized, embodied subjugation and segregation, including caste-driven taboos on touching, on using the same household items as one's employers, and on bodily proximity. These cultures of segregation have endured, albeit in changed forms, from precolonial and feudal to postcolonial times. As such, domestic servitude becomes a permanent constituent of identity that produces expectations of loyalty, deference, even self-abasement on one side, and varying degrees of obligation on the other.[34]

Umrigar's story is largely told from the perspective of Bhima, the longtime housekeeper of a middle-class Parsi widow named Serabai. At the novel's start, Bhima's orphaned granddaughter Maya, the first in the family to get a proper education, has gotten pregnant and dropped out of college. Fortunately, Sera is generous. She has sponsored Bhima's granddaughter through school, and she now proposes to help the girl obtain an abortion. Meanwhile, Sera's friends tease her for treating Bhima "like she is the Kohinoor diamond."[35] Sera, a survivor of domestic abuse, enjoys Bhima's nurturing presence but is careful to maintain limits on her relationship with her housekeeper. In Sera's home, Bhima drinks from a special glass "that is kept aside for her," and she "squats on the floor rather than use a chair."[36] When Bhima finally reveals that Maya's pregnancy was the result of being raped by Sera's son-in-law, Sera fires Bhima, choosing to believe her son-in-law's obvious lie over her servant's obvious truth.

The novel draws on and adapts the affirmative bildungsroman's form in its charting of the life arc of its protagonist Bhima, but it subverts that conventional structure in its construction of Sera as an upper-class foil to Bhima, whose life parallels yet diverges from Bhima's in certain ways that have to do with their social backgrounds. Through the intertwined parallelism of these two lives, the

---

[33] Raka Ray and Seemin Qayum, *Cultures of Servitude: Modernity, Domesticity, and Class in India* (Stanford: Stanford University Press, 2009), 3.
[34] Ray and Qayum, *Cultures of Servitude*, 26.
[35] Thrity Umrigar, *The Space between Us* (New York: Harper Perennial, 2007), 170.
[36] Umrigar, *The Space between Us*, 36.

novel suggests that unlike the protagonist of the affirmative bildungsroman, Bhima cannot come to terms with a social order that is so blatantly exploitative of women of her class. These differences in the way that both women experience the world are reflected in how Bhima and Sera view waged work. For Sera, an upper-class woman forbidden to work by her abusive husband, work is a mode of autonomy. Her husband forbids Sera to work as a form of control over her person and as a way to elevate his own status as the financial provider of the family. Umrigar presents these insights to the reader through the recounting of a conversation that Sera has with her friend Aban:

> Her best friend, Aban, had argued with her when she'd told her she was giving up her job at Bombay House. "No, yaar, in this day and age, a woman should be independent," she'd advised. At that time, swept up in Feroz's declaration that he was more than capable of supporting his wife, she had put Aban's words down to a simple case of envy. But Aban was right, she now realized. Today, she missed the simple routine of deciding what outfit to wear to work, the grand feeling of being swept up in the tidal wave of office workers as they poured out of the morning trains, the camaraderie that came from participating in the jokes and gossip that circulated around the office like unofficial memos, the satisfaction of doing a job that earned her praise from Mr. Madan. Never in her life had she experienced the heavy, oppressive feeling that now weighed on her as she sat in her bedroom and waited for Feroz to come home.[37]

What Sera misses about waged work is the freedom it gives her from her husband's tyranny. As Aban notes, work is a way for Sera to remain "independent." Sera's description of what she misses about it is thus replete with a desire to be in control of her own choices, including deciding what to wear and being able to exercise one's own individuality—whether it is participating in jokes or being proud of one's own work. The text presents the alternative to this life of choice and self-fulfillment as a life of being confined to her bedroom, waiting for Feroz to come home. When Sera does not work, she has no choices available to her—whether to do with the autonomy of her own physical body, or that of her mind. This gendered oppression is juxtaposed with its textual opposite: the freedom of waged work. As Sera sits in her room, the text describes her desperation:

> Time had never passed so slowly. At one point, she caught a glimpse of herself in the mirror and was shocked at the trapped, animal-like desperation she saw in her eyes. *A few months ago, I had a successful job, a good life, could come*

[37] Umrigar, *The Space between Us*, 78.

and go as I wished, she thought. And now I'm afraid to leave this room … She blinked her eyes, as if the gesture would somehow alter this strange reality that she found herself encased in.[38]

Sera is "oppressed" because she is not working. She is "trapped," "encased" because she cannot earn a wage outside the home. While *The Space between Us* here seems to participate in many of the same assumptions about waged work and freedom that Ellen Barry does, it nuances this link in its consideration of Bhima, for whom waged work represents something very different from an uncomplicated freedom.

Umrigar's representation of Bhima's experiences suggest that the freedom of waged work is relative, for it is largely determined by class; the only kind of waged work available to her as a member of the lower class is domestic servitude, which manifests itself through precapitalist cultures of servitude as they work alongside more modern ideas such as the fiction of "property in the person." The fiction of "property in the person," first illuminated by Marx, rests on the capitalist notion that a person's capacity for work—her abilities and attributes—are her "property," which suggests that these abilities and attributes are separate from the body and alienable from the self. In the process of conceptualizing a person's abilities as objects or commodities to be used, such an assumption objectifies and commodifies the person herself into a subordinate "other" who embodies subjugation and difference in the ways dictated by precapitalist cultures of caste and *jati* based bodily segregation.

Carol Pateman illuminates the ways that "property in the person" is an exploitative myth when she argues that while the employment contract seems to represent an equal exchange between a worker and his or her employer, in which money is exchanged for labor power (or the worker's capacity for work), labor power is in fact not separable from the person of the worker like pieces of property. The worker's capacities are developed over time and they form an integral part of her self and self-identity, constituting her will, understanding, and experience. This means that a person does not stand in the same relation to the property in her own person as she does to other types of property, because labor power is integral to personhood.[39] Since labor power is not something

---

[38] Umrigar, *The Space between Us*, 78.
[39] Carol Pateman, *The Sexual Contract* (Cambridge: Polity Press, 1988), 150–1. The lack of consensus over who owned the labor of a servant uncovers the complexities of the debate. The employer clearly owned the objects produced by his servant's labor, such as the dinner cooked, but what about the labor-power itself? Did a servant own her own labor-power, or did the master who hired the servant take ownership? Locke suggested that the employer owned the labor-power of the servant: "The grass my horse has bit, the turfs my servant has cut … become my property … the labor that was

that can be separated from the body, viewing it and using it as a commodity disguises the fact that the worker's entire being, especially within institutions like domestic servitude, is used in obedience of the employer. The relationship is one of subordination, while at the same time, through the device of contract and the fiction of property in the person, the parties are both misleadingly labeled as free and equal citizens. This embodied abjection enables the sustenance of the kinds of subjugation that buttress the globalized capitalist system.

Women like Bhima in the lowest strata of the economic ladder bear the brunt of this system. As the novel testifies, within the private sphere of the home, female domestic servants endure a triple subordination at the hands of the globalized economic system—subordination as a citizen, as a woman, and as a domestic servant. Pateman illuminates why this may be so in her theory of the sexual contract, which elaborates on the "social contract" theorized by Locke, Rousseau, and Rawls. Within social contract theory, the maintenance of the capitalist system itself, and indeed, of any modern society, requires that men give themselves up to public law, including employment contracts, in order to ensure the maintenance of the social order that allows them to live freely in the first place.[40] However, as Pateman elaborates through her notion of the "sexual contract," this sacrifice of the self to public law involves the male's retention of the right to rule the home in private. This means that both the public and private spheres depend on a sexual division of labor in which women are subordinated to men.[41] When paid domestic labor is introduced into this equation, housewives take responsibility as employers of the servant within the private sphere. This arrangement renders the domestic worker triply subjugated—by the terms of

---

mine removing them out of the common state they were in, has fixed my property in them." Another contemporary writer, John Vancouver, claimed that the ownership of labor-power could not be transferred. For Vancouver, "individual talent of labor or ingenuity was the untransferable stock of productive labor, whether of a corporeal or mental quality." See John Vancouver, *An Enquiry into the Causes and Production of Poverty, and the State of the Poor* (London: Philanthrophic Reform, 1796), 4–6. Employers seem to have favored the Lockean view. See John Locke, *The Second Treatise of Civil Government* (1690), https://www.gutenberg.org/cache/epub/7370/pg7370-images.html, chapter 5, "Of Property." Accessed April 2, 2022.

[40] Social contract theories originate in stories told to explain the formation of civil society and why citizens submit voluntarily to the state. The basic story tells of how inhabitants of the state of nature, each motivated purely by self-interest, agree to a social contract whereby civil society is created, and the behavior of each is regulated for the benefit of all. For instance, John Locke wrote:

> If man in the state of nature be so free as has been said: if he be absolute lord of his own person and possessions, equal to the greatest and subject to nobody, why will he part with his freedom ... because though in the state of nature he hath such a right, yet the enjoyment of it is very uncertain, thus social contract for mutual preservation of lives, liberties and estates.

See John Locke, *The Second Treatise of Civil Government* (1690), Gutenberg.org, chapter IX, "Of the Ends of Political Society and Government," Section 123.

[41] Pateman, *The Sexual Contract*.

the social contract that render all citizens subject to public employment laws, by the men who subjugate themselves to this contract only to rule their female dependents and children within the private sphere, and by the female employers of domestic servants who rule the private sphere by proxy while their men work in the public sphere.

*The Space between Us* is remarkable for its careful capturing of the tensions between the body as personhood and the body as property embodied in the figure of the female domestic servant. It is also exemplary in its exploration of what these tensions mean for the relationship between the employer and servant, illuminating the systemic material and cultural power structures, including economic and gender relations, which produce their behaviors. In particular, the novel consistently reveals the ways that the fiction of "property in the person" underpins the subordination and exploitation of Bhima by showing how Serabai conceptualizes Bhima's abilities and attributes as commodities to be used while being unaware of the ways that this translates into commodifying and objectifying Bhima herself:

> Bhima is in the kitchen, washing the dishes from last night's dinner. Viraf wanders in, adjusting his tie. "That's it," he says to no one in particular. "Next month, I'm buying a dishwasher. No point in poor Bhima slogging like this." Bhima looks up in gratitude, but before she can say a word, Sera speaks up "My Bhima can put your fancy dishwashers to shame. Not even a foreign-made machine can leave dishes as clean as Bhima can. Save your money." … And give it to me instead, Bhima thinks to herself … she needs a few seconds to fume. Sometimes she can't figure Serabai out. On the one hand, it makes her flush with pride when Serabai calls her "my Bhima" and talks about her proprietarily. On the other hand, she always seems to be doing things that undercut Bhima's interests. Like refusing Viraf baba's offer to buy a dishwasher. How nice it would be not to run her arthritic hands in water all day long. Bending over the sink to scrub the dishes has also begun to hurt her back, so that, at the end of the day, it sometimes takes half the walk home before she can straighten up.[42]

This passage reveals the idea of property in the person as a fiction, for Bhima's ability to wash dishes is clearly not simply a service she can rent out independently of her self. The references to Bhima's arthritic hands and hurting back call attention to the ways that Bhima's labor affects her whole person, so that her entire body is left marked—bent with arthritis—by her servitude. The

---

[42] Umrigar, *The Space between Us*, 25.

co-option of Bhima's entire person by Sera's employment turns Bhima herself into a dish washing machine appreciated only in terms of her capacity to perform household tasks. The "washing machine," then, becomes a metaphor for the commodification and objectification of Bhima.

The passage illuminates the disguised exploitation of Bhima and produces reader empathy not just through its content but its form, successfully integrating several streams of information that juxtapose different subjectivities—the point of view of the female employer, that of her female servant, as well as the men and women related to the two, all while privileging Bhima's. This textual strategy enables the novel to successfully illuminate the triple subordination inflicted on Bhima's person. Each of the three subjects in the passage function as symbolic representations of the hierarchies that oppress Bhima. Feroz, and then his son-in-law, Viraf, are the male patriarchs of the social contract, heading the private sphere even as they are subject to the laws of the public sphere. Viraf's mother-in-law Serabai runs the home on his behalf as part of the sexual contract, and both together wield authority over the domestic servant, Bhima. The insidiousness of this arrangement is masked by their seemingly generous, familial banter on Bhima's behalf. As the patriarch, Viraf offers to buy a washing machine, thereby effectively signposting Bhima's labor as a replaceable commodity even as such a gesture is masked by his seeming concern for Bhima's frail working body; as the matriarch, Serabai refuses the offer and seems to protect Bhima and her position as laborer by boasting about the quality of Bhima's work, even while this ignores Bhima's own frailties and fatigue. The third-person narrative represents these viewpoints only to center Bhima's own perspective by making it the only one expressed through her own consciousness and interiority. As a result, it becomes clear that Serabai's structural position as an employer who needs to extract as much labor as she can from Bhima's person overdetermines her personal relationship with Bhima. The economic transactionality of their relationship is why, Maryam Mirza argues, despite the commonality of the experiences of the female characters, class is still the "ultimately insurmountable barrier that condemns [these] women to fight their shared battles separately."[43]

Class differences and the nature of the labor contract are also responsible for an abuse of power between two other characters, Maya and Viraf. Under the unacknowledged assumptions of "property in the person," the servant will cede aspects of herself to her employer that go beyond her labor power, including the

---

[43] Maryam Mirza, *Intimate Class Acts: Friendship and Desire in Indian and Pakistani Women's Fiction* (Oxford: Oxford University Press, 2016), 23.

indiscriminate use of her body. Such an assumption of bodily ownership is most chillingly revealed in the sexual encounter between Maya and Viraf. The incident takes place following Viraf's request that Maya perform what should have been a simple labor chore upon his person, a massage, in just the way that the male "massagewallas at Chowpatty Beach" do. Umrigar is careful to highlight this act as a labor chore to Maya: "Her fingers found the knot of muscle and worked deftly to untie it. 'Dig deeper,' Viraf grunted. He turned slightly on his side and undid a couple more buttons to give her more room to work." Maya is doing her job here, an interpretation supported by the narrative voice's own labeling of the act as "work." Yet Viraf takes for granted that Maya is entirely available to service him, sexually and otherwise. The assumption that underlies the fiction of property in the person—that the labor performed by the body is alienable—translates into the entire self being thought of as alienable, which is why Viraf is able to use Maya's body in a way that constitutes a breach of her selfhood. Maya becomes nothing but labor power to Viraf, providing the satisfying of a bodily function, from the untying of the knot in his neck to sexual release at a time when his wife Dinaz is refusing to sleep with him: "Maya came to her senses before he did. While she lay frozen, rigid with terror and shame, he was still glowing, still limp with warmth and release. 'Been so long … ' she half-heard him say. 'Dinaz's pregnancy … so frigid … won't let me near her …' But she could barely hear what he was saying above the clanging bells of her own fear." Viraf's use of Maya as a commodity that satisfies a need in the same way that Bhima is a dish washing machine is apparent in his final words to her: "He was out the door when he turned back. 'Oh, one more thing,' Viraf said. 'Don't forget to wash the sheets, okay?'"[44] The careless nonchalance with which he throws this command her way testifies to Viraf's reduction of Maya to an embodiment of waged labor, whether a massage, sleeping with the boss, or washing incriminating evidence of rape off the sheets. Yet the narrative form consistently undermines this social understanding and invites empathy for Maya by privileging her own feelings at this moment. Viraf's sexual frustration is literally a background noise; what is foregrounded are the "clanging bells of her own fear," calling the reader's attention to the fact that what has happened is a rape. And, when Viraf leaves Maya, rather than walking out with him, the reader is left behind with Maya's crouched injured and fearful body, looking on at her "hurt, cowering look," and sharing the prospect of washing her virginal blood off her employer's sheets.

---

[44] Umrigar, *The Space between Us*, 390–6.

The sheet that can be washed to erase any evidence of wrongdoing is symbolic of the crime against Maya's person, which can easily be washed away within the world of systemic inequality she inhabits. Viraf rapes Maya with impunity and never has to pay for his crime because it is taken for granted that he has already paid under the assumption that Maya's entire self is up for sale along with her labor. The washable sheet signals the way that property in the person is a fiction that continually whitewashes what is actually at stake in the work of a domestic servant—the commodification and objectification of the person's entire self. But the metaphor also testifies to the porosity of the fiction, for it needs to be continually "washed clean" of violence in order to uphold the projected and questionable "truth" of the freedom and equality of the employment contract.

The novel subverts the conventional structure of the affirmative bildungsroman—in its neat accommodation of the individual to society—by refusing to depict a happy ending for Bhima. She stands at the shore, watching the waves, having just been fired by Serabai for accusing Viraf of raping Maya. The narrative ends with uncertainty, for Bhima has no waged work anymore. However, the tone of the novel is hopeful despite this, telling the reader that "it is dusk. But inside Bhima's heart is dawn." This ending complicates Barry's simplistic equation of waged work with freedom for women of Bhima's class in the global economy. Waged work for women of Bhima's class is the opposite of freedom. Bhima can only hope for freedom when she is free of her oppressive job. Bhima and Sera's discrepant experiences of waged work testify to how, in the new Indian economy, the majority of women do not work outside the home because they are ruled by patriarchal conventions that require them to spend their time on unpaid domestic work. The ones that do are largely the ones who have to—those, like Bhima and Maya, who occupy the lowest rungs of the social ladder. In their situations, freedom feels like being fired.

## *The Great Indian Kitchen*: Freedom as a Wealth of Choices

If "Big-City Dreams" reveals the predicaments faced by rural Indian women when they seek freedom in the global economy, and *The Space between Us* represents those faced by urban Indian women forced into the informal economy, *The Great Indian Kitchen* depicts how freedom may be defined for those that do not work—middle-class women at home. The film develops its notion of freedom through a return to the figure of Lakshmi, the Hindu Goddess of Wealth, suggesting alternative ideas of what a life lived freely could look like.

*The Great Indian Kitchen* tells the story of a newly married couple and follows their daily routines, conveying how the wife slowly discovers all of the housework expected of her. She spends her whole day in the kitchen cooking and cleaning as her husband and father-in-law practice yoga and sit around for hours reading the newspaper. When she asks her husband whether she can pursue her passion for dance by applying for a job as a dance teacher, he gently discourages her from doing so. Her father-in-law tells her: "that won't suit us, dear … Having a woman at home is very auspicious for the family."[45] This refers to the Hindu idea that the woman of the house is an embodiment of the goddess Lakshmi, and when she leaves, prosperity also leaves the household. Yet, the film quickly reveals that this ideal of the *grha Lakshmi* is an excuse for absolute control over the wife's time and labor.

In order to chart this control, the film presents a life-in-story that dispenses with the life arc of the affirmative bildungsroman. In fact, it dispenses with major plot points, for that would indicate progress, a movement forward, for the wife. Instead, the film suggests that there can be no progress when there is only domestic monotony; there can be no movement forward of a life when that life is constrained by an oppressive social order. The majority of the film is therefore composed of painstaking and repetitive close-up shots of housework, of vegetables being chopped, of dishes being washed. In one scene, the newlyweds hug in the kitchen; the husband is there on the pretext of depositing his teacup in the sink. The cuddle itself lasts five seconds. The shot of the wife picking up his teacup, rinsing it, applying soap, rinsing it again, and then drying it, lasts as long as the process would last in real life—over a minute long. The film lingers over repetitive household chores like this one on purpose, forcing viewers to share in the dreariness of the tasks, just as the women performing it do. The labor of cooking, cleaning, and then starting all over again for the next meal is a metaphor for the lack of choice women face in the way they spend their time. Domestic work becomes a symptom of the larger lack of individual freedom in the lives of women. This lack of freedom is not as dramatic as the physical imprisonment of women but happens by gradually constraining the number of choices that they have in their daily lives, determined through how they spend their hours. These women are not free, then, if we think back to the theorizing

---

[45] Jeo Baby, *The Great Indian Kitchen* (Kerala: Mankind Cinemas, 2021).

of freedom in the introduction, because their lives do not offer choices about the ways they can obtain self-fulfillment.

The film depicts this constriction of choice subtly. Male characters do not assert control explicitly, resorting to passive aggression instead. Most of it comes from the father-in-law who functions as a symbol of patriarchy. When the wife serves chutney with the meal, the father-in-law tastes it and asks: "Didn't you grind the chutney by hand?" She responds "No, I used the mixer." There is no outright admonishment here, just a disapproving look that achieves its purpose; next time, she grinds the chutney by hand. Similarly, the father-in-law asks her: "Did you cook the rice in the cooker?" When she responds affirmatively, he tells her: "Cook it on the fire next time okay?" The father-in-law can abhor modern, labor-saving machines like rice cookers only because the women of the household function like machines for him. The father-in-law does not yell when his wife does not bring him his toothbrush. He simply does not brush his teeth until she does. Similarly, he does not yell for her to bring him his shoes when he is leaving home. He simply does not leave until she does. Such preferences are justified in seemingly neutral terms: "Every family has its practices right?"[46]

This kind of passive aggressive patriarchy, the film suggests, is linked to more explicit and dramatic kinds of control. The backdrop of the film involves the Sabarimala Temple controversy, in which a temple in Kerala banned all women from entering its premises on the grounds that women of menstruating age are impure. This logic extends to the domestic realm, where the menstruating wife is told to sleep secluded on the floor of another room, keep herself and her washed clothes away from others, and then to purify everything that she uses with holy water. While the wife is confined in this way, her mere touch considered polluting, she listens to the radio, in which a journalist declares that "Women shouldn't see the court decision as just a matter of temple entry. It is a declaration of freedom. The declaration that we are slaves to nobody. They hope that they can chain women forever under their control in the house and kitchen." The film thus asks the viewer to consider how control over various facets of domestic routine are connected to more explicit and dramatic unfreedoms.

These forms of discrimination are linked because in both instances, women are not valued in and of themselves. What is valued is only the labor they perform for men. A menstruating woman is to be sidelined because she is not in any state that is useful to men: she is not pregnant, she is not as physically efficient at housework, and she is not as sexually consumable as when she is not

[46] Baby, *The Great Indian Kitchen*, 2021.

menstruating. The menstrual cycle is only impure waste, and women who are menstruating are therefore dirty and disgraceful, for women are worth only as much as what can be translated into value—whether reproductive, sexual, or domestic. *The Great Indian Kitchen* illuminates this status quo by suggesting that leftover food and the waste products of cooking and cleaning are a metaphor for the women themselves after their various forms of labor have been consumed. The parts of them that are not consumable can be spit out or discarded, just like vegetable peels, fruit skins, and dirty sink water.

This idea of the consumable woman is conveyed in the very first shot of the film where the soon to be wife is introduced to the viewers through shots of her joyful dancing. She is practicing the traditional dance from Kerala, Mohini Attam, and images of her obvious enjoyment and preoccupation are juxtaposed with shots of delicious foods being cooked in preparation for the meeting her household is arranging between her and her future husband. These foods are going to be consumed during the bride viewing. The juxtaposed shots of the food and the dancing virgin girl foreshadow that she too will be consumed by the marriage, her selfhood reduced to leftover waste products.

As the film progresses, the camera lingers over the waste products of the woman's labor to convey her transition to becoming waste. Her husband eats his meal and then spits out the skin of the various vegetables and fruit he is eating, leaving them on the tablecloth for his wife to clean up. Ants fester on the bucket of waste leftovers she collects and dumps in a pit outside every day. A few weeks into the marriage, the kitchen sink clogs up and the husband continually "forgets" to call a plumber. The wife lowers her hands into the dirty dish water to lift out whatever food particles she can and places a bucket underneath the sink to catch the dirty sink water as it leaks from the pipe. Every day, she wrinkles her nose as she cleans the drain and the space under the sink. At night, her husband mounts her for sex and all she can do is feel nauseated by the smell of the dirty dish water and cooking that lingers on her hands and naked skin. The wife's act of smelling her fingers and then wrinkling her nose during sex is symbolic: when she smells herself, she smells waste because that is what she has been reduced to. The parts of her that can be consumed—her labor power, her sex, her very skin— have been. Whatever remains of herself after her husband has consumed what he needs is considered to be waste by the patriarchal institution of marriage.

However, despite its critique of such domesticated femininity, the film does not equate waged work to freedom as Barry does, even while it invites a castigation of the father-in-law's denial of the wife's right to work as a dance teacher. There are only two women depicted throughout the main body of the film who work for a wage: the maidservant who comes to cook and clean while the wife is in menstrual confinement, and a teacher at the school the husband is also employed by. The first, like Bhima in *The Space between Us*, makes it clear that she works because she has to. She asks the wife: "What choice do I have? Who will feed my family if I take 3–4 days off?" The second, a teacher in the middle class like the wife's husband, hints that she is burdened by a double shift: waged labor as well as domestic work. This is revealed in an exchange between the husband and this female colleague when the husband steps out to buy lunch and it is revealed that his wife did not pack him one. The husband tells his colleagues: "she is a new bride, shouldn't we give her time to settle into her domestic duties?" His female colleague replies: "I wonder how long such niceties last?" suggesting that in her case they have not lasted.[47] The film's passing depiction of working women thus tallies with research suggesting that the rate of female labor force participation is dropping in India because Indian women are expected to prioritize domestic work and childcare above waged work, which enacts a toll on working women as well as those pressured to stay home. In other words, the film suggests that waged work by itself is not freedom without a change in the gendered roles and patriarchal attitudes that hinder women from achieving self-realization.

Instead of freedom as waged work, the film presents another ideal of freedom in the final scene of the film—the idea of freedom as a wealth of choice—a definition embodied by a more expansive invocation of Goddess Lakshmi than the patriarchal vision of the *grha Lakshmi*. The idea of freedom as wealth of choice is a contextual universalism because it is a local, culturally inflected idea of freedom that is to be applied universally; in the earthly realm, Lakshmi expresses herself as every girl and woman. In the "Song for the Glorious Lotus Goddess," (Kamalā Stotram), Lord Indra lauds Lakshmi:

> Every woman is an embodiment of you
> You exist as little girls in their childhood,
> As young women in their youth,
> And as elderly women in their old age.[48]

From the gods' point of view, all women are recognized as embodiments of Lakshmi. The final scene of *The Great Indian Kitchen* seeks to remind women of this through a depiction of the wife's life as a divorcee. She is now a dance teacher, and the final scene depicts a rehearsal that she is directing, to which

---

[47] Baby, *The Great Indian Kitchen*, 2021.
[48] Rhodes, *Invoking Lakshmi*, 134.

she arrives in her own car. As the girls dance to a feminist song about the power of womankind, the husband, now enjoying his second marriage, calls his first marriage a "rehearsal," leaving his empty morning teacup in the same place as before for his new wife to wash. His rehearsal taught him nothing except to enact patriarchal control more fully. His ex-wife's rehearsal, on the other hand, is a rehearsal for a fuller freedom through a choreographed hymn to the goddess Lakshmi. This dance song resists the narrowing of Lakshmi to a *grha Lakshmi* figure who represents only submissive domesticated wifehood:

> You are Earth's music, its form
> You personify valor.
> You are a flame that refuses to be put out.
> You light up this world!
> These worldly fetters. You escape them all.
> Bestower of life, Oh woman thee
> There are still many great stories left to narrate
> But time will not suffice
> Oh girl, march on!
> Enough with your grief.
> When you awaken the wisdom within
> your inner self,
> you are a relentless stream
> Spread on across this world!
> You are a woman, the strongest.
> Against the dust from your feet,
> even heaven pales
> Like the great sun and the dazzling stars
> Let this radiant face rule forever.[49]

The song is a paean to a culturally specific manifestation of the concept of individual freedom, or the individual ability to self-actualize in the absence of constraint. In the song, Goddess Lakshmi who lies within each woman symbolizes this contextual universalism of individual freedom. Being and becoming Lakshmi is a worldly and spiritual process. At a spiritual level, women can overcome external constraints because their divinity transcends the material world: "these worldly fetters. You escape them all." But the freedom represented by Lakshmi is also worldly, exemplifying a rethinking of autonomy as the capacity for meaningful choice between multiple material opportunities

---

[49] Baby, *The Great Indian Kitchen*, 2021.

**Figure 3** A still from the dance finale in *The Great Indian Kitchen*.

and modes of self-realization. Lakshmi in Sanskrit is derived from the root word *lakṣ* (लक्ष्), and *lakṣa* (लक्ष) is simultaneously the verb "to perceive, observe, know, understand" and the noun "goal, aim, objective," respectively.[50] Lakshmi means *know* and *understand* your goal, with the word "goal" referring to the four aims of a good Hindu life: the realization of *dharma* (morality), *artha* (material wealth), *kama* (sensual fulfillment), and *moksha* (spiritual transcendence) within the self. In other words, Lakshmi represents freedom through self-fulfillment via the capacity to realize one's goals within each of these four categories, through a multitude of pathways and life choices. When a woman does so, she will have fully embodied the goddess within herself, and achieved worldly as well as spiritual liberation, for one is not possible without the other.

The song lends depth to this contextual universalism of freedom as self-fulfillment by invoking one of the key attributes of the goddess, *sri*, or splendor, through the simile: "like the great sun and dazzling stars." Every woman must embody *sri* to become one with the divine Lakshmi who resides within her. One type of *sri* is wisdom, and the dance song enjoins women to "awaken the

---

[50] "lakṣ, लक्ष्." *Monier-Williams Sanskrit–English Dictionary* (Cologne, Germany: University of Koeln, 2015).

wisdom within your inner self" in order to achieve their *lakṣa*. One Hindu hymn celebrates this quality of wisdom in the following terms:

> O Auspicious One,
> You are sacrificial knowledge,
> Supreme knowledge,
> And secret, mystical knowledge.
> You are knowledge of the higher Self,
> O Goddess,
> And you are the one who confers liberation.
> You are metaphysics,
> You are the three Vedas,
> You are the arts and sciences,
> And you are the purveyor of justice.
> O Goddess, the entire world,
> With all of its pleasing and displeasing forms,
> Consists of your essence.[51]

Such invocations of Lakshmi as the different kinds of wisdom and knowledge essential to creation are a deliberate repudiation of the corrupting of the notion of *grha Lakshmi* by nationalist constructions of Hindu tradition. Prior to this corruption, the ideal of *grha Lakshmi* actually referred to the notion that the home was to be one space of sacred, ritualized action within which a woman could generate *Shakti*—the creative cosmic power of the goddess—that is part of her own essential being. The ideal of *grha Lakshmi*, in other words, is not meant to confine women to the home within a life of domestic servitude but to be one mode—of many—of embodying the goddess.[52] Similarly, Lakshmi is the bestower of life not because she represents women's reproductive role within a patriarchal understanding of motherhood but because she is the essence of existence. Cosmic creation itself is impossible without her. One aspect of Lakshmi's mythography asserts that creation proceeds from an infinite body of primordial water. Lakshmi is associated with this sap of existence; in "spreading on across this world," as the dance song enjoins women to do, they transform formless waters into organic life. As the goddess who sustains creation, Lakshmi benevolently embodies herself in time and space, pervading each realm to maintain harmony, fullness, and equanimity. When creation is in danger of losing its balance and falling into irreparable decay, she descends into the world,

---

[51] Rhodes, *Invoking Lakshmi*, 41.
[52] Rhodes, *Invoking Lakshmi*, 121.

manifesting in a specifically recognizable form. All prosperity, all that nourishes and ensures benevolent increase, is the expression of the auspicious Goddess Lakshmi, of every woman, indeed, of every human being that emanates from creation, which itself is a product of her cosmic energy.

The dance that the divorced wife's troupe performs in tune with this prayer song is a powerful and spiritual one, for the dance draws from folk forms performed on temple grounds to embody divinity within the self. The last scene, then, does not just invoke the goddess. It performatively seeks to bring her into being by enjoining women to embody her and the ultimate freedom that she represents. When they dance, the ex-wife's students strike the goddess pose, the *utkata konasana*, in their movements, a pose to help activate base energy centers that contain the life-force of *Shakti*—the essence of Lakshmi's creative force. They move their eyes from side to side in a bid to connect to their inner goddess. The role of dance teacher is symbolically important because it involves the protagonist teaching other girls how to realize their inner strength in line with a more expansive notion of freedom than the world offers her.

Through my analysis of these three texts, I have asked: How do we restore a fuller human that can critique both patriarchal domesticity and the systemic abuses of capitalism, charting a more capacious notion of individual freedom that transcends binaries? Barry's use of a bildungsromanian narrative arc represents the structural violence of capitalism as nothing more than an individual character-building struggle while reducing the individual herself to an empty vessel for capitalism. The human emerges necessarily impoverished by these contradictions. By contrast, Umrigar's adaptation of the bildungsroman form refuses to reconcile Bhima with the hegemonic structures of the informal economy within which she works, demonstrating the way that patriarchy and capitalism work together to oppress women of her class. The *Great Indian Kitchen*, meanwhile, pauses the life-in-story through its creative use of the cinematic form. It represents slow-paced domestic monotony to point us toward greater freedoms not restricted to waged or domestic work, expanding our imaginations regarding the various life choices that women embrace in order to gain freedom. Together, these texts offer multiple lives-in-story to complicate capitalist modernity's binary choices between domestic work and waged work, binaries that constrain the possibilities of freedom for countless women like my mother. In Chapter 2, I continue my analysis of how Freedom Inc. conceptualizes women's lives, and how women imagine autonomy differently, by focusing on Dalit women writers' struggles for equality.

2

# Dalit Women and the Quest for Freedom in Ambedkarite Life-Writing

Over a decade ago, during a vacation visiting my husband's family in Bangalore, I was introduced to some family friends of my mother-in-law. They were a wealthy elderly couple with a family business in jewelry and precious stones. I met them when we were invited to a lavish puja ceremony at their home. When it was over, we sat on silk cushions on the floor in the courtyard. A servant laid banana leaves in front of us, and another servant ladled out an extensive meal on to those leaves. There were endless South Indian dishes including a variety of different salads, coconut rice, curd rice, and lentil-based dosas with a spicy potato curry, tempered with mustard seeds and curry leaf. The meal was ended with steaming hot cups of sweet South Indian filter coffee. When we got home from that delicious meal, my mother-in-law sat down to a cup of tea and told me about the couple's marriage. "He had to travel a lot for business," she said. "And, even when he went abroad, his wife would go everywhere with him so that he never had to eat out." She exclaimed admiringly: "He had home cooked meals no matter where he was!" To my mother-in-law, this was a touching display of wifely devotion. My interpretation was very different. Newly married, I thought this was a ghastly story of patriarchal arrogance. In my estimation, the wife was a wealthy equivalent of a live-in servant, expected to cook for her husband not just in their own home, but wherever her husband went. Given that my husband and I were about to return "abroad" to the United States, I also had suspicions about why this story was being narrated to me in the first place.

It wasn't until this year that I had an epiphany, which hit me like a thunderbolt. "Were these family friends Brahmins?" I asked my husband desperately. "Yes," he said. "Why do you ask?" "Because," I exclaimed, "this is not just a story about patriarchy but about caste!" These family friends were Brahmins and he took his wife with him to cook everywhere he went because he was upper caste and did not want his food to be "polluted" by the touch of non-Brahmin cooks. I couldn't believe that it had taken me so long to grasp this fact, over ten years after I had first eaten at their home. As a person who sat in the middle to upper rungs of the caste system and grew up in Belgium, free of the daily orthodoxies of Brahmins as well as of the snubs borne by lower castes, I was blind to markers of caste discrimination because I had never suffered them myself. Caste was invisible to persons of privilege like me. This kind of ignorance, I now realize, allowed for the system's reproduction. Moreover, the caste system was harmful not just to lower castes but also to women of all castes; it was degrading to the Brahmin wife who had to function as her husband's personal cook and demeaning to an NRI Vaishnav like myself for whom she was being held up as an example of dutiful wifehood. The story taught me just how intertwined caste and patriarchy were—each system relied on the other, concretizing the term "Brahminical patriarchy," which was coined to describe just such an intersectional nexus of oppressions.

As I was pondering over these realizations, B. R. Ambedkar's writings came back to me. Bhimrao Ambedkar, or Bhima as his devotees call him, was British India's Minister of Labor, independent India's first Minister of Law and Justice, and the chief architect of the Constitution of India. He was a Dalit who earned his two PhDs in Economics at Columbia and the London School of Economics, and trained under the Pragmatist philosopher of education, John Dewey.[1] Ambedkar sought a society where caste and gender hierarchies were eliminated and where the French Revolution's ideals of "liberty, equality and fraternity" could be realized. He called this project a process of "reclaiming the human personality."[2]

I had read Ambedkar's writings only as stark documentations of a reality that I was historically and geographically removed from. But now I remembered how, in his attempt to reform caste hierarchies, Ambedkar repeatedly stressed how caste segregation relied on gender discrimination. Women, he said, were the gateways of the caste system, which also laid down a structure for the subordination of women. In his essay, "Castes in India," he outlined how endogamy—or a system of marrying only within one's own caste—was the essence of the caste system, and also of gender discrimination. Maintaining caste exclusivity, Ambedkar argued, is what led not just to practices like turning your wife into your personal cook but to the rise of Sati and child marriage as well. To

---

[1] Ambedkar studied with John Dewey while he was at Columbia and became deeply immersed in Dewey's ideas to the extent that he told his friends, "If Dewey died, I could reproduce every lecture verbatim." Ambedkar distilled his own egalitarian social vision and world view partly from Dewey's ideas of active inquiry and formal education, seeing these as necessary vehicles for realizing democracy, fraternity, and the Buddhist perception of respect and reverence for life.
[2] Ambedkar quoted in Dhananjay Keer, *Dr Ambedkar: Life and Mission*, 3rd ed. (Bombay: Popular Prakashan, 1971), 351.

liberate all Dalits, you had to liberate women. To liberate all women, you had to eliminate the caste system.

Such an assertion is not an obvious one and, in post-1990s India, liberation from caste is talked of in very different terms. The onus is not on reforming the institutions—like upper-caste patriarchy—through which caste is reproduced, but on the entrepreneurial initiative of Dalits themselves. In 2017, an *Indian Express* headline declared: "Meet Kalpana Saroj, Dalit Entrepreneur." Saroj is a Dalit businesswoman whose life is the "ultimate rags to riches tale."[3] The news story begins with her marriage at the age of twelve, which lasted only six months because of mistreatment by her in-laws. She faced so much stigma that she attempted suicide. When that failed, she worked at a hosiery factory for a measly 2 rupees a day. Eventually, she managed to secure a small government loan and bought some land, which enabled her to enter the construction business. Despite multiple death threats from upper-caste landowners and construction owners, Kalpana persevered and is now a millionaire. Milind Kamble, founder of the Dalit Indian Chamber of Commerce and Industry (DICCI), believes that Saroj's story exemplifies a boom in Dalit entrepreneurs after the neoliberal economic reforms in 1991. He told the *New York Times* that out of the 100 members of DICCI, only one was in business before the liberalization. "We are fighting the caste system with capitalism," he declares triumphantly.[4] He might also have declared, given its implicit presence in this story, that "We are fighting patriarchy with capitalism!" For, according to this story, Saroj escaped caste as well as child marriage through capitalist initiative.

In this regard, the bildungsroman of Saroj's life in these news stories is carefully curated to represent capitalism as the route to freedom from caste, gender, and poverty. This story of Freedom Inc. begins in her childhood where she is assailed by the forces of caste and gendered oppression in the form of an abusive child marriage. After her attempted suicide, she reaches an ultimate low point and there is no other place to go but up. She takes control of her own life story and meets each obstacle head-on, finally emerging triumphant as she rides on the cresting wave of free market capitalism, which ultimately delivers her safely to shore. This is a familiar tale, repeated by many other voices in the Indian media who claim that entrepreneurship offers freedom from caste. Within this story,

---

[3] Tarishi Verma, "Meet Kalpana Saroj, Dalit Entrepreneur Who Broke Corporate Hegemony," *The Indian Express*, June 12, 2017.
[4] Milind Kamble in Lydia Polgreen, "Scaling Caste Walls with Capitalism's Ladders in India," *New York Times*, December 21, 2011.

Saroj goes from having no autonomy to absolute autonomy, with the transition only being possible because she embraces entrepreneurship.

Yet this story overlooks the fact that a miniscule percentage of enterprises—9.8 percent—are owned by Dalits even while Dalits constitute 16.14 percent of the Indian population. Moreover, 98 percent of those are small enterprises, with a revenue of only $80 a month.[5] The overwhelming majority of Dalits remain poor and their entrepreneurship is limited to businesses like selling vegetables on a roadside pavement for tiny profits. And given these realities, Saroj's narrative of absolute autonomy should be regarded not as an example of, but an exception to, the contemporary Dalit reality.

This chapter juxtaposes the exceptional story of the female Dalit entrepreneur to the burgeoning literary field of the Dalit life narrative, which insists on the intertwined nature of caste and gender oppression and contests both jointly. I read two memoirs by Dalit women, Shilpa Raj's *The Elephant Chaser's Daughter* (2017) and Yashica Dutt's *Coming Out as Dalit* (2019). Both texts contextualize Dalit women's decisions toward a better life situation by depicting the intertwined caste and gender hierarchies that bind them. These hierarchies form the contextual scaffolding of the story structures, as Charles Taylor would put it, within which their decisions toward liberation are taken. In positing a more nuanced idea of autonomy through this attention to context, these memoirs make use of an older notion of individual freedom grounded in B. R. Ambedkar's legacy of struggle on behalf of Dalits. For Ambedkar, individuals could not be truly free within a fundamentally discriminatory society. He therefore stressed the importance of reforming discriminatory institutional structures until a common good that included Dalits and women could be achieved. To that end, he saw individual freedom as "individuality in and for the common interest," revising other prominent ideas of individual freedom. For example, while J. S. Mill's meditations on liberty defined freedom as a private arena in which the state could not interfere, Ambedkar recognized that the state's interference in "private" matters such as religious patriarchy would be necessary. The state would need to eradicate the constraints that upper castes posed to Dalit, as well as female self-rule, and forcefully institute the mechanisms—such as an integrated education system—that would enable a common interest that was inclusive to all. Dalits who succeeded in penetrating spaces of privilege would face a responsibility toward consolidating a common

---

[5] Kathryn Lum, "Why Are There So Few Dalit Entrepreneurs? The Problem of India's Casted Capitalism," *Conversation*, January 18, 2016.

interest that included Dalits and women by bringing more of their lower-caste brethren into shared spaces. This rethinking of freedom as a contextual universalism—as an idea of universality derived from the particularities of Dalit experience—restores the importance of social context and equal opportunity more fully to the idea of individual freedom, while shifting away from Freedom Inc.'s myopically individualistic focus on liberation from caste through entrepreneurship.

In what follows, I track the continuing power of the discourse of Freedom Inc. for Dalit liberation and suggest that while government bodies in the neoliberal state promote such a notion, various Dalit texts and memoirs interrogate this link. These texts adapt the structure of the coming-of-age tale in the way they follow individual lifespans into adulthood. Yet, even as they do so, these life narratives refuse to follow the logic of the bildungsroman's traditional adaptation narrative. Instead, such Dalit life-writing disrupts the intertwined oppressions of the caste and gender system by taking up Ambedkar's notion that education rather than entrepreneurship is the vehicle through which freedom can be realized for Dalit women. B. R. Ambedkar's idea of individual freedom as "individuality operating in and for the common interest" animates Dalit life-writing's emphasis on education to posit a more nuanced version of autonomy than Freedom Inc.'s myth of absolute autonomy.

## Freedom Inc.: Freeing Dalits from Caste through Entrepreneurship

How do Dalits achieve freedom from caste? For many Dalit leaders, the answer is entrepreneurship. DICCI's tagline for Dalits is: "Be Job Givers—Not Job Seekers," declaring that it exists to "promote entrepreneurship among Dalits as a solution to their socio-economic problems," to "fight caste with capital."[6]

Other scholars have confirmed this vision of freedom from caste through capitalism. Political Science scholar, Devesh Kapur, in *Defying the Odds: The Rise of Dalit Entrepreneurs*, writes that "while markets may not transcend caste, they mitigate its social salience."[7] He elaborates that because of market capitalism, "a dehumanizing social system is slowly but surely giving way" and compares

---

[6] DICCI, "Developing SC/ST Business Leadership," https://dicci.in/about-dicci/ (accessed September 1, 2021).
[7] Devesh Kapur, Chandra Bhan Prasad, and D. Shyam Babu, *Defying the Odds: The Rise of Dalit Entrepreneurs* (New Delhi: Random House, 2014), Location 71.

**Figure 4** Still from the DICCI website showing the organization at an event with PM Modi.

these social changes to those brought about by the introduction of industrial capitalism to nineteenth-century Europe: "Historians are likely to look back and compare the sheer magnitude of these changes to ... the decline of serfdom and feudalism in Europe and Latin America."[8] Kapur's words here implicitly gesture to the end of history narrative, implying that India, stuck in the "waiting room of history," is only just now, due to liberalization, going through the kinds of dramatic progress that Europe went through centuries ago.

Within this conception of freedom as economic liberalization, the individual acts alone within the free market, achieving freedom through self-help and entrepreneurship. Kapur supports this analysis with chapters that each focuses on a different Dalit entrepreneur, detailing their journey from childhood to successful adulthood. Notably, only one of these chapters focuses on a Dalit woman entrepreneur. Of this, the text only notes that "there are regrettably few women entrepreneurs, an illustration of the continued deep gender inequalities in Indian society, including within Dalit communities."[9] Since Kapur equates individual freedom to entrepreneurship, and there are very few Dalit women entrepreneurs, his schema effectively leaves out Dalit women from the quest for freedom entirely.

Kapur's celebration of Dalit male entrepreneurs who have supposedly achieved freedom from caste follows the affirmative bildungsroman's form of the

---

[8] Devesh Kapur, Chandra Bhan Prasad, and D. Shyam Babu, *Defying the Odds*, Location 82.
[9] Kapur et al., *Defying the Odds*, Location 89.

successful adaptation narrative. Within this structure, the individual comes to terms with the society in which they live, achieving success within that society's parameters, and thereby perpetuating its logics. This capacity to adapt to social inequalities by individually transcending them is why Slaughter writes that "the affirmative bildungsroman is a fundamentally conservative genre, confident in the validity of the society it depicts, and anxious to lead both the hero and reader toward a productive place within that world."[10] This affirmation of society is apparent in Kapur's celebration of the Dalit "school of hard knocks," which has the advantage of producing "grit," enabling Dalits to cultivate the drive necessary to succeed in entrepreneurship:

> The experiential school of hard knocks is their true classroom of learning. Indeed, degrees from elite institutions may well make their recipients risk-averse, avoiding the types of occupations or sectors they believe are not "good enough" for them. But for this group, having so little to begin with and the determination to make something of their lives means that they have fewer inhibitions. They are willing to try entrepreneurial opportunities in areas as wide-ranging as trading in wholesale vegetable markets, construction or recycling, where the working conditions are rarely air-conditioned offices in swank office buildings. Indeed, the same is the case with manufacturing, where the heat and dust, labour issues and inspectors, among other factors, have meant that the scions of more privileged social groups lack the stomach to rough it out, leaving these spaces as opportunities for those willing to roll up their sleeves.[11]

In Kapur's analysis, success in entrepreneurship is hard won, achievable only by those who are not arrogant enough to expect comfortable working conditions. Dalits who want freedom from caste must be willing to put up with "heat and dust," and to "rough it out." A Dalit, unlike an upper-caste Indian with social privileges, is more likely to "roll up" his sleeves and achieve something, thereby winning "greater self-confidence and resilience." For Kapur, this process resonates with Ambedkar's perceptive insight that "self-respect is the most vital factor in life. Without it, man is a cipher … It is out of hard and ceaseless struggle alone that one derives strength, confidence and recognition."[12] Moreover, Kapur appreciatively notes, for successful Dalit entrepreneurs, this hard struggle does not produce resentment because

---

[10] Joseph Slaughter, *Human Rights Inc. The World Novel, Narrative Form, and International Law* (Fordham: Fordham University Press, 2007), 180.
[11] Kapur et al., *Defying the Odds*, Location 115.
[12] Kapur et al., *Defying the Odds*, Location 136.

their dreams outweigh their memories. They certainly, occasionally, glance back, but for the most part they are focused on driving forward knowing that one can't drive too far if one is obsessively focused on looking back. While Dalit intellectuals continue to focus on the past to make sense of the present, Dalit entrepreneurs look at the present to create opportunities for new futures … While powerlessness is pervasive, some transcend it, creating agency by prying open the pores and cracks of the Indian "system."[13]

Kapur describes the Dalit path to freedom, then, in terms of individuals not being "obsessively focused" on difficulties, thereby "transcending" caste. The result is that, while his celebration of individual Dalit entrepreneurs is inspiring and captures the hard work that each put into achieving success, he does not examine the constraints that lead to the majority of Dalits failing to realize their ambitions. It seems that within dominant cultural narratives of adaptation like this one, the individual must accept singular responsibility for both his present marginalization and his future assimilation. In Kapur's stories, Dalit entrepreneurs, always male, are solely responsible for their success, which depends on intangible qualities like possessing dreams and the correct attitude.

Isiah Berlin's distinction between positive freedom and negative freedom is illuminating here on what adaptation narratives like Kapur's overlook. For Berlin, positive freedom refers to self-mastery, asking not what we are free from, but what we are free to do in accordance with our own will. Negative freedom, on the other hand, is freedom from interference, the absence of external constraints. Berlin defines negative freedom as "simply the area within which a man can act unobstructed by others. If I am prevented by others from doing what I could otherwise do, I am to that degree unfree; and if this area is contracted by other men beyond a certain minimum, I can be described as being coerced, or, it may be enslaved … coercion implies the deliberate interference of other human beings within the area in which I could otherwise act."[14] Berlin's words here are significant because they point to the ways in which narratives like Kapur's focus on the positive freedom possessed by Dalit entrepreneurs at the expense of recognizing their lack of negative freedom. For focusing on the negative freedom of Dalits would require acknowledging the various constraints that prevent Dalits from achieving self-mastery.

---

[13] Kapur et al., *Defying the Odds*, Location 138.
[14] Isiah Berlin, "Two Concepts of Liberty," in *Four Essays on Liberty* (Oxford: Oxford University Press, 1969), 16.

This book is about those few who, through a combination of grit, ambition, drive and hustle—and some luck—have managed to pull themselves up by their own bootstraps (although the metaphor does not work for many of them who did not have shoes growing up!). These are inspirational stories that are hopefully also aspirational for the millions of young Dalits—and indeed, other poor and socially marginalized groups—who are trying to make something of their lives and who have to navigate between the Scylla of low aspirations that lead to resignation and the Charybdis of unattainable high aspirations that breed frustration and despair when they are not met.[15]

For Kapur, Dalit entrepreneurs succeed because they "pull themselves up by their own bootstraps" without succumbing to "resignation," "frustration," and "despair." There is no focus on the need to reform the various obstacles that prevent millions of others from being free. In talking about the affirmative bildungsroman, Slaughter calls such a framing "the discursive mechanics of hegemony—the means by which a particular group's formulation of common sense comes generally to be taken for granted as the natural and received shape of the world."[16] In this case, that common sense is the hegemonic one of neoliberal capitalism.

How is this version of Freedom Inc., one in which individuals possess the agency to assimilate themselves into hegemonic formulations of common sense, different from other visions of freedom for Dalits? And are these other versions of freedom also unapologetically gendered as male? In the next section, I explore these questions through B. R. Ambedkar's conception of individual freedom as it was harnessed toward the goal of eradicating the intertwined institutions of caste and gender oppression.

## Ambedkar's Idea of Caste and Gender Liberation: Intertwined Freedoms

In recognition of the co-consolidation of caste and gender hierarchies, Ambedkar's focus on reform was always two pronged. This was apparent in his attempt to pass The Hindu Code Bill, which focused on abolishing the practices of Brahminical patriarchy. The bill sought to give women an absolute right over property, eradicate endogamy, give women access to divorce, and relieve women

---

[15] Kapur et al., *Defying the Odds*, Location 157.
[16] Slaughter, *Human Rights Inc.*, 199.

of the threat of polygamy. However, the bill kept getting tabled in the Parliament with promises to address it "at a later point in time." Ambedkar resigned in protest and, in his speech, lamented that

> The Hindu Code was the greatest social reform measure ever undertaken by the legislature in this country. No law passed by the Indian legislature in the past or likely to be passed in the future can be compared to it in point of its significance. To leave inequality between class and class, between sex and sex, which is the soul of Hindu society, untouched and to go on passing legislation relating to economic problems is to make a farce of our Constitution and to build a palace on a dung heap. This is the significance I attached to the Hindu Code. It is for its sake that I stayed on, notwithstanding my differences.[17]

Individual freedom for Ambedkar was linked to eradicating hierarchies between "classes"—here referring to castes—and sexes. Without addressing these deeply intertwined hierarchies, India would only "build a palace on a dung heap."

If caste and gender hierarchies were the social mechanisms that oppressed Dalits, what did freedom look like? Ambedkar answered this question by harnessing various contextual universalisms that he brought into transnational engagement with each other in the context of the Dalit struggle in colonial India. His composite idea of freedom included Enlightenment notions of "liberty, equality, fraternity," through which Ambedkar envisioned the Mahad tank satyagraha[18] as the Dalits' own "Declaration of Independence"; Buddhist notions of equality, articulated through the idea that one's responsibility for oneself was in actuality a responsibility for the entire *sangha* or community; the medieval poet Kabir's *nirguna* concept of equality realized through the insistence that "all of creation" contained the same essence of divinity within; and American Pragmatism's notions of individual freedom as a tool with which to ensure human flourishing. Pragmatism assessed the value of ideas and beliefs in terms of the success of their practical application, and the measure of that success was to be how far they lent themselves to the creation of a democratic society of informed and engaged inquirers who would promote common human interests.[19] To this

---

[17] B. R. Ambedkar, "Dr Ambedkar and the Hindu Code Bill," in Vasant Moon (ed.), *Dr. Babasaheb Ambedkar, Writings and Speeches Vol. 14, Part 2* (Mumbai: Education Department, Government of Maharashtra, 1995), 1325.

[18] The Mahad Satyagraha or Chavdar Tale Satyagraha was a satyagraha, or "movement for truth" led by B. R. Ambedkar on March 20, 1927 to allow untouchables to use water in a public tank in Mahad.

[19] American Pragmatism is a philosophical school that contends that most philosophical topics—such as the nature of knowledge or being—are all viewed and judged in terms of their practical uses and successes. Ambedkar was most influenced by Dewey's version of Pragmatism, within which democracy was the highest form of ethical being, and all propositions were to be judged in terms of their consequences—particularly in terms of their efficacy in advancing democratic forms of life.

**Figure 5** Photograph of a statue of Ambedkar atop a model of the Indian Parliament. Shankar S., https://www.flickr.com/photos/shankaronline/24074287337/in/photostream/.

end, John Dewey defined individual freedom as "individuality in and for the common interest." Dewey was Dr. Ambedkar's intellectual mentor at Columbia University and Dewey's rethinking of individual freedom animated Ambedkar's idea of progress as social justice. Ambedkar's statues all over India point forward in line with this ideal.

I explore the legacy of two of these intertwined Ambedkarite contextual universalisms on Dalit notions of freedom—the Pragmatist idea of individual freedom as "individuality operating in and for the common interest" and the Buddhist notion that one's responsibility for oneself was in actuality a responsibility for the entire *sangha* or community. The first referred to individual freedom as the agency possessed by an individual within a context where one's interests—as a woman and as a Dalit—coincided with the larger common interest of the society as a whole. The individual, within this conception of freedom, was always already embedded in the social. The definition of freedom as "individuality operating in and for the common interest" was essentially an assertion that positive freedom, the capacity to act on one's will, cannot exist without negative freedom, the capacity to "act unobstructed by others." This is because, when balanced toward social justice, positive and negative freedom constitute a society where one's will synergizes with the will of others, producing a common interest that gives free play to everyone's individual agency, including that of women and Dalits. Such a freedom is realized through the availability of a number of different life pathways not just for upper castes or for men but for Dalit women too.

The impossibility of having positive freedom without negative freedom is what Ambedkar meant when he argued, at the Round Table Conference convened by the British prime minister in 1930 to discuss the future of India, that "the constitution may give me certain rights, but I know that 99 percent of the people in India are not going to allow me to exercise those rights. What is the use of those paper rights to me unless the constitution provides that if anyone infringes my rights he is liable to certain penalties?"[20] Ambedkar argues here that when constraints exist and negative freedom is compromised, as in the caste system, positive freedom is rendered impossible. An individual cannot be truly free where one group has "interests of its own which shut it out from full interaction with other groups."[21] In this context, upper caste patriarchies oppressed Dalit women doubly. A Dalit man could never be allowed to have the same common interest as that of an upper-caste man. And a Dalit woman could never be allowed to share the common interest of upper castes or of Dalit men.

To bring about freedom as "individuality in and for the common interest," Ambedkar increasingly came to rely on Dewey's notion of endosmosis, a term used to describe the interaction between different social groups. For Arun Mukherjee, endosmosis "conveys fluidity, channels through which groups and individuals in a democracy are linked and are, so to say, irrigated or suffused with the nutrient of each other's creative intelligence."[22] The concept "provides for the privacy of the individuals but does not enclose them within impermeable walls." A society that contains group identities but insists on their permeability is what produces shared common interests and therefore allows all members of any group to be free. Dewey writes that without a "large variety of shared undertakings and experiences, the influences which educate some into masters,

---

[20] B. R. Ambedkar in "Dr. Ambedkar at the Round Table Conference," in *Dr. Babasaheb Ambedkar's Writings and Speeches, Vol. 2*, Vasant Moon (ed.) (Bombay: Education Department, Government of Maharashtra, 1982), 538.

[21] B. R. Ambedkar, "Annihilation of Caste with a Reply to Mahatma Gandhi," in *Dr. Babasaheb Ambedkar's Writings and Speeches, Vol. 1*, compiled by Vasant Moon (Bombay: Education Department, Government of Maharashtra, [1936] 1979), 52.

[22] Arun P. Mukherjee, "B. R. Ambedkar, John Dewey, and the Meaning of Democracy," *New Literary History*, 40 (2), India and the West (Spring 2009): 352.

educate others into slaves ... a separation into a privileged and a subject class prevents social endosmosis."²³

Ambedkar used Dewey's concept of endosmosis to complain that in India there is no porosity between social groups that would allow the development of a common interest:

> in other countries, there is, at the most, a hyphen between the governing class and the rest. In India, there is a bar between the two. A hyphen is only separation; but a bar is a severance with interests and sympathies completely divided ... the distinction between masters and slaves, between privileged and unprivileged continues hard in substance and fast in colour. On the other hand, where there is social endosmosis, there is a mental assimilation which makes the governing class more flexible, its philosophy less anti-social.²⁴

Ambedkar rued India's lack of endosmosis, lamenting that "caste in India is exclusive and isolated. There is no interaction and no modification of aims and objects. What a caste or a combination of castes regard as 'their own interest' as against other castes remains as sacred and inviolate as ever."²⁵ The result is that "there is no common plane on which the privileged and the subject classes can meet. There is no endosmosis, no give and take of life's hopes and experiences. This separation has caused the educated to become slaves and created the psychological complex which follows from a slave mentality." In the upper castes, on the other hand, "isolation and exclusiveness" creates "the anti-social spirit of a gang."²⁶

As a counterpoint, Ambedkar lays out his social vision of freedom through the development of a common interest in *Annihilation of Caste*:

> In an ideal society there should be many interests consciously communicated and shared. There should be varied and free points of contact with other modes of association. In other words, there must be social endosmosis. This is fraternity, which is only another name for democracy. Democracy is not merely a form of Government. It is primarily a mode of associated living, of conjoint, communicated experience. It is essentially an attitude of respect and reverence towards fellowmen.²⁷

---

[23] John Dewey, *Democracy and Education* (Michigan: University of Michigan Press, 1916), 97–8.
[24] B. R. Ambedkar in "What Congress and Gandhi Have Done to the Untouchables," in *Dr. Babasaheb Ambedkar's Writings and Speeches*, Vasant Moon (ed.) (Bombay: Education Department, Government of Maharashtra, 1979), 232–3.
[25] Ambedkar, "What Congress and Gandhi Have Done," 191–3.
[26] B. R. Ambedkar in *Dr. Babasaheb Ambedkar's Writings and Speeches*, Vasant Moon (ed.) (Bombay: Education Department, Government of Maharashtra, 1991), 285.
[27] B. R. Ambedkar, "Annihilation of Caste with a Reply to Mahatma Gandhi (1936)," in *Dr. Babasaheb Ambedkar's Writings and Speeches*, Vol. 1, compiled by Vasant Moon (Bombay: Education Department, Government of Maharashtra, 1979), 57.

Democracy itself is only possible in a society with endosmosis because individual freedom, without which democracy cannot exist, is only realized where there is fraternity, associated living, and the common interests that flow from that conjoint, communicated experience. In other words, democracy and individual freedom only exist when each individual's will is realized in and through the common interest of the social whole, producing a magnificent concert between positive and negative freedom. This idea, within which Dalit liberation is only achievable by reforming the social fabric in which individuality is performed, is a far cry from DICCI's account of Freedom Inc.: of individual freedom as isolated self-reliance and absolute autonomy on the part of special men.

For Ambedkar, education was one of the central keys to endosmosis and therefore to achieving freedom as "individuality in and for the common interest."[28] This conviction was reflected in his founding of the People's Education Society in 1945 as well as of multiple educational institutions for lower castes. Ambedkar's commitment to education as a vehicle toward freedom was also apparent in his enshrining of the right to a free education within the Indian constitution. For Ambedkar, women would be the subjects and vehicles of this pursuit of an integrated education because their well-being would lead to the well-being of their children and therefore to that of the whole Dalit community. In an address to the All-India Depressed Classes Women's Conference, Ambedkar thus told women not to marry off their daughters. Instead, he enjoined: "Give education to your children. Instill ambition in them." Education would lead to a removal of the Dalit "*nuangand* (inferiority complex) which has stunted their growth and made them slaves to others, to create in them the *jaaniv* (understanding) of the significance of their lives for themselves and for the country, of which they have been cruelly robbed by the existing social order. Nothing can achieve this except the spread of higher education."[29] In the absence of the reform of upper-caste patriarchy from above, Dalit women would have to work to realize their self-will, their positive freedom, from below. Education would enable them to realize this freedom.

Yet education was also to be a vehicle for negative freedom because Ambedkar's Pragmatist notion of achieving "individuality in and for the

---

[28] Ambedkar's focus on education is also not surprising given its unusual prominence in his family life. His grandfather and father were associated with the military of the East India Company government, which made education compulsory for its soldiers. While children studied in the day, adults studied at night schools. The Mahar platoon had its own school and Ambedkar's father was a headmaster there for fourteen years. All of the women and children in his family could read. Using the tool of education, they sought to fashion the new Dalit *stree–purush* into full human beings.

[29] B. R. Ambedkar quoted in *Janata*, September 15 and 22, 1951.

common interest" was married to the Buddhist ideal that one's responsibility for oneself was in actuality a responsibility for the entire *sangha* or community. For when a Buddhist entered the *sangha* "he became one with the rest like rivers entering the water of the ocean."[30] Ambedkar conceptualized *navayana* Buddhism as a process of recognizing that one's own spiritual and worldly practice was for the benefit of everyone, because "ultimately self-and-other are not two." This meant that while working to realize their own self-will, individual Dalits would also use their education to eradicate the constraints to freedom experienced by other members of the community. This is why Ambedkar constantly asked: "Are the educated helping with the progress of the community?"[31] He worried that educated Dalits had become selfish after availing themselves of education and employment opportunities, and had forgotten about the efforts of others that had made their education possible. During his speech at the Bombay Presidency Depressed Classes Youth Conference, held on February 12, 1938, he declared: "education is like a sword, and being a double edged weapon it is dangerous to wield ... an educated person without *sheel* (moral character) and *saujanya* (humility) is more dangerous than a beast."[32] In actively working to remove constraints from the environments of other Dalits, educated Dalits had a moral responsibility to steer their freed wills toward the creation of a society ruled by a common interest, which by definition would include everyone.

Ambedkar's intertwining of these various contextual universalisms produced a vision of freedom that remains aspirational in post-1990s India, more than seventy years after he was writing. In what follows, I analyze the documentary *Daughters of Destiny* (2017), about girls at a Dalit school called Shanti Bhavan (Abode of Peace), alongside two Dalit life narratives: Shilpa Raj's memoir, *The Elephant Chaser's Daughter* (2017), written by a Dalit schoolgirl who attended Shanti Bhavan, and Yashica Dutt's *Coming Out as Dalit* (2019), written by a Dalit journalist who recounts her experiences attending elite Indian institutions where Dalits are sidelined and marginalized. Each of these texts points out the absence of negative freedom that defines Dalit lives alongside a wish to fix this lack by creating a society where one bears a responsibility for the well-being of the entire *sangha*, thereby achieving a society defined by the common interest. In doing so, these texts show that Ambedkar's universalizing legacy of freedom remains alive and well.

---

[30] B. R. Ambedkar, *The Buddha and His Dhamma*, annotated and edited by Aakash Singh Rathore and Ajay Verma (New Delhi: Oxford University Press, 2011), 222–3.
[31] B. R. Ambedkar quoted in *Janata*, July 26, 1952.
[32] B. R. Ambedkar quoted in *Janata*, February 26, 1938.

## Freedom in Context: *Daughters of Destiny*, *The Elephant Chaser's Daughter*, and *Coming Out as Dalit*

*Daughters of Destiny* is a celebration of a pioneering school for Dalit children, focusing on the lives of Dalit girls. The school, Shanti Bhavan, was founded in 1997 in Bangalore by the Indian-American businessman Abraham George. It is a boarding school that accepts twenty-four preschool students a year and provides free education, food, and housing through twelfth grade. Because of the scope of its responsibilities toward its pupils, Shanti Bhavan can only take one child from a single Dalit family. It is both an educational institution and a social experiment: a demonstration that Dalits can thrive academically when given the right resources, and an attempt to pull Dalits out of poverty by preparing children for jobs that can support their extended families and communities. *Daughters of Destiny*, which the writer and director Vanessa Roth shot over the course of seven years, follows five girls of different ages—one who enters as a four-year-old, and others who are already graduating and embarking on jobs. Roth returns to them over the years, observing and interviewing these young women as they aim for financially beneficial careers.

Shanti Bhavan's mission is realizing the individual freedom of its students through an educational vision that is very close to Ambedkar's, for the school nurtures its students with a long-term view toward creating a society defined by a common interest, and doing so through an awareness that one's responsibility to oneself is actually the responsibility for the well-being of the entire *sangha*. Shanti Bhavan thus strives to achieve a common interest by preparing its Dalit students to pull up their Dalit family members rather than perpetuating the separate spheres common to a hierarchical society. According to the school's website, 97 percent of alumni are employed full-time and give 20 to 50 percent of their salaries to their families and villages.

Shilpa Raj is a student at Shanti Bhavan and one of the subjects of *Daughters of Destiny*. She is also the writer of a memoir, *The Elephant Chaser's Daughter*, about her experiences there. Raj's memoir enshrines Ambedkar's idea of individual freedom as it is worked out through the span of one life—that of a Dalit girl child. The memoir provides the text for some of the documentary's voiceover commentary and covers a lot of new information not included in the documentary about her life story as it winds in and out of Shanti Bhavan. We learn that Raj's parents' home is in the village of Thattaguppe, Karnataka. Her father is an elephant chaser, employed by the government to help protect the villagers from the elephants who wander in from the surrounding forests, hoping to eat the sugarcane planted on the forest edge. It is a dangerous and tenuous job but better than his previous pastime of illegally brewing and selling liquor, which led to police raids, arrests, and bribes needing to be paid. Other Dalit villagers work for upper-caste landowners as farmworkers or domestics. They are illiterate and live in constant debt, grappling with high levels of alcoholism and domestic violence. Shilpa's sister, Kavya, is a victim of this violence—she falls into the company of two hoodlums from the village, who stalk her, seduce her, and then run away with her. She is found dead a few months later.

This was the kind of life that Shilpa had to look forward to until the appearance of a Blue Jeep in 1997, which was sent into the village from Shanti Bhavan to select children for admission. Shilpa recounts how her father insisted that Shilpa be tested as a candidate, seeing her as a ticket out of generations of cyclical poverty. Indeed, in this wish, he shared in Dr. George's Ambedkarite aspirations for the school and its children. In line with this vision, Shilpa expresses an idea of individual freedom as "individuality operating in and for the common interest." She does so by recounting the lack of negative freedom that hurts her family members, producing caste and gender constraints that even lead to her sister's death. And she tries her best to live so as to uplift the *sangha*, harnessing her own individuality toward the creation of a common interest that could mitigate some of those constraints.

*Daughters of Destiny* and *The Elephant Chaser's Daughter* take the bildungsroman as a structural guide for their form and content. However, unlike the affirmative bildungsroman, the form of these texts is modified to express Dalit women's dissatisfactions with the social order and marked by the quest for a common interest that includes Dalit women. Here I take a cue from Debjani Ganguly, who points out that Dalit life narratives are often productively read as variations of the bildungsroman because both genres involve the journey of a protagonist from childhood to maturity, encountering in the process many hurdles and setbacks amidst an often intractable social ethos.[33] Ganguly invokes what Franco Moretti calls the capaciousness of the bildungsroman, their capacity to provide, in a functional rather than strictly formal sense, a measure for all narratives of individual development and modern subject formation. "Even those novels that clearly are not

---

[33] Debjani Ganguly, "Dalit Life Stories," in *The Cambridge Companion to Modern Indian Culture* (Cambridge: Cambridge University Press, 2012), 148.

bildungsroman or novels of formation," writes Moretti, are perceived by us against this conceptual horizon of individual development in relation to a larger social world "so that we speak of 'failed initiation' or of a 'problematic formation.'"[34] Similarly, Ganguly claims a functional equivalence between Dalit life narratives and the bildungsroman because "like the novel in the bourgeois public sphere of 19th century England, contemporary Dalit life narratives play a critical role in enabling ex-untouchable castes to imagine a coherent community of oppressed individuals, formed in the hellfire of caste persecution, and emerging, in the process, as 'persons' in their own right."[35] This narration of her journey toward becoming a "person in her own right" is why Shilpa Raj claims, by the end of her memoir, that "the word untouchable will have no meaning for me."[36]

I speak earlier in the text of a modified bildungsroman also because, as Ganguly points out, Dalit life stories are not simply successful adaptation narratives, with the individual coming to terms with the society in which they live. Rather, they come closer to Slaughter's notion of the "dissensual bildungsroman." The latter both affirms the egalitarian imaginary of a democratic society and exposes the disparities and paradoxes that prevent some from partaking of that imaginary. It does so by "placing an ambivalent double-edged marginality at the center of the field of bildungsroman possibilities."[37] This marginality is double edged because it "neither accepts the grossly compromised terms of enfranchisement nor rejects them outright; instead, it holds onto the ideal of harmonious integration even as it narrates the unfulfillment of the promises of human rights and idealist bildung."[38] The term "dissensual" comes from Jacques Ranciere's account of political dissensus after the French Revolution, in which French women were "subjects that did not have the rights that they had."[39] Slaughter calls this a "double-demonstration ... that protests the protagonist's exclusion from the public realm of rights, yet articulates this protest within the normative genre of the rights claim."[40] As Judith Butler has written, "one with no authorization to

---

[34] Franco Moretti, *The Way of the World: The Bildungsroman in European Culture*, trans. Albert Sbragia (London: Verso, 2000), 15.
[35] Ganguly, "Dalit Life Stories," 149.
[36] Shilpa Raj, *The Elephant Chaser's Daughter* (CreateSpace Independent Publishing Platform, 2017), 230.
[37] Slaughter, *Human Rights, Inc.*, 181–2.
[38] Slaughter, *Human Rights, Inc.*, 181.
[39] Ranciere quoted in Slaughter, *Human Rights, Inc.*, 181.
[40] Slaughter, *Human Rights, Inc.*, 181.

speak within and as the universal nonetheless lays claim to its terms" in order to "demand that the universal ought to be inclusive of them."[41]

The dissensual bildungsroman is interesting to me in the context of Dalit women's life-narratives because as a literary form it performs Ambedkarite notions of individual freedom as individuality operating in and for the common interest. In laying claim to rights, the Dalit woman writer engages in an exercise of positive freedom that asserts her entitlement to act in accordance with her individual will. However, in narrating the countless obstacles to realizing that individuality, the Dalit woman also simultaneously points out her lack of negative freedom by representing the ways that this will is denied her. She thereby points to the necessity of a society governed in and for the common interest so that her individual will, and those of her family and community, is realizable. Shilpa Raj's complaint about being left out of one's rights, voiced in the language of rights, is a dissensual exercise in building "individuality in and for the common interest," marrying positive and negative freedom by recognizing the ways that Dalit women's contexts constrain their wills.

This double-edged marginality—the simultaneous possession of and dispossession from universal rights—is symbolically represented by the way that the lives of girls at Shanti Bhavan straddle two spheres. The first is the world of their school where they are taught that they are the subjects of universal rights and where, as Shilpa notes, "everyone is created equal."[42] She writes that "the upbringing I had in Shanti Bhavan brought me self-confidence and self-worth … I will not entertain the thought that I am intrinsically inferior to anyone else."[43] This is a rights claim that allows her to overcome her family's insistence that she marry her uncle. The second sphere that students like Shilpa occupy is the world of their villages, in which they encounter domestic and sexual violence steeped in Brahminical patriarchy. Rights are nonexistent here. The tension between the two spheres is illustrated in Raj's recounting of caste discrimination during a vacation from Shanti Bhavan. When she enters the home of a high-caste landlord with her father, he tells her, "We can't enter the kitchen." Shilpa realizes that his hesitation stems from his knowledge that lower castes are not allowed in upper-caste spaces. Yet Shilpa ignores his warning because "courage stemmed from what I had learnt at school—that everyone is created equal."[44] The

---

[41] Judith Butler, "Sovereign Performatives in the Contemporary Scene of Utterance," *Critical Inquiry* 23 (Winter 1997): 368.
[42] Raj, *The Elephant Chaser's Daughter*, 227.
[43] Raj, *The Elephant Chaser's Daughter*, 227.
[44] Raj, *The Elephant Chaser's Daughter*, 227.

language of rights allows Shilpa to transcend caste discrimination even as she is subjected to it, resulting in the dissensual tension that Slaughter speaks of.

Raj's memoir harnesses this dissensual tension in its affirmation of the universal rights claim even as it simultaneously points to its failures of implementation. The tension is illuminated particularly through the figure of her sister, Kavya. Dwelling on Kavya's tragically short life allows Shilpa to claim her own rights and her positive freedom while pointing out that her community is denied them. Shilpa, shielded by Shanti Bhavan, enjoys negative freedom from caste and gender constraints. Kavya, on the other hand, is continuously deprived of the right to act on her own will because she lacks negative freedom; her life is formed in and through caste and gender constraints in a world where a common interest between her and upper castes, or between her and other Dalit men, is impossible.

Kavya thus acts as a foil to Shilpa, for she represents what would become of a will to freedom without the accompanying absence of gender and caste constraints. Shilpa is careful to establish Kavya's will to freedom early in the narrative, telling the reader that her sister had positive freedom of "her own making": she "was truly free in the village, not because she was given any freedom by our parents, but by her own making. Even as a child she would wander about like a gypsy, and you wouldn't know whether she was with friends or strangers. But she carried herself with an air of utter confidence, keeping any inner fears to herself."[45] Despite this will to freedom, Kavya meets a tragic end because of her lack of negative freedom. She does not receive the same opportunities as Shilpa, a fate that Shilpa calls "karma," "the fate that is written on one's forehead," because it is one that seems inescapable. Speaking of Kavya's murder/suicide at the hands of two village goons who, it is implied, sexually harass her, Shilpa writes:

> Kavya had met her karma and, for some unknown reason, I had been spared the misfortune of my sister. My feet turned numb. I tried to stand up but my legs felt weak. Sitting down again, I stretched my legs but my body was stiff with anxiety. It felt strange that I had survived this far. The odds were stacked against me and yet my path had been a charmed one until now. There was nothing I had done to deserve it. I couldn't explain fate having taken me in a different direction. It all began one day when I was four years old and a blue jeep pulled into my village.[46]

---

[45] Raj, *The Elephant Chaser's Daughter*, 5.
[46] Raj, *The Elephant Chaser's Daughter*, 9.

Shanti Bhavan's blue jeep represents a freedom from the "karma," or the constraints, that Kavya dies of. Realizing this, Shilpa asks fearfully: "Could I be destined to a life of hardship and indignity for no fault of mine?" before realizing that Shanti Bhavan precludes such an end for her. "The culmination of my schooling brought me hope. Standing in the middle of the pathway that day, I knew I had been given much to prepare me for the outside world and I felt confident that my future would be what I would make of it. For the first time, I felt I was in control of my life."[47] Shilpa's schooling allows her an environment in which she can have both positive and negative freedom, which render her "in control of my life." Meanwhile Kavya, like millions of other Dalit girls, does not have any control over her circumstances and her life trajectory. Significantly, Kavya's is not the story of one individual. Shilpa notes that:

> The hardships Kavya faced in her short life, and her sudden death, are not uncommon. There are millions of girls like her among the lower castes—butterflies without wings—growing up in families troubled by domestic violence and danger ... there is no escape for them. Women in these families have little or no control over their destinies; they suffer innumerable cruelties and lead lives regulated strictly by men. This way of life is not something I am prepared to accept as a natural order. Kavya's short life was like the intertwining patterns of rangoli she taught me to draw upon the sand, and now she had vanished into the earth. The thought that she could have gone to college, become a teacher or a doctor, travelled the world, and fallen in love with a man who would be a caring partner to her, if only she had had the opportunity I received, added to my crushing guilt and sadness.[48]

Shilpa's words about Kavya point to the interchangeability of her sister's fate with countless other individuals who suffer similarly, and also with others who live more charmed lives. In pointing out this wasted potential, Shilpa also suggests that ensuring negative freedom—which amounts to "opportunity"—is key to realizing a common interest where the individuality of millions of girls like Kavya is allowed to find its way. *Daughters of Destiny* and *The Elephant Chaser's Daughter* both approach the problem of Dalit freedom by highlighting how Shanti Bhavan removes the various constraints that Dalit girls face, thereby allowing them to act on their own wills and to live a life where their individual interest is accounted for within the larger common interest.

---

[47] Raj, *The Elephant Chaser's Daughter*, 240.
[48] Raj, *The Elephant Chaser's Daughter*, 247.

**Figure 6** Shilpa talks about her sister Kavya in *Daughters of Destiny*, Season 1, Episode 3.

The creation of a society where "individuality in and for the common interest" prevails, Raj argues, is only possible if, following Ambedkar, one takes on responsibility for the entire *sangha* or community. Ambedkar married both these contextual universalisms because they were deeply related. And Raj's memoir as well as *Daughters of Destiny* focus on the way that Shanti Bhavan encourages its students not only to work for their own freedom but also to eradicate the various constraints faced by their Dalit communities, through financial and other kinds of support. This means, as one of the Shanti Bhavan teachers puts it, that

> Shanti Bhavan children have a mission. That's how they're different from every other child. Their mission is very clear cut: they have to uplift their families. They have to bring education to as many children as possible, which we hope will be a hundred in their lifetime and they have to uplift their caste, community and their village.[49]

Dr. George adds that his students, and the school as a whole, exist toward one common purpose—the eradication of the caste system: "One thousand years of suffering must now end finally. That's why we run Shanti Bhavan." Like Ambedkar, Dr. George rues those educated Dalits who do nothing for their community, insisting that Shanti Bhavan seeks to "create a solid value system" defined by a priority to uplift other Dalits so that they may raise yet more Dalits from their communities.

---

[49] Vanessa Roth, *Daughters of Destiny*, Cause and Effect Media, 2017.

As Dr. George puts it, "I want them to recognize that they were beneficiaries of other people's generosity, or kindness or help. And they cannot walk away from helping someone else."[50] Raj's memoir internalizes this mission, which is apparent in her recounting of Dr. George's graduation day speech at Shanti Bhavan:

> "'You will transform your families in many ways, bring comfort and dignity to their lives, and offer them choices they have never had,' he said."[51]

Dr. George here aims to offer Dalits a version of individual freedom defined and actualized through a variety of life choices and opportunities not just for his pupils but for the entire communities from which they come. Shilpa Raj takes this message to heart, telling her readers:

> For my part, I am determined to help my family, community, and anyone else who is in need. Having experienced the kindness and generosity of strangers all through my life, I firmly believe my obligations to society reach well beyond my blood family … . I was now to be the architect of my future with the knowledge and confidence to free my family from the bondage of poverty. I was free to follow a road my ancestors never even set foot on, redirecting our assumed fate like a large boulder in the middle of a river, diverting its flow.[52]

Shilpa's words speak to her recognition of her own positive freedom. She calls herself an "architect" who is "free" to choose her own path but, significantly, this "freedom" is inseparable from the achievement of negative freedom for all those around her, compelling her to harness her own individuality toward the common interest. Just like Ambedkar, whose Buddhism spoke of the individual becoming "one with the rest like rivers entering the ocean," Shilpa conceptualizes herself as an individual who must work towards creating a common ocean of humanity constituted by the inclusion of each individual river. After graduating, she thus aspires to be the "large boulder" that ensures that each individual river in her community does not become a lone tributary flowing in the wrong direction, but rather a manifestation and confirmation of the ocean of a common interest. This marriage of Ambedkar's Pragmatist notion of individual freedom with his Buddhist notion of one's responsibility to the community means that Shilpa's "knowledge and confidence" will lead to not only her own freedom but also that of her community.

*Daughters of Destiny* shows that Shilpa is not an exception in its representation of the way that other pupils define individual freedom. Like

---

[50] Roth, *Daughters of Destiny*.
[51] Raj, *The Elephant Chaser's Daughter*, 235.
[52] Raj, *The Elephant Chaser's Daughter*, 230.

Shilpa, Kartika shares in Dr. George's aspirations of building a society marked by a common interest that includes Dalits. Kartika is the daughter of a bonded laborer on a quarry, who carries heavy loads of stone for a living. Her mother and siblings live in a tiny mud hut covered with tarp at the edge of the quarry. Kartika aims to become a human rights lawyer so that she can alleviate the hardships that her own family, and others like them, face. Sitting in her law classes, Kartika reacts with horror when she hears of a case involving a farmer who had his tongue cut off for asking for better wages and living conditions. The camera zooms into her face as she describes her feelings:

> Immediately I thought: that could have been my mom, my brother. I was very fascinated with the lawyer who came over because he had the power to help him. And that is how I became interested in law. I can help bring about equality. My heart says that I want to do human rights related work and just work for people who are being discriminated against and who don't have the power to represent themselves.[53]

Another student, Manjula, acknowledges how much easier it is to simply stop thinking about her family and their troubles, but also recognizes her responsibility to take on the burden of helping them: "When I was younger I was really afraid about my mom and about all her problems … [I thought] why is she telling me all her problems? I don't want to be burdened by all this. But now I understand that it is essential for me to be burdened by this." Manjula elaborates: "Dr. George is constantly helping us, trying to move us into the right path. I realize that this is my set course and I can't vary from it."[54]

These last words point to a potential conflict between the individual freedom of Shanti Bhavan students and their quest to achieve that freedom for all members of their communities. Even as Manjula has been given the means to act according to her individual will, she must use that will to work for her community, not varying from that "set course," words that continue Ambedkar's river metaphor to suggest a lack of free choice rather than an abundance of it. In the introduction, I suggested that one of the metrics through which individual freedom should be measured is according to whether an individual acts in an environment that offers a rich array of choices for self-actualization and flourishing. At first, Manjula's words would suggest that, according to this metric, Shanti Bhavan has constrained her rather than freed her. However, read alongside Shilpa Raj's story of self-becoming as it is juxtaposed with Kavya's stunted life, it becomes clear

---

[53] Roth, *Daughters of Destiny*.
[54] Roth, *Daughters of Destiny*.

that the students of Shanti Bhavan have many more opportunities for flourishing available to them than they would if the school did not exist. This, by itself, does not validate Dr. George's Ambedkarite philosophy of individual freedom. Rather, what makes Shanti Bhavan's ethos a sustainable form of individual freedom, as I note in my introduction, is that it acknowledges the ways that an individual is co-constituted through her relationships and circumstances within a community and cultural context. Dr. George's Ambedkarite approach to raising autonomous individuals is built on the knowledge that because the individual does not exist independently of her community, an action's autonomy arises out of a process of engaging with and reflecting on these grounds.

*Daughters of Destiny* juxtaposes these conflicting ideas of individual freedom in its depiction of a Shanti Bhavan pupil, Preetha, who perceives herself as an individual in opposition to the community that has produced her. Unlike Dr. George, Preetha does not recognize a continuity between achieving individual success and creating a society where her family members and village community can do so too. The film is careful to provide a nuanced picture of Preetha's situation, showing that Ambedkar's vision of freedom puts tremendous pressure on some Shanti Bhavan students. This is the central drama of *Daughters of Destiny*, one that is apparent in the documentary's juxtaposition of the Ambedkarite vision of individual freedom possessed by Dr. George, and that possessed by some of his Dalit students, including Preetha.

Preetha's idea of a free life as a musician is often irreconcilable with the vision of working toward the common interest. Dr. George discourages her from pursuing her musical dreams because such an interest will most likely not lead to a lucrative career path that would enable her to help others:

> When I told Dr. George that I'm not interested in studying economics, history or political science he said it will give you good job opportunities. Go ahead and do it. We have to do what Dr. George tells us to do, because we know that we can't pay for our college education, and I really wanted to go to college, at least get a degree. I still don't feel that freedom. I can't do what I want to do cause of the power he has over us ... I am very very fond of Dr. George. But as I grow up, I don't like the control and I don't like that he tells me what to do all the time.[55]

Preetha's words speak to the way that Dr. George's aspirations on her behalf, which cohere with his aspirations for her whole downtrodden community, act as constraints, resulting in her not being able to "feel that freedom." She feels that she

---

[55] Roth, *Daughters of Destiny*.

cannot act on her will, her positive freedom, because she feels stifled by Dr. George and therefore looks forward to graduating and moving away from Shanti Bhavan:

> When I was in tenth grade I used to wait to graduate and get out of the clutches of Shanti Bhavan. Dr. George had a lot of control over us, like, every single thing that we did. It's like: everything's wrong. It used to be so frustrating. Dr. George doesn't know this but now I feel that if I want to be a musician or singer it'll be a little easier. Because in Bangalore I see a lot of people interested in doing that and they invite you. Saying, come just try this. This can be, like, maybe a start for my singing career.[56]

Preetha does not experience freedom as "individuality in and for the common interest" because she wishes for an autonomy that is unconstrained by a concern for others, that is limited to what Ambedkar would label her own "selfish" interests. In this respect, Shanti Bhavan's Ambedkarite ethos is in conflict with what Preetha, and a dominant strand of post-liberalization Indian culture, considers individual freedom. This latter discourse of Freedom Inc. speaks of an autonomy separated from the context within which a Dalit girl like Preetha acquires that autonomy in the first place. This context free autonomy is reflected in her college counselor's words "Can you just do what you want to do? Because at the end of the day you need to be happy more than anybody else for that matter." Individual freedom here is a purely individual concern, ignoring the way that individuality is only realizable within one's contexts and communities. Shanti Bhavan's Ambedkarite vision of individual freedom, meanwhile, marries the aims of the individual to the transformation of an entire society. It aims to do this through endosmosis; after Shanti Bhavan, these children are expected to have the prowess to live and succeed in upper-caste worlds, and to turn these worlds into places that are no longer upper caste, that are instead marked by the common good. That this may be too idealistic a vision is also suggested in Yashica Dutt's memoir, *Coming Out as Dalit*.

In *Coming Out as Dalit*, Dutt weaves a narrative of her own personal experiences as a Dalit in Indian education, right from school to higher education. She also employs the techniques of the dissensual bildungsroman, affirming her own claim to rights while showing how she is systemically denied them when she "comes out as Dalit." The educational institutions she attends are very different from Shanti Bhavan, for rather than functioning as vehicles of endosmosis, they are impermeable walls within which Dalits can only fit by pretending that they

---

[56] Roth, *Daughters of Destiny*.

are not Dalit. In *Coming Out as Dalit*, "passing" as upper caste is a practice that serves as a reminder of the way that rights that claim to be universal are in fact not. The act of passing is a metaphor for the denial of rights to Dalits and is thus not a radical act. Pretending to be upper caste to lay claim to rights upholds the very hierarchies that deny those rights to other Dalits. It achieves the opposite of realizing Ambedkar's vision of freedom as "individuality operating in and for the common interest," and of the Buddhist notion of one's responsibility for the self as being one's responsibility for the entire *sangha*.

Thus Yashica expresses her own shame at "passing" and admires Rohith Vemula for staying true to Ambedkar's vision and of bravely laying claim to his Dalit identity due to his belief in caste equality. Vemula was a Dalit who suffered caste-based persecution at Hyderabad University, which led to him committing suicide:

> When news of his suicide broke in the mainstream media in January 2016, my own Dalit identity was deeply buried beneath layers of convent education, urban upbringing and a hardened resolve to avoid engaging with anything related to caste … We had many things in common, but one very vital thing was different. Unlike me, Rohith did nothing to bury his Dalitness. Instead, he used it as a shield to stand up for his fellow Dalit students in Hyderabad University against the caste based prejudice of members of the administration.[57]

Yashica's memoir is penance for passing, penance for laying claim to rights given to upper castes while not working to expand those rights to other Dalits. Her act of writing is an act of "coming out as Dalit," of claiming her Dalitness just as Rohith did:

> After I came out as Dalit, I no longer had anything to hide. Everything about my life was connected to a larger narrative. Everything that I had done so far or that had happened to me was somehow related to my caste. But I didn't want to tell just my story. I also wanted to tell the stories of all those Dalits that the media and society at large had ignored. Through their accounts and by making sense of my own life, I have tried to piece together a larger picture of what casteism looks like today.[58]

These words point to Yashica's recognition that "coming out as Dalit" means that she is finally free, for her individual will has now been harnessed for her community, for a common interest. Her life story, now representative of the trials and tribulations faced by other Dalits, works toward recognizing and

---

[57] Yashica Dutt, *Coming Out as Dalit* (New Delhi: Aleph Book Company, 2019), xiv–xv.
[58] Dutt, *Coming Out as Dalit*, ix.

eradicating the constraints that other Dalits face, thereby going some way toward realizing the common interest that Ambedkar wished for. The memoir narrates how Yashica "comes out" so as to exist as a Dalit in *savarna* spaces, thereby claiming endosmosis through her memoir and clearing the way for other Dalits to do so as well. In this sense, her dissensual memoir also refuses the adaptation narratives of the affirmative bildungsroman, for rather than adapting to a caste-based social world, her existence within it as an out and proud Dalit troubles that world and reveals its murky edges, its pretensions toward equality and freedom. Like other dissensual bildungsromane, her story affirms these rights only to show that Dalits like her have been left out of them.

These examples of Dalit life-writing all harness Ambedkar's legacy of marrying multiple disparate yet like-minded contextual universalisms in the service of freedom. In contrast to Freedom Inc., which leaves out Dalit women almost completely, Ambedkar's notion of freedom as "individuality in and for the common interest" addresses itself to Dalit women as achievable through educational endosmosis. Each of these texts insists on achieving individual rights through a focus on collective rights for its female subjects. These memoirs thus adopt the structure of a coming-of-age tale in the way they follow individual children's life spans into adulthood. But, rather than depicting adult children who have been groomed to make their way in one world, comfortable within its hierarchies, they point to the way that these children exist uneasily at the borders of many worlds and are primed to transform the structures that create that uneasiness. These memoirs testify to the possibility that even if my mother-in-law's Brahmin friends continue to cook at home to avoid contamination, their son may have to cook and eat with Dalit women at colleges like St Stephens, and work with them as colleagues. By modulating and disrupting the affirmative bildungsroman's uneasy contract between the individual and the society, these stories lend new depth and life to Ambedkar's legacy of Dalit freedom.

This chapter has charted how Freedom Inc.'s discourse of entrepreneurial empowerment fails to live up to its promise for most Dalit women, who consequently turn to other ontologies of individual freedom for sustenance. But in Chapter 3, I consider how Freedom Inc. *does* hold sway among underemployed young men, and among women of the middle and upper classes, through a love for self-help books. In yet another instantiation of gendered capitalism, the genre of self-help crafts dominant masculinities molded by Freedom Inc. but, through literary fiction, also destabilizes them by pointing to other more expansive iterations of individual freedom; the genre encodes patriarchal behaviors but also holds out ways of realizing agency for those who possess little of it.

3

# Underemployed Young Men and the Quest for Freedom in the Self-Help Novel

Shortly after getting married in Bombay, my husband and I traveled to Bangalore to visit his parents. Every morning I would find my mother-in-law armed with a pencil and a self-help book. By 8 a.m. she would prepare a steaming kettle of water and multiple tea bags and sit at the head of the large glass dining table. Then she would read continuously for three hours as she sipped her tea, getting up every now and then to tinker with something in her bedroom or kitchen. Her favorite titles included popular classic American self-help books like Napoleon Hill's *Think and Grow Rich*, George Samuel Clason's *The Richest Man of Babylon*, Susan Jeffers's *Feel the Fear and Do It Anyway*, Brian Tracy's *Eat That Frog*, and Dale Carnegie's *How to Win Friends and Influence People*, but also non-American titles like Don Miguel Ruiz's *The Four Agreements*.

My mother-in-law was thrilled that I too was a reader but didn't quite understand why I mostly chose to lose myself in novels. And I didn't understand what she got from her self-help books. She was a strong character when I got to know her, disciplined, organized, and always possessed with a plan for herself (and for everyone around her too!). In short, she seemed to be the last person in need of self-help. But her penchant for self-help began to make more sense when my husband began to tell me her life story. She hadn't always been a confident self-possessed individual. She had been married off through an arranged marriage at the age of eighteen to a man she didn't know. Her husband was the third son of a wealthy businessman. Branches of her father-in-law's famous biscuit factories spanned the subcontinent, making the family name a household one. She found herself part of a large extended family with a whole host of domestic rules and gendered expectations of a young wife. Her husband was kindhearted and loving but also rule driven and a micro-manager. Not yet sure who she was herself, she found herself stifled and weighed down by a constricting hierarchical family ethos. After the death of her father-in-law who had neglected to leave a will, a family feud over the sizable inheritance began, and she and her husband were forced to leave home and fend for themselves. That was when she began to read self-help and to join self-help personality development courses, which she credits with turning her into the strong-willed, financially independent woman she is today. She achieved that financial independence by wisely investing her husband's precarious small business earnings into Bangalore's real-estate boom of the 1990s. She used the business management skills she was reading about and adopted the determined masculine assertiveness that the self-help books taught.

My mother-in-law's successful and single-minded self-transformation is why she would be astonished that self-help is an increasingly discredited genre among cultural critics, who argue that it reduces the self to an easily marketable brand, primed for maximum revenue generation, and that it is individualist to a fault. The freedom offered by self-help, according to these critics, is an illusion, for it relies on the myth of absolute autonomy, conceiving of the individual as completely independent of the social relations and ties that produce her choices.[1] The illusion works by obscuring structural and cultural constraints to individual agency such as, for instance, the limitations produced by patriarchy. While these criticisms are important, they exist alongside my mother-in-law's use of self-help as a tool of genuine empowerment. In response, my mother-in-law would say that self-help's deliberate ignoring of social ties and constraints was exactly the model of freedom that a woman like her needed. I can hear her voice as I write this, asking: how can one simply discount the struggle, guided by self-help, that she went through? What about the fact that turning herself, her husband, and her three boys into independent revenue streams was exactly what she needed to do to survive?!

I begin with this story to capture the contested terrain that the genre of self-help, and the notions of masculine freedom that it pedals, inhabits in India today. It is indeed the case, as I will show, that individual freedom has been reinterpreted in contemporary South Asia to mean the ability to be anyone, and that this transformational self-making is carried out with the end of generating a profit. It is also true that the genre of self-help has accompanied and reinforced this shift in the meaning of freedom. Yet the literary critic Beth Blum would not be surprised by my mother in-law's turn to self-help during

---

[1] See for instance Daniel Nehring, Emmanuel Alvarado, Eric C. Hendriks, and Dylan Kerrigan, *The Politics of Self-Help: Transnational Popular Psychology and the Global Self-Help Industry* (London: Palgrave Macmillan, 2016).

difficult times. Blum sees the emergence of self-help not as a giving up of more expansive kinds of freedom but as "a defense of a specific mode of reading—for agency, use, well-being, and self-change."[2] With Blum, I ask: is it fair to say that entrepreneurial masculinity is the only model of freedom that this genre pedals, or that it is as simplistic, self-serving, and unrealistic as its detractors would suggest? In this chapter I explore the contemporary refashioning of individual freedom as entrepreneurial action through self-help literature. But I also explore the way that the genre provides other models of being free and being human, especially when it is critiqued by and incorporated into the contemporary bildungsroman.

I begin by exploring the self-help genre's existence in India today before investigating the kind of self-help books that my mother-in-law read, the kind that have been much critiqued for defining individual freedom as entrepreneurial agency. I focus on two nodes of this definition of Freedom Inc. First is the idea that one has freedom when one is free of one's social relations and contexts. Second is the notion that one has freedom when one has the agency to transform the self into a revenue stream. This two-pronged notion of Freedom Inc. is elaborated by self-help literature such as Robin Sharma's *The Monk Who Sold His Ferrari* (1999). While such books pedal the myth of absolute autonomy, the genre is harnessed and critiqued by literary bildungsromane like Aravind Adiga's *The White Tiger* (2008). Spurred on by my mother-in-law's story, in the second part of the chapter, I complicate the idea that all self-help literature in India necessarily reduces freedom to only a singular notion of entrepreneurial agency. Rather, the genre, and the literary fiction that makes use of it, also points to other more expansive iterations of individual freedom. Mohsin Hamid's novel, *How to Get Filthy Rich in Rising Asia* (2013), for instance, incorporates the Sufi tradition's emphasis on freedom as transcending the self to decenter entrepreneurial self-help's narcissistic inclinations.

## Self-Help in the New India

Significantly, self-help is one of the most popular genres in India today. Nielsen BookScan, a major market research company that gathers media statistics internationally, documents the rise in the sales of self-help books in India from

---

[2] Beth Blum, *The Self-Help Compulsion: Searching for Advice in Modern Literature* (New York: Columbia University Press, 2020), 8.

about 230,000 to 274,000 by 2014.³ This increasing popularity is reflected by the bestseller lists on Amazon.in and flipkart.com, the two biggest booksellers in India. During the month of December 2020, three out of the five bestselling books on Amazon were on self-help. The remaining spots among the top ten on both sites are typically occupied by textbooks or by the odd Chetan Bhagat novel. On both sites, only one non-English book—a Hindi textbook—made the list.

It is not, then, an exaggeration to say that Indian readers with an internet connection—now about 50 percent of the population or about 687 million users—are largely reading self-help and largely reading it in English. As the cover photo of this book testifies, self-help books also account for a large proportion of pirated books sold at traffic signals in urban centers all over India.⁴

What accounts for the rise in sales of self-help? The genre's popularity does seem to speak to a hunger for advancement and self-betterment, just as it did in nineteenth- and early-twentieth-century Europe when industrial modernity—urbanization, secularization, the division of labor—created a vacuum that self-help strove to fill. Historians discuss these and other factors as part of "the turmoil of the turn of the century," which led to the rise of the "therapeutic ethos."⁵ Now too, India's aspirational middle classes find themselves undeniably anxious and obsessed with economic advancement, so much so that they think that telling someone that they have a "middle class mentality" is an insult rather than a compliment.⁶ The anxiety is heightened by India's downward economic spiral given that elites (i.e., the top 10%) are accumulating wealth at a greater rate than the rest, and that rather than growing, most of India's middle class may be shrinking in size.⁷ This economic stagnation means that it is not just anxiety but also desperation that may propel India's educated middle classes to read self-help. As Craig Jeffrey notes in *Timepass*, a large proportion of India's educated male youth suffer from being in limbo; pervasive underemployment because of the lack of job opportunities has propelled young men into situations of chronic

---

³ "Nielsen Bookscan. 2015. Bespoke Book Sales Data Report," Quoted in Daniel Nehring, Emmanuel Alvarado, Eric C. Hendriks, and Dylan Kerrigan, *The Politics of Self-Help: Transnational Popular Psychology and the Global Self-Help Industry* (London: Palgrave Macmillan, 2016), 89.
⁴ India is a country where studies estimate 20–25 percent of books are pirated. Ariel Bogle, "The World of Indian Book Piracy," https://www.mhpbooks.com/the-world-of-indian-book-piracy/ (accessed August 2021).
⁵ T. J. Jackson Lears, "From Salvation to Self-Realization: Advertising and the Therapeutic Roots of the Consumer Culture 1880–1930," *Advertising and Society Reviews*, 1 (2000): 2 quoted in Beth Blum, *The Self-Help Compulsion: Searching for Advice in Modern Literature* (New York: Columbia University Press, 2020), 8.
⁶ See Meghalee Mitra, "'Paise Nahin Hai': How Middle Class Mentality Builds Character and Makes You Happy," https://www.arre.co.in/social-commentary/middle-class-mentality-indian-families/, July 23, 2018 (accessed August 2021).
⁷ See "India's Missing Middle Class," *The Economist*, January 11, 2018.

waiting during which they can only dream of building lives for themselves.[8] It is not, then, difficult to understand the popularity of self-help; the genre offers the promise of transformation, limitless growth and opportunity, and more importantly the idea that the power to succeed lies solely in one's own control precisely at a time when circumstances seem to prove the opposite.

## Freedom Inc. in Contemporary Self-Help

The reading of self-help, a genre that appears to grant people complete control of their circumstances at a time when they have little of it, suggests that the genre works as a placebo to offer hope to those without hope. However, it does nothing to transform the structural conditions that produce their devastating life circumstances. Innumerable critics including Daniel Nehring and Sabine Maasen have thus lambasted self-help as a neoliberal tool that contributes to the precaritization of social life by selling the illusion that individuals have complete ability within themselves to succeed.[9] I explore the credibility of this argument through Robin Sharma's *The Monk Who Sold His Ferrari*, which follows in the tradition of early self-help authors, such as Samuel Smiles, Napoleon Hill, and Dale Carnegie, in its reconception of individual freedom as entrepreneurial agency.

Sharma's website declares that his book is a number 1 international bestseller that is now published in over forty-two languages. It boasts that "Robin Sharma is one of the top leadership experts in the world, with his work embraced by rock stars, royalty, billionaires, and celebrity CEOs. With over 20,000,000 books sold, clients such as Starbucks, Nike, GE, The Coca-Cola Company, NASA, and Microsoft are using his leadership methods to drive real growth + top performance."[10] *The Monk Who Sold His Ferrari* and the spate of titles in this series style themselves as spiritual helpers to transform people into business leaders and entrepreneurs. The title refers to an exhausted and disillusioned millionaire CEO, Julian, who after suffering a heart attack, sells his Ferrari,

---

[8] Jeffrey Craig, *Timepass: Youth, Class and the Politics of Waiting in India* (Stanford: Stanford University Press, 2010).
[9] See Daniel Nehring, Emmanuel Alvarado, Eric C. Hendriks, and Dylan Kerrigan, *The Politics of Self-Help: Transnational Popular Psychology and the Global Self-Help Industry* (London: Palgrave Macmillan, 2016). See also Sabine Maasen, Barbara Sutter, and Stefanie Duttweiler, "Self-Help: The Making of Neosocial Selves in Neoliberal Society," in Sabine Maasen and Barbara Sutter, *On Willing Selves* (London: Palgrave Macmillan, 2007).
[10] Robin Sharma, https://www.robinsharma.com.

**Figure 7** Cover image of *The Monk Who Sold His Ferrari*.

and goes off to find himself in the Himalayas through "ancient" wisdom. There he meets monks who teach him lessons about how to live, lessons that also happen to be lessons in how to be a good entrepreneur. The self in Sharma, reduced to monk as CEO, defines freedom as entrepreneurial agency. One who possesses this kind of freedom is first conceptualized as free of social relations and structures, enabling him to be an empty receptacle for the timeless spiritual wisdom of ancient religions. And second, he is possessed of limitless agency to transform himself into a revenue stream, a goal that is presented as being continuous with that timeless spiritual wisdom.

Within the first node of this definition of freedom, the self is imagined as unembedded from any social processes and institutional frameworks. The self is an individual alone. As Heidi Rimke phrases it, self-help "negates the inherent sociality of being."[11] Instead it posits a "thin self," which is also a desocialized, atomized self, one struggling with purely personal challenges to accomplish purely individual objectives.[12] There is no sense here that the self is constructed in and through social relationships. Freedom here means being free from social, interpersonal ties, a definition that is both descriptive and prescriptive. Sharma tells his readers: "Read every day something no one else is reading. Think every day something no one else is thinking. It is bad for the mind to be always part of unanimity."[13] In other words, one is and should strive to be completely unique. One should avoid acknowledging that one is constituted by one's contexts and interrelationships.

In *The Monk Who Sold His Ferrari*, the embodiment of this unembedded self is the entrepreneur, a figure who is a natural extension of the "thin self." Indeed, from the time of its origins, the word "entrepreneur" has been associated with self-reliance, as in the influential writing of Jean Baptiste Say: "The knife grinder's craft requires no occupancy of land; he carries his stock in trade upon his shoulders, and his skill and industry at his fingers' ends; being at the same time adventurer, capitalist, and labourer." Like other entrepreneurs, the knife grinder is also:

> often ... his own technical expert, in so far as a professional specialist was not called in for special cases. Likewise he was often his own buying and selling agent, the head of his office, his own personnel manager, and sometimes, even

---

[11] Heidi Rimke, "Governing Citizens through Self-Help Literature," *Cultural Studies*, 14 (1), 2000: 62.

[12] Such a thin self, Nehring et al. contend, is a central ideological component of an international (neo)liberal regime that furthers the precaritization of social life. *The Politics of Self-Help*, 158.

[13] Robin Sharma quoting Christopher Morley in Robin Sharma, *Leadership Wisdom from the Monk Who Sold His Ferrari* (Carlsbad, CA: Hay House, 2003), 225.

though as a rule he of course employed solicitors, his own legal advisor in current affairs.[14]

For Say, the entrepreneur is free in the sense of being completely self-reliant, for he is materially and socially unembedded—he has "no occupancy of land" and "carries his stock in trade upon his shoulders."[15] According to the economist Joseph Schumpeter, this freedom as unembeddedness is what enables the entrepreneur to be innovative; the entrepreneur is the carrier out of "new combinations … and loses that character as soon as he has built up his business, when he settles down to running it as other people run their businesses." These descriptions characterize the entrepreneur as an "individual" first. He is on "his own." He dabbles in what is "new," and this renders him a "risk taker."[16]

Because he is unembedded, the entrepreneur's freedom is intelligible not through his social relations and contexts but through rational introspection, which properly orchestrated means that the individual is alone responsible for determining the course of his own life, provided that he undertakes a course of systematic modification and self-improvement projects. This self-improvement proceeds through a few major assumptions that recur in self-help. Chief among them is the idea that success, happiness, and empowerment are the result of positive thinking and of the cognitive orientation of individuals; they have nothing to do with history, biography, or the social, and anyone can achieve them as long as they believe in their ability to attain their goals. Sharma thus tells his readers that "belief creates the actual fact. Our expectations create our reality. Success in business and in life is a self-fulfilling prophecy. Thoughts have power—never forget this timeless natural law." In line with this, Sharma includes an epigraph: "you are the master of your thought, the molder of your character, and the maker and shaper of condition, environment, and destiny."[17]

The idea that you make and shape your own destiny has implications for the way that Sharma defines free choice:

> Every day, you have a choice as to which path you will take. Take one path, and it is certain to take you to one destination. Choose another, and it will take you

---

[14] Jean-Baptiste Say, *A Treatise on Political Economy* (Auburn, AL: Ludwig von Mises Institute, 2008), 78.
[15] Say, *A Treatise*.
[16] Joseph A. Schumpeter, *The Theory of Economic Development: An Inquiry into Profits, Capital, Credit, Interest, and the Business Cycle*, translated from German by Redvers Opie (New York: Oxford University Press, 1961), 66.
[17] Sharma, *Leadership Wisdom from the Monk Who Sold His Ferrari*, 31.

to an entirely different place. If there's one thing the sages taught, it's that ... the level of your success will, at the end of the day, boil down to what activities and initiatives you have chosen to focus on. What people you have chosen to surround yourself with.[18]

Such an explanation ignores the larger structural factors—class, gender, race, sexuality, economics, education—that embed the self in certain ways in society and that produce certain choices for some but not for others. Moreover, Sharma's theory of freedom as choice is not just the result of overlooking one's embeddedness within sets of social relations but of actively believing that these social contexts do not matter. Thus, Sharma admonishes his readers: "Accusing the times is but excusing ourselves." Instead, he suggests that every individual will have an "incredible barrage of choice coming at us" and that one must respond by having a "predetermined game plan. If you have one, you will have created a framework that will allow you to select only those choices that will advance your purpose. You will begin to be the master of all the choices rather than their servant. A plan relieves you of the torment of choice."[19] Such a directive to identify one's dreams and goals and to formulate action strategies on their basis does not just ignore the limited choices that disadvantaged individuals face. It also produces what Micki McGee calls a belabored self. This self is constantly open to improvement. One must "continually work on himself in efforts to remain employable and re-employable ... self-improvement is suggested as the only reliable insurance against economic insecurity."[20]

The idea of the "game plan" set by an "endlessly belabored self"[21] leads us into the second node of self-help's redefinition of freedom. If one is free of social relations and structures of all kinds, one has no limitations and one possesses absolute agency to transform the self into a revenue stream. According to Llana Gershon, this idea of the self is "a move away from the liberal vision of people owning themselves and their labor power as though they were property," as in the Lockean idea of "property in the person" that we encountered in Chapter 1. Instead, the self as revenue stream relies on the idea of people owning themselves as though they were a business.[22] In this sense, the self comes to be understood as a collection of potentially useful traits, the development of which can be

---

[18] Sharma, *Leadership Wisdom from the Monk Who Sold His Ferrari*, 164.
[19] Sharma, *Leadership Wisdom from the Monk Who Sold His Ferrari*, 180.
[20] Micki McGee, *Self-Help, Inc. Makeover Culture in American Life* (New York: Oxford University Press, 2005), 13, 16.
[21] McGee, *Self-Help, Inc. Makeover Culture in American Life*, 12.
[22] Llana Gershon, "Neoliberal Agency," *Current Anthropology*, 52 (4), August 2011: 539.

invested in. These skills can then be mobilized in competition or cooperation with other individuals and are only limited by the rationality of the market.[23] Self-management involves the skillful enhancement of those traits that are most beneficial to this enterprising self. An early example of this shift is indicated in Napoleon Hill's injunction in *How to Sell Your Way Through Life* ([1939] 2010), in which Hill enjoins readers to "sell your personality. You must do it!"[24] In line with seeing the self and other people as revenue streams, Sharma encourages the CEOs he addresses to see employees as "assets" who need "developing." They are "bundles of human potential just waiting to be unleashed for a worthy purpose."[25] The next sentence clarifies what this worthy purpose might be, for if people are helped to "work and live at their highest levels, the profits are certain to come."[26]

This two-pronged rethinking of freedom as an unembedded self with the ability to act willfully to transform oneself into a revenue stream reduces more capacious concepts of freedom to a much narrower idea of Freedom Inc. Because the self is free only by virtue of being unembedded, this self is unable to focus on the larger structural conditions that produce his immediate choices. He has only the agency to maximize his own functionality within these immediate contexts. He does not have the freedom to reject or reimagine those contexts altogether. This is why, "instead of asking whether there is another game in town other than (neoliberal) capitalism, the thin self often uses its agency to ask how we can adjust our moods and emotions to better suit capital accumulation."[27] In other words, within the discourse of Freedom Inc. we possess agency as entrepreneurs of the self, but not the freedom to be anything other than entrepreneurs.

The two-pronged idea of freedom as entrepreneurial agency is encapsulated in the cultural environment of post-1990s India, as seen in a 2018 credit card advertisement. The advertisement features a high-flying entrepreneur, a businessman who provides the voiceover for a video of himself at work. However, interspersed among these images are also shots of his young wife and child left home alone without him, dejected and waiting, or sitting next to him ignored, as he closes deals on the phone or works on his laptop. The voiceover that plays alongside these images describes freedom as an unceasing life of motion that is free because it is free of obligations, of the demands of family, of relationships. Indeed, his only role is of being a revenue stream:

---

[23] Gershon, "Neoliberal Agency," 540.
[24] Napoleon Hill, *How to Sell Your Way Through Life* (New York: Wiley Books, [1939] 2009), 7.
[25] Sharma, *Leadership Wisdom from the Monk Who Sold His Ferrari*, 72.
[26] Sharma, *Leadership Wisdom from the Monk Who Sold His Ferrari*, 47, 229.
[27] Nehring et al., *The Politics of Self-Help*, 161.

My business is my passion, my office my heaven. My friends and family call me ATM because I work 24/7. My bag is always packed because I travel back to back. I travel on business every other day. My real home is in fact a hotel or a home stay. Even when I am out enjoying a meal it's usually over, you know, a business deal. And on weekends when out on family trips I'm on the phone discussing new partnerships, meetings, town halls, seminars, and workshops. I may stop for fuel, but business never stops.[28]

This description of himself as an ATM, an automated money machine, is followed by a pause and the question: "So, what do my loved ones have to say about my frequent absences?" The camera responds by panning into his young daughter's smiling face as she sits in a fancy speedboat with her mother and yells "YAAAAAAAAYYYY!" The voiceover continues: "Because my passion helps me take my family to great places thanks to my jet privilege membership. Your passion can take you places too. Simply become a Jet Privilege member and discover many ways to earn and use JP miles."[29] By the end of the advertisement, the image of freedom as an unembedded and individualized passion to earn, free of interpersonal relationships, prevails. The images of the entrepreneur's wife and child looking sad at his repeated absences are replaced by shots of their jubilation at being taken on expensive holidays due to the entrepreneur's Jet Privilege credit card membership.

I give this example as a way of demonstrating just how widespread such a notion of entrepreneurial masculine freedom has become. And I do so in conjunction with an analysis of how self-help has accompanied and reinforced such an entrepreneurial idea of individual freedom. It is no wonder, then, that literary fiction has picked up on the power and popularity of the self-help genre as a vehicle to ponder the question of what freedom and fulfillment look like in post-1990s India.

## Critiquing Freedom as Entrepreneurial Agency in *The White Tiger*

Aravind Adiga's *The White Tiger* tells the story of its main character as he goes from poverty to business ownership and wealth. However, Balram's journey toward embodying entrepreneurial freedom is far from a triumphant one. As the story unfolds, Balram's narration of his life veers into a horror story. For in order

---

[28] Dentsu India, Jet Privilege advertisement, India, https://www.youtube.com/watch?v=gp3BP84tbuw.
[29] Dentsu India, Jet Privilege advertisement, India, https://www.youtube.com/watch?v=gp3BP84tbuw.

to embody entrepreneurial freedom, he becomes a chauffeur to the son of a rich landlord, murders this boss, steals a huge sum of money from him, becomes a fugitive of the law even as he is certain his family has been hunted down and killed in revenge, and then adopts the name of his murdered boss to launch his new business. Through this sordid story, the novel challenges self-help's idea of freedom as entrepreneurial agency in both its form and content.

The novel critiques the self-help genre's assumptions about individual freedom by literalizing them and carrying their meaning to an extreme. Balram becomes an embodiment of the thin self, insofar as this means deliberately unembedding himself from all the relations and social ties that once made him who he is. Balram also becomes free in the sense of turning into a revenue stream, but, ironically, that freedom means that he lives as a fugitive. Through the horrific results of literalizing the thin self, the story critiques entrepreneurial agency, and twists the form of the affirmative or adaptation bildungsroman, in which typically the protagonist begins his journey at odds with the society within which he lives but ends it reconciled with social mores. Conversely, for Balram, individuation and entrepreneurial freedom can only be achieved by forever severing his bonds with the society in which he lives in the most extreme of ways. In this sense, the novel borrows the conventions of self-help and its insistence on an extreme individualism only to turn these ideas on their head.

Very quickly, the novel reveals that the first node within the idea of the entrepreneur's freedom—the ability to act alone, unembedded and unaffected—is impossible. The novel does so by first depicting the way that characters are produced by their social contexts and relations and then by representing the extreme brutality involved in severing the ties that constitute oneself during the journey to become an entrepreneur. To the first end, Adiga's narrator Balram reveals his own constitution in and through a particularly Indian socioeconomic context. He does so through a self-help letter he writes to a Chinese premier to educate him on how to become an entrepreneur, a form of address that frames the novel and gives the story its epistolary form:

> When you have heard the story of how I got to Bangalore and became one of its most successful (though probably least known) businessmen, you will know everything there is to know about how entrepreneurship is born, nurtured, and developed in this, the glorious twenty-first century of man ... See, when you come to Bangalore, and stop at a traffic light, some boy will run up to your car and knock on your window, while holding up a bootlegged copy of an American business book, wrapped carefully in cellophane and with a title like: TEN SECRETS OF BUSINESS SUCCESS! or BECOME AN ENTREPRENEUR

IN SEVEN EASY DAYS! Don't waste your money on those American books. They're so yesterday. I am tomorrow.[30]

Significantly, Balram stresses that his story is a departure from the self-help books that pervade India's cultural fabric, the traditional American self-help titles of Dale Carnegie and Napoleon Hill included. For these titles ignore what it takes to be an entrepreneur in this particular context, that of Bangalore. This attention to the individual's constitution in and through his own particular social context is also apparent in a passage in which Balram complains about the way he is depicted on his Wanted poster following his murder of his employer. "There's no mention of my school in the poster, sir—that's a real shame. You always ought to talk about a man's education when describing him. They should have said something like, the suspect was educated in a school with two foot long lizards the color of half ripe guavas hiding in its cupboards."[31] Here, Balram provides a contradictory celebration of absolute individuation in his insistence that the protagonist is the "rarest of creatures—the White Tiger," while also acknowledging that such individuation is actually impossible, because the individual can only be a sum of his social constitution, in this case of the brutal structural inequality and poverty that produces a murderer.

Adiga makes a similar point about the centrality of social context to individuation in a passage where Balram celebrates his schoolteacher's desecration of a government program instituted to provide free uniforms to village children:

> the schoolteacher hadn't been paid his salary in six months. He was going to undertake a Gandhian protest to retrieve his missing wages—he was going to do nothing in class until his paycheck arrived in the mail. Yet he was terrified of losing his job, because though the pay of any government job in India is poor, the incidental advantages are numerous. Once, a truck came into the school with uniforms that the government had sent for us; we never saw them, but a week later they turned up for sale in the neighboring village … No one blamed the school teacher for doing this. You can't expect a man in a dung heap to smell sweet. Every man in the village knew that he would have done the same in his position. Some were even proud of him, for having got away with it so cleanly.[32]

The schoolteacher's corruption, which Balram calls entrepreneurship, is produced by the structural poverty and corruption of his village surroundings.

---

[30] Aravind Adiga, *The White Tiger* (New York: Free Press, 2008), 4.
[31] Adiga, *The White Tiger*, 28.
[32] Adiga, *The White Tiger*, 28.

Once again, this celebration of entrepreneurship can only happen through a recognition that one's identity as an entrepreneur of corruption is inseparable from the failures of the social context within which one lives. Both these examples—Balram's murder of his boss and the schoolteacher's thefts—suggest that one does not *choose* to become an entrepreneur in this context of inequality and limited opportunities. One is forced to become one. Entrepreneurial freedom, then, contains its own antithesis.

The novel also critiques the idea of the thin self who is unmoored from one's contexts by pushing Balram to the extremes necessary to remain faithful to it, and then lets the reader judge whether the resulting severing of ties is worthy of celebration. For instance, Balram continuously deprives himself of the company of his family and friends to attain the ideal of entrepreneurship. For Mrinalini Chakravorty, the novel uses the stereotype of the slum to index the loss of community that Balram subjects himself to, for the "slum limns how communities of affection" fall outside the "kinds of desire, acquisitiveness, and individual ambition Balram adopts." Chakravorty notes how the only moments of levity in the novel are tied to episodes when he risks connecting with other people within his social class, suggesting that "slum life contains values that are always in surplus of the kinds of motivational capitalist creed" that drive Balram's progress. In one example, Balram drives past a slum where he sees families sitting together in an intimacy that seemed "so complete—so crushingly complete." As Chakravorty puts it, the pathos in these moments of community and human sociality "expressively defy the momentum of Balram's entrepreneurship," highlighting all that Balram must give up in his quest to become the thin self of globalization's modernity.[33]

All that Balram must give up to attain the thin self is clearest in his metaphor of the rooster coop, which he uses to describe and critique the Indian family unit:

> The greatest thing to come out of this country … is the Rooster Coop. The roosters in the coop smell the blood from above. They see the organs of their brothers … They know they're next. Yet they do not rebel. They do not try to get out of the coop. The very same thing is done with human beings in this country.[34]

Familial loyalty and love become weaknesses in the logic of the rooster coop because if a servant attempts to escape or disobeys his employer, the superior's

---

[33] Mrinalini Chakravorty, *In Stereotype: South Asia in the Global Literary Imaginary* (New York: Columbia University Press, 2014), 112–13.
[34] Adiga, *The White Tiger*, 147.

family punishes the servant by murdering or brutally torturing his family. Balram thus realizes that to create a better life and "break out of the Rooster Coop," one must be willing to sacrifice everything, including attachment to morals and to one's family. Becoming an entrepreneur is to literally become a thin self—divorced from one's attachments and relations—even to the point of destroying those one loves. Balram confirms that:

> only a man who is prepared to see his family destroyed—hunted, beaten, and burned alive by the masters—can break out of the coop. That would take no normal human being, but a freak, a pervert of nature. It would, in fact, take a White Tiger. You are listening to the story of a social entrepreneur ... I could gloat that I am not just any murderer, but one who killed his own employer (who is a kind of second father), and also contributed to the probable death of all his family members. A virtual mass murderer.[35]

The "social entrepreneur" must be a "virtual mass murderer" and he must regard that as a good thing; he must "gloat" about it. The only kind of social relations that a thin self is allowed are perverse: he takes responsibility not for fellow human beings but for corpses.

> Murder a man, and you feel responsible for his life—possessive, even. You know more about him than his father and mother; they knew his fetus, but you know his corpse; only you know why his body has to be pushed into the fire before its time, and why his toes curl up and fight for another hour on earth. Now, even though I killed him, you won't find me saying one bad thing about him. I protected his good name when I was his servant, and now that I am (in a sense) his master, I won't stop protecting his good name.[36]

In depicting this perverted version of loyalty, the novel critiques entrepreneurial agency through a rewriting and subversion of the affirmative bildungsroman's form. For instead of the protagonist reintegrating into society and embodying its human relationships and entanglements, he promotes an existence alone: "All that remains to be told is how I changed from a hunted criminal into a solid pillar of Bangalorean society."[37] This denouement, which would have completed the story arc of the adaptation narrative, never materializes because the only relationship allowed within Freedom Inc. is that of employer and employee:

---

[35] Adiga, *The White Tiger*, 37.
[36] Adiga, *The White Tiger*, 39.
[37] Adiga, *The White Tiger*, 283.

> Once I was driver to a master, but now I am a master of drivers. I don't treat them like servants—I don't slap, or bully, or mock anyone. I don't insult any of them by calling them my family either. They're my employees, I'm their boss. That's all. I make them sign a contract and I sign it too, and both of us must honor that contract. That's all. If they notice the way I talk, the way I dress, the way I keep things clean, they'll go up in life. If they don't, they'll be drivers all their lives. I leave the choice up to them. When the work is done I kick them out of the office: no chitchat, no cups of coffee. A white tiger keeps no friends. It's too dangerous.[38]

The employees too are "free" but only insofar as they have the "choice" to honor the employment contract and imitate Balram's own inclinations: "If they notice the way I talk, the way I dress, the way I keep things clean, they'll go up in life." While the discourse of Freedom Inc. presents itself as absolute freedom, it is always mired within a situation of constraints, and one that precludes a full embodying of humanity. For its freedom is only available to the thin self who is free of relationships, who partakes in "no chitchat, no cups of coffee."

If the novel critiques the first node of entrepreneurial agency as freedom from one's ties and social relations in its form and content, it also explores and refutes the second node I outline earlier in the text—the idea that the self possesses endless agency to remake itself into a revenue stream. The idea of self as revenue stream is mocked through Balram's recounting of his own journey to continually transform himself. Inspired by his childhood hero, Vijay, who also rose from a humble background to achieve success in the upper echelons of Indian society, Balram dedicates himself to self-improvement, so much so that he is willing to destroy who he once was. He sees identity as fluid and malleable, a fact articulated through the many name changes he employs throughout the story. Ultimately, even murder is an "act of entrepreneurship" because it allows Balram to literally remake himself into his master, Ashok. He adopts a new name each time he moves up within India's social hierarchy—Munna, Balram, Ashok. This endless remaking of the self is why Balram tells the reader early on that he doesn't have a name, thereby negating the very self he is creating.

The novel strengthens its critique of endless self-making by showing the way that it is rigidly gendered, for it relies on embodying a certain kind of masculinity. Balram must not just fashion himself into an entrepreneur but into a particular kind of man. An effeminate Balram as servant is juxtaposed with the ultra-masculine Balram as entrepreneur, suggesting that women—even rich

[38] Adiga, *The White Tiger*, 302.

ones—fall at the bottom of the social hierarchy. The gendering of entrepreneurial capitalism through an alpha-masculinity means that the effeminate Balram serves his master Ashok as a wife, and narrates this story of domination in the genre of a love story:

> Mr Ashok's face reappears now in my mind's eye as it used to every day when I was in his service—reflected in my rearview mirror. It was such a handsome face that sometimes I couldn't take my eyes off it. Picture a six-foot-tall fellow, broad shouldered, with a landlord's powerful, punishing forearms, yet always gentle (almost always—except for that time he punched Pinky madam in the face) and kind to those around him, even his servants and driver.[39]

Ashok is described as possessed of a dominant masculinity, sexually attractive and powerful, yet capable of brutality. As a servant Balram falls in love with this model of masculinity, seeking to belong to it in the way that women supposedly desire being possessed by men. Laying eyes on his master above him on a balcony in a parody of Romeo and Juliet, Balram recounts: "I saw a figure on the terrace, a fellow in long loose white clothes, walking around and around, lost deep in thought. I swear by God, sir—I swear ... the moment I saw his face, I knew: *This is the master for me*" (emphasis in original). The satirical scene brings to mind a Bollywood romance of a lover pining for his beloved on a balcony above. Yet such a romance is a perverse metaphor for the master–servant relationship, because Balram, a male servant, must style himself as an effeminate wife who relates to Ashok as his lord and master: "I knew it was my duty to be like a wife to him. I had to make sure he ate well, and slept well, and did not get thin. I made lunch, I served him, I cleaned up."[40] The analogy means that Ashok's dominant masculinity exists at the top of two intersecting hierarchies—that of gender and class. I am reminded again of my mother-in-law, who could only reconceive herself as a free person by appropriating such a mode of dominant masculinity. She styled herself as an upper-middle-class entrepreneur not through a reconceived womanhood but by appropriating the symbolic capital of patriarchy. This is why she began to insist that she replace her husband at the head of the table, occupying his seat during meals. Balram, though a man himself, must overcome his position as a servant by also assuming an alpha-masculinity that his social class has not afforded him. Reading Balram's journey toward entrepreneurial freedom as a quest for dominant masculinity makes

---

[39] Adiga, *The White Tiger*, 38.
[40] Adiga, *The White Tiger*, 50.

sense if one considers the significance of the novel's central figure of the "white tiger." The tiger, as Ravinder Kaur points out, has long functioned as a symbol of India in colonial discourse and, in the New India, also signifies the nation's strong potential as an emergent economy within optimistic development discourse. The tiger as a symbol of the Indian economy's newfound ferocity and vigor relies on a rhetoric of "corporate masculinity" embodied through the "fashioning of hyper-masculine bodies."[41] Balram's quest to embody entrepreneurial freedom by becoming a white tiger references just such development discourse, relying on the construction of a dominant masculinity in which women and lower classes are equally subordinated. In its satirical upending of such a notion, the novel reveals that this is a freedom that paradoxically relies on the unfreedom of others.

My claim in this section that the novel is critiquing a model of freedom as entrepreneurial agency has been resisted by critics such as Swaralipi Nandi, who argues that Balram's individuation at the cost of the social fabric is evidence that Balram—and by extension the novel itself—is an agent of the free market. Balram's purpose is to train other white tigers. By the end of the text, he aims to transform other young men into entrepreneurs who attain success through individuated self-making by launching a school in which they are taught Balram's version of entrepreneurship. Nandi concludes that since it is capitalism that enabled Balram's transformation and hard-earned freedom, the novel's anxiety about Balram's actions is "resolved with Capitalism emerging as the novel's hero."[42] Balram's dream of starting a school to train other entrepreneurs becomes "a humane replacement for India's corrupt welfare state, taking on the state's duty of providing for those on the margins."[43] However, such an interpretation ignores both Adiga's claims on the novel's behalf[44] as well as the novel's satirical critique of the entrepreneurial idea of freedom and of the thin self that exercises

---

[41] Ravinder Kaur, "The Market Hunters: Corporate Masculinity and the Art of Opening the Economy," https://ravinderkaur.net/the-market-hunters-corporate-masculinity-and-the-art-of-opening-the-economy/, August 14, 2020.

[42] Swaralipi Nandi, "Narrative Ambiguity and the Neoliberal *Bildungsroman* in Aravind Adiga's *The White Tiger*," *Journal of Narrative Theory*, 47 (2), Summer 2017: 297.

[43] Nandi, "Narrative Ambiguity and the Neoliberal *Bildungsroman* in Aravind Adiga's *The White Tiger*," 297.

[44] In Adiga's own statements on *The White Tiger*, he claims that the novel is penance for the exclusions in his triumphant writing about India's economic state during his past career as an international finance journalist. For Sarah Brouillette, the novel is metatextual when its narrator ironically models his triumph over psychological adversity. For such a modeling could just as easily reference Adiga's own work as a finance journalist, in which he strove to "keep the 'bad news'" out of his work, and then as a writer of literature tried to recover from the pathologies this caused by making "bad news … the essence of his concern." Sarah Brouillette, *Literature and the Creative Economy* (Stanford: Stanford University Press, 2014), 85.

it. The two critical nodes of this notion—that an individual is free because he is alone, unembedded from social ties and relations, and that he is free because he possesses agency to endlessly remake the self into a revenue stream—are both upended by the end of the text.

Sarah Brouillette supports this interpretation of the novel when she argues that Adiga's satire highlights the contradictions within the neoliberal discourse of self-help. The latter continues "generalizing and globalizing the rhetoric of the free-floating agent of enterprise throughout all social strata, disseminating it even to those for whom this particular trajectory might seem a kind of sick joke."[45] Indeed, as books like *The Monk Who Sold His Ferrari* show through their exemplification of self-help, and as Adiga shows through his literary critique of it, the model of the self in self-help is an abstraction that, through myths like the "free-floating agent of enterprise" whose life is "devoid of suffering," buttresses and obscures all kinds of hierarchies. However, it is precisely these obscurations that render it appealing to its readers. Madhavi Gokhale argues that books like the one by Sharma peddle a pseudo-spirituality, offering language that is sanctioned by "divine" authorship and embellished with the metaphorical imagery of transcendental experiences; to the sufferer, it offers the rhetoric of consolation; to the ambitious, a magical formula for realization of desires."[46] But, as Stewart Justman suggests, this magic world is a "fool's paradise." "Self-help uses the rhetoric of liberation, telling of emancipation from oppression, not the details of freedom."[47] These details, as *The White Tiger* shows, may include murder but one would never know it from fable-like self-help narratives. "Neatly packaged and processed, the life-stories of the self-help genre go down easily, like coated pills."[48]

Even as I agree with these general characterizations of most books in the genre, I began this chapter with the story of my mother-in-law's painstaking self-transformation because the liberation that self-help offers need not always be a fool's paradise. Sometimes, the genre's lessons must be determinedly internalized for those who find their immediate situations difficult to navigate. In what follows, I suggest that it would be a mistake to over-generalize about self-help's detrimental version of Freedom Inc. both because it is used by diverse actors

---

[45] Sarah Brouillette, *Literature and the Creative Economy* (Stanford: Stanford University Press, 2014), 94.
[46] Madhavi Gokhale, "The Implications of Simplification in 'Inspirational Literature,'" *International Journal of Social Science and Humanity*, 2 (5), 2012: 403.
[47] Stewart Justman, *Fool's Paradise: The Unreal World of Pop Psychology* (New York: Ivan Dee, 2005).
[48] Justman, *Fool's Paradise*.

such as my mother-in-law for variegated ends related to self-realization and because the genre itself is multifaceted, which is why it has been appropriated by literary fiction. South Asian novels seem to be reacting to the thin self not only by critiquing its assumptions as Adiga's *The White Tiger* does, but by adapting it to pose a different kind of freedom instead. Mohsin Hamid's *How to Get Filthy Rich in Rising Asia*, for instance, uses the self-help genre to free the self, but constitutes this self through communities and networks of relations. In Hamid's estimation, the novel wields narrative as a mode of democratically constituting the self and its ability to do so also reconceives the individualism of the self-help genre. The kind of self that emerges is constructed through a co-creative process that implicates the reader, author, and narrator within itself.

## Freedom as Transcending the Self through Love: A Sufi Contextual Universalism

*How to Get Filthy Rich in Rising Asia* is a story written in the form of a self-help book. Each chapter in the novel is framed in terms of particular self-help goals (e.g., "Get an Education," "Don't Fall in Love," "Work for Yourself") that are also the practical steps one needs to take to become "filthy rich." The book charts the life journey of its male protagonist—"You"—from his childhood till his death as an old man. The journey involves him falling in love with a neighborhood "pretty girl" who he does not end up marrying. It also involves marrying a woman he does not love, making a lot of money through crooked practices, bankruptcy, suffering from heart disease, reuniting with the pretty girl, and finally dying as an old man. This story is recounted, I argue, to suggest that humans exist through their links with other people. They do not exist as individuals but in aggregations, like "the fingers on one hand, the toes on one foot … shoals of fish or flocks of birds or indeed tribes of humans."[49] Through this central assumption, the novel recuperates and refutes understandings of self-help as inherently individualistic both through its content and its form.

Hamid constructs this story arc to redefine freedom as a mode of transcending the self through one's loving relationships with others. In an interview he notes that this concept of freedom comes from a particular literary lineage of the Sufi love poem in his hometown of Lahore, Pakistan:

---

[49] Mohsin Hamid, *How to Get Filthy Rich in Rising Asia* (New York: Riverhead Books, 2014), 14.

> In Pakistan the dominant literary form is the Sufi love poem. Sufism is a mystical tradition within the Muslim tradition ... Sufis refer to love as a way of understanding the universe, of transcending yourself, and of looking at life and the divine. And the way that this Sufism is communicated is through epic love poems often told to a "You," the Beloved.[50]

Hamid, here, is referring to a contextual universalism, which imagines love as a universal essence that resides within each and every person. Love is a synonym for the divinity that runs through every being, connecting them to each other. When one recognizes this divinity in another through love, one transcends the self and becomes one with the universe and with the divine. Thus William C. Chittick defines a Sufi as someone who "transcends his own individual self and reaches God,"[51] which is conceptualized as attaining the greatest freedom. As Hamid notes, this sentiment has been expressed in mystical verse for thousands of years through addresses to the beloved, the divine, referred to in intimate terms through the second person as "you."

For Hamid, Sufi poetry is an important counter to prevalent forms of me-centered self-help because it seeks to transcend the self by subsuming that self within the divine fabric of the universe. By harnessing Sufi poetry to this end, Hamid notes that he is positing a counter-version of self-help that is over a thousand years old: "So I was wondering down a path that has existed for a very long time but isn't too common in the novel form."[52] Moreover, this notion of freedom as self-transcendence through love helps Hamid to rethink the discourse of Freedom Inc. found in contemporary self-help:

> Self-help today is a problematic term because so much of self-help is a kind of narcissistic thing. It is all about "me." And, of course, what all of the great humane humanistic spiritual and philosophical traditions converge on is that it is important to transcend the self. So self-help is actually about self-mitigation.[53]

For Hamid, post-1990s self-help is narcissistic because the genre depicts a thin entrepreneurial self, interested only in turning oneself into a revenue stream. In another interview, he notes:

---

[50] Chicago Humanities Festival, Mohsin Hamid: *How to Get Filthy Rich in Rising Asia*, https://www.youtube.com/watch?v=0EaIkSNAsWU.
[51] William C. Chittick, *The Sufi Doctrine of Rumi* (Bloomington, IN: World Wisdom, 2005), 9.
[52] Chicago Humanities Festival, Mohsin Hamid: *How to Get Filthy Rich in Rising Asia*, https://www.youtube.com/watch?v=0EaIkSNAsWU.
[53] Chicago Humanities Festival, Mohsin Hamid: *How to Get Filthy Rich in Rising Asia*, https://www.youtube.com/watch?v=0EaIkSNAsWU.

> I moved back to Pakistan in 2009 and saw this uber-money-obsessed and money-vulnerable society, which was significantly transformed from 1989, when I had left to go to college. So, in *How to Get Filthy Rich in Rising Asia*, I tried to juxtapose this new religion of money against an almost Sufi-like second-person narrative about the Beloved, in order to compare an older wisdom against a currently prevailing ethos. I was trying to figure out what one can do against this crushing imperative—of money at all costs—to see if there is a way to possibly transcend it and if literature could play a role in aiding that.[54]

In remaking self-help in the image of spiritual notions of freedom found in Sufi Mysticism, Hamid defends and develops the practice of reading as a tool to achieve well-being and self-development. This is apparent in his novel, which uses the self-help genre to implicate the reader in the story being told, thereby performing notions of loving collectivity and guiding the reader on how to most fully embody and appreciate transient experience. While the title suggests it is about the ultimate goal of entrepreneurial freedom—how to turn oneself into a revenue stream and thereby get "filthy rich in rising Asia"—the novel very quickly reveals its true hand. Freedom is reimagined here as a capacity to transcend the self by defining oneself through one's networks of relations, networks that include the reader who, as is typical of the self-help genre, is imagined as being in direct conversation with the author. In the process, Hamid points to the various metatextual devices within self-help texts that have the potential to remake freedom into co-constitution. Ultimately, the protagonist's—and through him, the reader's—formation through meaningful relationships—romantic and filial—are more important life lessons than his advice about how to become "filthy rich."

The novel depicts the co-constitutive, embedded, connected nature of human life by pointing out that human beings are not absolute, unique individuals but interchangeable with one another. This is why the protagonist is never named but only referred to in the second person as a "you" that refers to the reader and the protagonist simultaneously. As Angelia Poon notes, this is a "different inflection of the more orthodox triangulated relationship of narrator–reader–character as the reader is denied the safety of distance, becoming as well the conjoined object of satire" and an integral part of this triadic journey of self-making.[55] Indeed, with the use of "you," the reader is forcefully implicated in everything

---

[54] Chicago Humanities Festival, Mohsin Hamid: *How to Get Filthy Rich in Rising Asia*, https://www.youtube.com/watch?v=0EaIkSNAsWU.

[55] Angelia Poon, "Helping the Novel: Neoliberalism, Self-Help, and the Narrating of the Self in Mohsin Hamid's *How to Get Filthy Rich in Rising Asia*," *The Journal of Commonwealth Literature*, 52 (1), 2017: 142.

that happens in the novel, including in the protagonist's more questionable actions. The rhetorical act acquires a coercive, interpellative power. Far from collaborating with Freedom Inc.'s ultimate emphasis on unique individuality, on the "thin self," Hamid presents a protagonist (and reader) so embedded in their textual and extra-textual contexts and relations that they cannot possibly be unique. This means that even the poor working-class protagonist's experiences are described in terms of experiences that the literate, probably middle-class reader identifies with:

> Your anguish is the anguish of a boy whose chocolate has been thrown away, whose remote controls are out of batteries, whose scooter is busted, whose new sneakers have been stolen. This is all the more remarkable since you've never in your life seen any of these things.[56]

Hamid does not pose these analogies of anguish to convince the relatively well-off reader that the reader's despair at being denied batteries or chocolate is commensurate to the privations experienced by the poor protagonist. Rather the point seems to be that the protagonist experiences emotion in the same way as the educated, richer counterparts reading his story. What distinguishes them from each other is simply the circumstances of their birth. No inherent difference defines the two. Each is constituted by their contexts and the networks they find themselves in, which is why they would in fact be interchangeable with each other if they were born into each other's situations. As Hamid notes in an interview, charting the life of this lower-class protagonist allowed him to "imagine what it was like to be someone. I could now think that anybody is somebody's child. It was a way of widening empathy."[57]

In pointing out the interchangeability of different human beings in terms of their emotional capacities, the novel directly contradicts the contemporary self-help genre's prize assumption that "choice or desire or effort" is all it takes to succeed. Rather, what makes you "you" is almost entirely a product of chance and circumstance. Even among siblings, mere chance—like the order of one's birth—determines one's life situation. "You's" individuality cannot be extricated from his circumstances as a third child.

> There are forks in the road to wealth that have nothing to do with choice or desire or effort, forks that have to do with chance, and in your case, the order of

---

[56] Hamid, *How to Get Filthy Rich in Rising Asia*, 4.
[57] Chicago Humanities Festival, Mohsin Hamid: *How to Get Filthy Rich in Rising Asia*, https://www.youtube.com/watch?v=0EaIkSNAsWU.

your birth is one of these. Third means you are not heading back to the village. Third means you are not working as a painter's assistant. Third also means you are not, like the fourth of you three surviving siblings, a tiny skeleton in a small grave at the base of a tree.[58]

Similarly, the novel points to other limiting structural conditions that are outside one's control, and that have a determining power on the choices one makes, or rather, is meted out. A particularly notable limiting circumstance is that of gender. The protagonist recognizes that his freedom depends on being born male when he contrasts his own life with that of his sister:

> Your sister has worked as a cleaning girl since shortly after your family moved to the city, your father's income unable to keep up with the rampant inflation of recent years. She was told she could go back to school once your brother, the middle of you three surviving siblings, was old enough to work. She demonstrated more enthusiasm for education in her few months in a classroom than your brother did in his several years. He has just been found employment [sic] as a painter's assistant, and has been taken out of school as a result, but your sister will not be sent there in his stead. Her time for that has passed. Marriage is her future. She has been marked for entry.[59]

The sister's agency will fall solely within the limiting framework of marriage. If one is female, one is subject to being targeted for "entry," which suggests a victimizing sexual penetration, a reduction of the self only to one's reproductive worth. One's social contexts and ties, one's place within networks—including the family you are born into, and the gender you belong to—constitute the nature of one's choices and agency.

This acknowledgment of the determining nature of context enables Hamid to pose a more nuanced account of individual freedom. The novel suggests that one must be cognizant of one's limiting contexts so as to be able to act within them effectively:

> As you lie motionless afterwards, a young jaundiced village boy ... it must seem that getting filthy rich is beyond your reach. But have faith. You are not as powerless as you appear. Your moment is about to come. Yes, this book is going to offer you a choice.[60]

---

[58] Hamid, *How to Get Filthy Rich in Rising Asia*, 33.
[59] Hamid, *How to Get Filthy Rich in Rising Asia*, 28.
[60] Hamid, *How to Get Filthy Rich in Rising Asia*, 93.

The protagonist here is "not as powerless as you appear" because he learns how to enact his freedom by actively reflecting on the contexts and interrelationships that have shaped him. He recognizes and finds ways to work through his own limiting circumstances by actively distinguishing between the choices available to him. This, in turn, allows him to avoid the more malevolent systems of inequality and hierarchical interrelationships that he encounters. For example, Hamid notes that for a brief time "You" is a member of a large political organization on the protagonist's university campus. This organization "sells power … When combined with those at other institutions around the city, the street filling capability of these young people becomes formidable, a show of force in the face of which unwanted laws, policies, and speech must tremble."[61] Yet, the protagonist enacts a nuanced version of individual freedom when he realizes that this kind of network curtails choice, that it cannot be the nexus through which one's will can be orchestrated, because it ignores the emotional fabric of ties that constitutes him. "You" discovers this when his mother dies and he is forbidden to mourn her:

> At the university, members of your organization urge you not to mourn too much or for more than the prescribed period. They say that to do otherwise is to reject what fate has decreed. Instead they tell you to focus your energies on the tasks you are assigned, to recognize your comrades as your true family, and to act through the organization to fulfill your destiny as your mother has fulfilled hers. But these suggestions strike you as scripted and uncompelling.[62]

The network that such a large-scale organization offers squelches freedom by insisting that it replace other kinds of ties, those defined by love, such as that between the protagonist and his mother. Instead, the organization insists on absolute paths decreed by "fate" and "destiny." That these represent the antithesis of acting freely is confirmed by the protagonist's naming of these life paths as "scripted."

The novel, then, points out the embeddedness of human life and freedom within networks, and the limitations to individual agency that these networks pose, but it also distinguishes between different kinds of networks so as to offer a more capacious version of freedom than the self-help genre's notion of entrepreneurial agency. What distinguishes the two types of networks mentioned earlier is that one is driven by power, and the other by love. The kind of small-scale collectivity driven

---

[61] Hamid, *How to Get Filthy Rich in Rising Asia*, 61.
[62] Hamid, *How to Get Filthy Rich in Rising Asia*, 72.

by love produces empathy, because it makes one's experience comprehensible in terms of other peoples' experiences, and helps the self belong to a network of relations through which his life is constituted and can derive meaning.

It is not just the novel's content but its form that defines individual freedom as agency that is enacted through one's networks of co-constitution, illuminating the ways that the novel, its author, its narrator, its protagonist, and its reader are all co-created by their relationships with each other.

> Like all books, this self-help book is a co-creative project. When you watch a TV show or a movie, what you see looks like what it physically represents … But when you read a book, what you see are black squiggles on pulped wood or, increasingly, dark pixels on a pale screen. To transform these icons into characters and events, you must imagine. And when you imagine, you create. It's in being read that a book becomes a book, and in each of a million different readings a book becomes one of a million different books, just as an egg becomes one of potentially a million different people when it's approached by a hard swimming and frisky school of sperm.[63]

The novel operates on two levels of dialogue—one level narrates the plot and the second, like this passage, provides another level of commentary in which it knowingly comments on its own workings. Through this metatextuality, the novel calls the reader's attention to the process of its own creation as well as the protagonist's and reader's self-development through co-constitution, insisting all the while that the novel, its author, its protagonist, or its reader, do not exist by virtue of individual effort alone. Rather they become their own unique individual selves—"a book becomes one of a million different books" and "an egg becomes one of potentially a million different people" depending on who it forms a relationship with.

This idea of "co-creation" or co-constitution being central to the act of reading self-help is why the novel's protagonist and its reader are both addressed as the second person "you." For if the protagonist's selfhood is produced by the reader and the author working together, the protagonist's self is in some sense also the reader and the author's self. The reader is interchangeable with the author and both are interchangeable with the protagonist. All of them could be "you," separated only by circumstance, by the sheer chance of which sperm approaches which egg. The interchangeability of the author/narrator/protagonist/reader is confirmed by the narrator's injunction that "for our collaboration to work … you must know yourself well enough to understand what you want and where

---

[63] Hamid, *How to Get Filthy Rich in Rising Asia*, 97.

you want to go. Self-help books are two-way streets, after all. Relationships." The "collaboration" between author, reader, and protagonist are "relationships" within a network that co-constitutes everyone within it.

If the reading self is continually dependent on their co-creation through this textual network, the self in the land of self-help is a slippery one. This is why Hamid writes that "a self-help book is an oxymoron. You read a self-help book so someone who isn't yourself can help you, that someone being the author." The self is an oxymoron because it is coproduced by someone who is not the self. Yet this slipperiness is "good. Slippery can be pleasurable." Slippery can be pleasurable because it renders the self the responsibility of someone more than just the self—a fact which conversely amounts to the greatest freedom—that of living one's life as part of a larger whole.

How does this emphasis on the self as a product of co-constitution rethink the form of the affirmative bildungsroman? Hamid uses the form to depict a very different kind of bildung than the genre's typical compromise between an individual and society. "You" is not a passive individual who comes to adapt to social norms and injunctions. Rather, because he and the reader and the author are constituted by, and constitutive of, his own story, he is also a creator of the social context within which his story takes place. He is both the individual and the society. This means that his will, and that of the larger community within which he lives, is in concord. He therefore possesses the ultimate freedom; he is an agent. And, as an agent, he models self-transcendence through co-constitution as an inherently empathetic act. This is apparent at the end of the text, when the aim of becoming filthy rich in rising Asia is replaced by a very different goal: that of recognizing the truth of co-constitution in a world that seeks to deny it. To do this, he must imagine his life through that of others. He must embody empathy:

> As you create this story and I create this story, I would like to ask you how things were. I would like to ask you about the person who held your hand when dust entered your eye or ran with you from the rain. I would like to tarry here awhile with you, or if tarrying is impossible, to transcend my here, with your permission, in your creation, so tantalizing to me, and so unknown. That I can't do this doesn't stop me from imagining it. And how strange that when I imagine, I feel. The capacity for empathy is a funny thing.[64]

This passage suggests that the self's greatest existential truth is that he exists in and through other people. This is the novel's greatest intervention, and Hamid stresses

---

[64] Hamid, *How to Get Filthy Rich in Rising Asia*, 214.

this point by highlighting the narrator/protagonist's words through the use of the first person "I" for the first time in the novel. In this passage, the "I" is allied with the "you," so that it is unclear who—the protagonist, the narrator, the author, or the reader—is implied by each pronoun. The syntax merges "you" and "I" into one, performing the truth of the self's co-constitution through form and content. In doing so, Hamid suggests that this idea of the self is not just inherent to Sufi poetry, but to the novel and to self-help. For the novel also relies on the practice of untethering—"to transcend my here"—which means detaching oneself from one's own situation to imagine one's life through the narrated experiences of other people. Moreover, Hamid suggests that this process of untethering is inextricably linked to empathy, for imagining leads to feeling.

In line with this vision, the novel ends with a transcending of the particularity of the self for interchangeability and universality. "You" has now reached the end of his life, surrounded by his relations, as he lies in a hospital bed:

> And you are ready to die well, ready to die like a man, like a woman, like a human, for despite all else you have loved, you have loved your father and your mother and your brother and your sister and your son and, yes, your ex-wife, and you have loved the pretty girl, you have been beyond yourself, and so you have courage, and you have dignity, and you have calmness in the face of terror, and awe, and the pretty girl holds your hand, and you contain her, and this book, and me writing it, and I too contain you, who may not yet even be born, you inside me inside you, though not in a creepy way, and so may you, may I, may we, so may all of us confront the end.[65]

"Your" love pushes "you" "beyond yourself" so that "you" contains other "yous." Hamid humorously notes that he does not mean this in "a creepy way," for this perpetual interconnectedness, at the end, is life's most profound truth. As Poon points out, the novel juxtaposes the time–space compression enacted by the protagonist's remembering of his loving relationships with the time–space compression enacted by globalization in the service of markets. In the protagonist's case, the kind of connection being celebrated is the "capacity for imagination, which allows us to truly traverse time and space by providing us an experience of sympathy and an occasion for contemplating solidarity" as well as the way that one's life is measured and produced through one's loving relationships. This interconnectedness is a truth that is a rewriting of the Sufi mystic Rumi's poetry into the novel form:

---

[65] Hamid, *How to Get Filthy Rich in Rising Asia*, 222.

> The minute I heard my first love story
> I started looking for you,
> not knowing how blind that was.
> Lovers don't meet somewhere.
> They're in each other all along.⁶⁶

The love spoken of here is a radical Sufi love through which one connects with the divinity that runs through the universe and through each being. "You" is both particular but universal, because the "you" is not just a man but also "a woman," "a human." The "you" is interchangeable and is defined not by the process of getting filthy rich in rising Asia but by one's love for others. Love is a bond that constitutes "you" and everyone "you" has loved, which is why "I contain you and we" and everyone else. Together and through our love for one another in Sufi mysticism, the "I," the "you," the "me," the "we," the "all of us," make up the divine essence of the universe.

I am arguing here that Hamid does not do away with the genre of self-help but rather recuperates and remakes it in line with an older spiritual universalism of freedom that relies on transcending the self through one's loving relationships with others. The ground of this freedom is the recognition that these others are not 'other' at all, but co-constitutive of the self. The novel performs this universalism through its form, rewriting the adaptation bildungsroman's conservative remodeling of Freedom Inc. through the Sufi love poem, which Hamid sees as the first ever form of self-help. The form of Hamid's novel performs this message of freedom through love, presenting the reader with a story structure—complete with its connections and multiple ties—within which the self and the world are mutually intertwined and inextricable. Such a reimagining of freedom is why Hamid declares in an interview that "the very act of writing is a loving act."⁶⁷

When my mother-in-law began to read self-help books, she too imagined her reading of them as a loving act. For she was attempting to remake herself for the sake of her sons' futures, which had suddenly been unanchored from the safety of the large extended family network. Thus, ironically, even as she consumed Freedom Inc.'s version of entrepreneurial freedom, her enactment of it was a co-creative act of survival. I deliberately highlight the messiness and ambivalence of her journey—hers was simultaneously a feminist mode of self-fashioning that relied on the myth of absolute autonomy and a submission to a

---

⁶⁶ Coleman Barks, *Rumi's Little Book of Love and Laughter Teaching Stories and Fables* (Newbury Port, MA: Hampton Roads Publishing, 2016), Poem 1246—Rumi.
⁶⁷ Chicago Humanities Festival, Mohsin Hamid: *How to Get Filthy Rich in Rising Asia*, https://www.youtube.com/watch?v=0EaIkSNAsWU.

patriarchal model of entrepreneurial alpha-masculinity. It was simultaneously a process of discovering her individuality and also a process of intertwining her life more fully with that of her husband and children. And yet, through this contradictory self-fashioning, she created a myriad of selves enmeshed in various different networks richer and more freeing than the limiting ties of the patriarchal extended family. The freedom she created out of the self-help genre's myth of absolute autonomy was one that could not be reduced to a life of absolute autonomy. Her journey, alongside Adiga and Hamid's adoption and creative re-constitution of self-help, presents a more complex engagement with the genre and its possibilities, despite itself.

Previous chapters have focused on the way that a gendered capitalism in the new India promotes particular waged or entrepreneurial femininities and masculinities through the discourse of Freedom Inc. The process of exploring this gendering has thrown into relief the contextual universalisms of individual freedom and gendered being that complicate and counter Freedom Inc. through storytelling. Chapter 4 more explicitly explores how capitalist masculinities and femininities position men and women in relation to one another, particularly in the domain of romantic love.

4

# Chasing Freedom through Romantic Love in Popular and Literary Fiction

I was nineteen when I happened to meet my future spouse, Rahul. It was summer in Belgium, where I grew up as a Non-Resident Indian (NRI), and I was home from college for the holidays. The chemistry was such that we kept in touch for a number of years through long-distance Skype calls and furtive flights to see each other during vacations. We found ourselves falling in love and finally decided to broach the subject of getting married with our families. I come from a conservative Hindu family within which no one had yet had a "love marriage." What this means is that all previous marriage matches in the family had been introduced and vetted by the family elders before being okayed or rejected by the prospective bride or groom. Since I was choosing my own spouse, this accepted way of doing things presented a series of questions about how things would go when I broached the subject with my parents. Somewhat naively, I believed that I would simply introduce my parents to Rahul, they would approve, a wedding date would be scheduled in consultation with his parents, and we would get married. But when I told my parents that I wanted to marry Rahul, they asked me for all the information they considered relevant (his professional, regional, religious, and family background), read over this "biodata" carefully, and then, seemingly satisfied, simply informed me that we would talk about marriage when Rahul had graduated from graduate school and had found a job. I was taken aback. I didn't think the biodata criteria they were so interested in had anything to do with the kind of person Rahul was. I was also completely surprised that this was not going to be a simple "we approve" or "we don't approve" communication. Finally, I didn't think it fair that we would have to wait until *they* considered us ready to marry.

When Rahul was about to graduate, I brought up our wish to marry again with my parents, and this time, my father, the oldest of eight siblings, decided that he would reach out to Rahul's parents and would begin talking to his numerous brothers and sisters about the prospect of my marriage. My father's conversation with Rahul's parents and his trip to meet them in Bangalore, India, however, was similarly nonconclusive. As conversations with the entire extended family about Rahul's suitability dragged on, I grew more and more frustrated. As far as I was concerned, I had already made the decision to marry, and no one else had the right to pretend that that decision was not mine to make. After multiple arguments with my parents in which my father told me that it was important to him that all his brothers and sisters felt comfortable with this marriage, Rahul and I decided that we would continue to see and to love each other, whether married or not.

One day in December, over three years after I had first broached the topic of marriage, my father called me. I was in Ithaca, NY, working toward my PhD at Cornell University. Rahul was finishing his PhD at Carnegie Mellon. The Christmas vacation was about to start. "Book a flight," my father said. "We've spoken to Rahul's parents and to everyone in our family, and we've booked you a wedding venue. Your wedding will be on the 22nd of December." And this is how I was married. It was a gigantic wedding with all of my cousins and relatives present. As soon as the wedding was over, Rahul was embraced as part of my huge extended family. Today, he is as enmeshed in this close network of kinship relations as if he had been born into them.

I relate this experience because of what it reveals about the difference between distinctive kinds of love. For me, my love for Rahul and my desire to marry him was an autonomous decision that had to do with our compatibility with each other. It did not concern anyone else. For my parents and extended family, this kind of love did not exist, or at least it didn't matter. This is why my parents went about converting our "love marriage" into an "arranged marriage." For them, love and marriage were not acts of individual autonomy but collective decisions. Years later, when I read the sociologist Eva Illouz on the changing nature of love, my parents' views began to make sense to me. Illouz refers to non-modern notions of love through her definition of "character," which is the capacity to mold oneself to a moral purpose that transcends individual desires and interests, confirming one's obligations to others. "Character" requires that the self's reputation and honor is regulated by public rules of conduct toward others—including those one courts. Who we love is also thus the one who holds us accountable to a moral code that transcends both. In the context of love and courtship, character designates the fact that both lovers derive their personal sense of value directly from their capacity to enact moral codes and ideals, even when they go against their own self-interests or result in the lovers' potential separation. Love here is not instrumental; it does not serve one's own interests. Rather it is part of the moral dimension that organizes emotional life, which is also simultaneously public and collective. My parents were acting on this character-driven notion of freedom and love when they were trying to make sure that Rahul's family and mine held the same agreed on moral codes and when they made sure that everyone in the extended family had been both informed and consulted regarding our match.

Such an idea of love seems vastly outdated today, as it did to me when I struggled to bring my parents to respect my decision to marry Rahul. I did not realize, then, that they already did respect it but needed to make sure the community and kinship relations in which they were embedded did too. Yet, surprisingly, my own understanding of love as an autonomous decision made in recognition of a deep emotional connection between two individuals seems just as outdated today as my parents' ideas of love. For in post-1990s India, the kind of love that is ascendant in popular and literary discourse is increasingly a fungible commodity. Romantic love, in the texts I read in this chapter, is an emotion that is separable from the self and subject to a process of self-evaluation and rational judgment. It is evaluated because it must fulfill a function; it is instrumental, existing as a means to an end, and that end is increasingly to confirm a revenue generating entrepreneurial alpha-masculinity. When Freedom Inc. is gendered as masculine, it emphasizes the ability to transform oneself into a competitive, revenue stream. The extent of one's successful self-transformation toward this kind of individual freedom is evaluated through one's ability to acquire a romantic partner, and one's emotion for that partner is therefore also a means to an end; a measurement of one's own financial success. In this way, the realms of romantic love and work are linked to each other. The competitive man achieves the prize of freedom and of romantic love by commodifying components of himself, including his emotions.

I read Chetan Bhagat's popular novels, *One Night at the Call Center* (2005) and *Half Girlfriend* (2014), as well as Netflix's enormously popular reality show *Indian Matchmaking* (2020) to explore the Freedom Inc. version of love. I then turn to other conceptions of love captured in Vikram Seth's *A Suitable Boy* (1993) and Manju Kapur's literary novels, *Difficult Daughters* (1998) and *Custody* (2011). In Bhagat, women are positioned as objects to be won by the "better man"; the "half girlfriend" only becomes a "full one" when the hero successfully petitions the Bill Gates Foundation to donate money to rural India, or when he resigns from a call center serving "power-hungry, uncouth" Americans and becomes a successful entrepreneur instead. Women in these texts are not the subjects of freedom but solely the vehicles through which men can measure the success of their own self-transformation into free subjects, with freedom becoming a synonym for revenue-generating capacity. Acquiring the object of one's "love" is a way of confirming the self's status as a successful man who can compete in an economic and romantic marketplace. Vikram Seth's *A Suitable Boy* and Manju Kapur's novels, *Difficult Daughters* and *Custody*, represent another notion of individual freedom built upon character-driven ideas of love that I now recognize as part of my parents' ontologies of freedom. Together these texts point to the changing nature of individual freedom in India as charted through the lens of romantic love. I ask: what constraints are built into these different kinds of "freedom?" What sacrifices must be made? How must the self be shaped?

## Freedom Inc. in the Novels of Chetan Bhagat

Chetan Bhagat is the most popular English language writer in India today. He initially turned to writing as a break from his international investment banking career. Together, his eight novels have sold millions of copies and almost all have inspired Bollywood films. He is actively read by millions and hailed as "the biggest-selling English-language novelist in India's history."[1] He writes in a simple colloquial English that makes itself available to readers who regard English as a second language. In fact, he has even expressed the wish that his novels function as language learning tools for rural and urban Indian youth. His stories are plot driven love stories and often appear simplistic—as if they are written to be made into Bollywood rom-coms. They contain mostly flat characters and avoid literary registers of symbolism and metaphor.

For Ulka Anjaria, Bhagat's novels represent a "new provincialism" from the vantage point of India's small towns rather than its big cities, "offering an imagination of national futurity" that is based in India and not abroad.[2] As such, they are written for an audience of youth based in the small towns, many of whom, as Craig Jeffrey has shown, are stuck in situations of endless waiting for fulfilling and sustainable employment. But despite its provincial setting, Bhagat's writing offers an aspirational vision that revolves around India's place in the global economy. The stories embrace a free market capitalism, revolving

---

[1] Donald Greenlees, "An Investment Banker Finds Fame Off the Books," *New York Times*, March 26, 2008, https://www.nytimes.com/2008/03/26/books/26bhagat.html (accessed March 10, 2021).
[2] Ulka Anjaria, "The New Provincialism," in Ulka Anjaria, *Reading India Now: Contemporary Formations in Literature and Popular Culture* (Philadelphia: Temple University Press, 2019), 28.

around individual empowerment and entrepreneurialism, while denigrating government led welfare initiatives like farm subsidies. In his speeches and newspaper columns, Bhagat has made clear that individual innovation directed within the global economy is the only path to national development. His novels have overwhelmingly male protagonists who succeed when they transform themselves into revenue streams but do so in a way that elevates India's position within the global economy. In an echo of Gurcharan Das's representation of India's economic liberalization as its true era of independence, Bhagat represents this version of individual freedom as the only route toward national freedom. This coupling of individual freedom with national liberalization is also apparent in two of Bhagat's novels, *Half Girlfriend* and *One Night at the Call Center*.

*Half Girlfriend* is about Madhav Jha, a rural boy from a village in Bihar, India's most backward state. The novel describes Madhav's trouble fitting into St. Stephens, an elite Delhi college, because he cannot speak fluent English. He nevertheless gains admission through the sports quota and falls in love with the rich and beautiful Riya Somani. When he asks Riya to be his girlfriend, she refuses but agrees to be his "half girlfriend." Frustrated, Madhav tries to get her to prove her commitment by delivering an obscene ultimatum for her to either sleep with him or "get lost." Disgusted, Riya refuses to talk to Madhav anymore and marries her childhood friend. Heartbroken, Madhav returns to Bihar, where he helps his mother run her school. The school's lack of amenities or funds drives Madhav to appeal to the Bill Gates Foundation for help. To convince Gates, who is due to visit Bihar, Madhav has to prepare a speech in English, the language that is his Achilles' heel and the source of his insecurities. Seeking help from an English coaching center, Madhav happens to run into Riya, who is now divorced. Riya helps him learn English and to prepare a successful speech that wins Madhav the funding he seeks. However, when he finishes delivering the speech, Riya is gone. She leaves a note stating that she is in the last stage of lung cancer and has only three months left to live. Madhav is heartbroken. One day, three years later, he comes across one of Riya's old journals in which she reveals that she faked her cancer because of a confrontation with Madhav's mother, who didn't want her son to marry a divorcee. Madhav flees to New York to find her. They are happily reunited and return to Bihar, where they marry and run his school together.

*One Night at the Call Center* begins with a frame story that recounts a train journey from Kanpur to Delhi. During the journey, the narrator meets a beautiful girl who tells him a story about six youth working at Connexions Call Centre in Gurgaon, Haryana. Each character in the story, including the male protagonist,

Shyam, needs to confront and remediate an aspect of themselves or their lives that they are dissatisfied with. For Shyam, this aspect is his unrequited love for his coworker Priyanka, who has recently gotten engaged to an NRI from the United States who earns a good salary working for Microsoft. Shyam is also dissatisfied with his boss, Bakshi, a bossy, unfair manager who continues to take credit for all of Shyam's work. Vroom, Shyam's friend and coworker, is similarly exasperated by call center work, tired of the verbal abuse he has to endure from racist American clients. One night the coworkers receive a phone call from God, who advises each to take charge of their own lives and guides them on the best way to work through their dissatisfactions and to achieve their dreams and goals. As a result, Shyam gets Priyanka and the entrepreneurial career he always wanted.

Bhagat's novels define their version of masculinized individual freedom by setting up a dichotomy between unfree men defined as "losers" who are trapped within a nexus of constraints that they cannot overcome, and men who successfully construct themselves as entrepreneurs of their lives. The "loser" is one who possesses no capital; he fails to sell himself in exchange for money or social respect and therefore must also give up the prospect of love. The winner, the free man, is one who manages to turn himself into a revenue stream. Each novel sets up a bildungsromanian structure beginning with a "loser" at odds with his social order and rejected by the girl he desires. After a journey of overcoming obstacles, the "loser" becomes a hero and is rewarded with the girl. In line with this basic plot structure, *One Night at the Call Center* ends triumphantly with the following words:

> I used to feel I was a good for nothing non-achiever. But that is not true. After all, I helped save lots of jobs at a call center, taught my boss a lesson, started my own company, was chosen over a big catch NRI groom by a wonderful girl and now I even finished a whole book. This means that i) I can do whatever I really want ii) God is always with me and iii) there is no such thing as a loser after all.[3]

The protagonist, Shyam, attains freedom—"I can do whatever I really want"—because he achieves an income stream that is not dependent on a boss who buys his labor. Rather his income depends on his own management of his self as capital. This is confirmed by his boast that he has "started my own company" and "finished a whole book." Shyam here is entrepreneur of himself, "being for himself his own capital, being for himself his own producer, being for himself the source of [his] earnings."[4] As a result, Shyam is "chosen over a big catch NRI

[3] Chetan Bhagat, *One Night at the Call Center* (New Delhi: Rupa Publications, 2014), 253.
[4] Michel Foucault, *The Birth of Biopolitics* (London: Palgrave Macmillan, 2008), 226.

groom by a wonderful girl."⁵ The last words of the passage "there is no such thing as a loser after all," are aimed at Bhagat's many small-town underemployed male readers, giving them the confidence that they, like Shyam, may have thought of themselves as "losers" but can also succeed in transforming themselves.

Bhagat represents Shyam's success in terms of him having won the ultimate freedom—"I can do whatever I really want." But, in reality, this seemingly broad conception of freedom is a narrow one, reduced to the freedom to compete, the freedom to earn, the freedom to produce oneself according to what will be rewarded by the market. Freedom Inc. ignores the ways that such freedom is still governed by the constraints of the market as well as the discursive constraints that shape a subject. What kinds of choice and rationality now govern and constrain the self? What kinds of gendered constellations of value must he adhere to in order to be seen as free? What kinds of conditions, disguised as "freedoms," must he submit to?

As the quote given earlier and the structure of the novel confirms, one important constraint is that of a compulsory and competitive heterosexuality. The male entrepreneur's success is measured by whether he is sexually rewarded by the girl of his choice by the end of the novel. What, then, does it mean to be an entrepreneur in relation to love? If the competitive self is an income stream, the components of the self are what can be commodified in order to generate that income stream. Within this framework, the ontology of emotions undergoes a drastic change. Eva Illouz writes that emotions, including love, are now understood as objects of rational analysis that can be detached from the subject for control and clarification. Such an emotional ontology makes intimate relationships evaluable according to abstract criteria so that they are transformed into cognitive objects that can be compared with each other and be subjected to a cost–benefit analysis. Illouz writes that "when we use commensuration to help us decide things, value is based on the trade-offs we make between different elements of the decision. Indeed, the process of commensuration makes intimate relationships more likely to be fungibles, that is, objects which can be traded or exchanged."⁶ Emotions and romantic relationships become exchangeable consumer choices, which stand in as metrics for the successful attainment of Freedom Inc.

Bhagat's characters compare and trade intimate relationships, and therefore romantic emotions, just as if they are commodities. Within this consumer model

---

⁵ Bhagat, *One Night at the Call Center*, 253.
⁶ Eva Illouz, *Cold Intimacies: The Making of Emotional Capitalism* (Cambridge: Polity Press, 2007), 36.

of choice as individual freedom, Shyam's girlfriend Priyanka faces constant pressure from her mother to marry well. Via marriage websites like *shaadi.com*, Priyanka encounters marriage as an economy of abundance, where the self must choose and maximize her options, using techniques of cost–benefit analysis and efficiency. She finally chooses to marry an NRI Indian man, Ganesh, who works for Microsoft and is "well settled"[7] in the United States because this would be a more profitable choice. Shyam is hurt but understands, asking: "How am I going to succeed against Mr. Perfect Match Ganesh? A house with a pool, a car that costs more than ten years of my salary, freaking working for the world's top company … . No way I could ever buy a Lexus. Maybe a Maruti 800, one day but that's about it."[8] Shyam knows that he just cannot compete. He must let Priyanka go because he has not yet achieved the epitome of competitive masculine freedom:

> My job was going nowhere, with Bakshi bent on sucking every last drop of my blood. Maybe he was right—I just did not have the strategic vision or managerial leadership or whatever crap things you are supposed to have to do well in life. Maybe Priyanka's mom was right too—her daughter was stuck with a loser.[9]

In Bhagat, the word "loser" signifies an incomplete man, one who has not yet transitioned to a competitive state of being able to do "whatever I really want," and therefore one who has no choice but to forego his love interest. He can do nothing but acknowledge to Priyanka that "I can't offer you what Mr Microsoft can."[10]

Despite its generation of sympathy for Shyam the "loser," the narrative perspective does not contest this economized account of romantic love or of what counts as freedom. All the characters leverage the idea that the romantic encounter should be the result of the best possible choice of mate, who is himself the man who has best commodified himself to generate an income that can buy other commodities. A coworker tells Priyanka: "Marry him sooner, you get to drive the Lexus sooner."[11] And Priyanka herself defends her mother's pressure on her to choose the most profitable groom:

> She married my dad who was just a government employee only because he seemed like a decent human being. But her sisters waited to marry better

---

[7] Bhagat, *One Night at the Call Center*, 232.
[8] Bhagat, *One Night at the Call Center*, 242.
[9] Bhagat, *One Night at the Call Center*, 128.
[10] Bhagat, *One Night at the Call Center*, 242.
[11] Bhagat, *One Night at the Call Center*, 126.

qualified boys and they are richer today. Her concern for me comes from there. She is my mother. It is not as if she does not know what is good for me. I want someone doing well in his career as well.[12]

Priyanka's word choices here acknowledge her slippage between the man she considers a "decent human being"—a category that usually encompasses values, emotions, and morality—and the man who is likely to end up "richer." The phrasing she uses to describe her mother: "She married my dad who was just a government employee only because he seemed like a decent human being. But her sisters waited to marry better qualified boys and they are richer today" suggests, through the use of the words "but" and "seemed" that the actual "decent human being" is the one who is "better qualified," who will end up "richer." Under Freedom Inc., the definition of "decent human being" itself changes from an ethical register to an economic one.

These passages in Bhagat resonate with Eva Illouz's account of neoliberal love as a market, which turns the search for a partner into an economic transaction:

> it transforms the self into a packaged product competing with others on an open-ended market regulated by the law of supply and demand; it makes the encounter the outcome of a more or less stable set of preferences; it makes the process of searching constrained by the problem of efficiency; it structures encounters as market niches; it attaches a more or less fixed economic value to profiles—and makes people anxious about their value in such a structured market and eager to improve their position in that market.[13]

The result of the economization of love is that Shyam must have his masculinity confirmed in both the private sphere—that usually concerned with romantic emotion—and the public sphere of economic exchange. Both spheres become intertwined with each other, each mirroring the other, absorbing each other's mode of action and justification, and ensuring that "instrumental reason be used in and applied to the realm of emotions and, conversely, making self-realization and the claim to a full emotional life become the compass of instrumental reason."[14]

This account of romantic love as a fungible commodity applies to the way both men and women perceive romantic prospects. When Vroom describes his girlfriend's complaints about him, he notes that she thinks that he does not "know what love is" because he "cares for cars and bikes more than girls … ."[15]

---

[12] Bhagat, *One Night at the Call Center*, 131.
[13] Illouz, *Cold Intimacies*, 88.
[14] Illouz, *Cold Intimacies*, 112.
[15] Bhagat, *One Night at the Call Center*, 116.

Vroom's response is not a denial of this equation between cars, bikes, and girls but an analogy about women's similar approach to love: "That is such an unfair comparison. It's like asking women what they care for more, nice shoes or men. There is no easy answer."[16] This is not a line delivered ironically; the narrative trajectory of the novel confirms that men and women, and their emotions, are as commodities to each other. This means that Priyanka finally chooses to give up her Microsoft NRI groom and marry Shyam not because she begins to believe in an idealized version of love as noninstrumental, holistic, and free of worldly interests. Rather she chooses Shyam because while he "may not be successful now, it doesn't mean he doesn't have the potential."[17] These words confirm the ways that a competitive heterosexuality commodifies love into a fungible available only to the man who best transforms himself into an income stream. Priyanka accepts Shyam as her husband because she is making a financial bet on his eventual profitability that she hopes will pay off.

Bhagat adds yet another constraint to the crucible within which freedom must be formed. A truly free man—one who can "do whatever I want"—has to be self-interested in a way that is also patriotic. Whether one gets the girl depends not just on how well one generates an income stream but also on one's potential for moving the nation forward toward freedom. Within the "end of history" narrative exemplified by Gurcharan Das among others, individual freedom depends on national freedom, which itself depends on how successfully capitalism has spread to that nation. Bhagat inverts this equation; the progress of the male citizen toward freedom becomes a synecdoche for the progress of India as a whole. Thus Priyanka clarifies her choice to marry Shyam through an analogy between him and India, a nation that is poor but has a lot of potential. It is patriotic for Priyanka to choose Shyam because his potential will carry India forward:

> "Shyam, you know how Vroom said just because India is poor doesn't mean you stop loving it?" Priyanka said.
>
> "What?" I blinked at the change of topic. "Oh yes. And I agree, it is our country after all."
>
> "Yes, we love India because it is ours. But, do you know the other reason why we don't stop loving it?"
>
> "Why?"

---

[16] Bhagat, *One Night at the Call Center*, 116.
[17] Bhagat, *One Night at the Call Center*, 242.

"You don't because it isn't completely India's fault that we are behind. Yes, some of our past leaders could have done things differently, but now we have the potential and we know it. And as Vroom says, 'one day we will show them.' I thought, this is the same as my Shyam, who may not be successful now, but it doesn't mean he doesn't have the potential. And it sure as hell doesn't mean I stop loving him."[18]

"Potential" here refers to Shyam's capacity for a patriotic masculinity that can uplift the nation if the hero chooses the right kind of work. Call center work is the wrong kind of job because it puts one in a subservient position as an individual, as a man, and as a citizen of a nation within a global hierarchy. For Bhagat, the racism a man faces in the job becomes an index of his subservience as an individual, as a man, and as a citizen of India. Take, for instance, this exchange between Vroom and an American client who berates him on the phone:

"'So what did you have to do to get this job? Fucking degree in nuclear physics?'"

"Sir, do you need help with your cleaner or not?" Vroom said.

"C'mon son, answer me. I don't need your help. Yeah, I'll change the dust bag. What about you guys? When will you change your dusty country?"

"Excuse me, sir, but I want you to stop talking like that," Vroom said.

"Oh really, now some brown kid will tell me what to do—"

William Fox's voice stopped abruptly as I cut off the call. Vroom didn't move for a few seconds. His whole body trembled and he was breathing heavily. Then he placed his elbows on the table and covered his face with his hands. Then he banged a fist on the table.

"Damn," he screamed and kicked hard under the table. Vroom stood up and his six-foot-plus frame towered above us.

"Guys, there are two things I cannot stand," he said and showed us two fingers. "Racists. And Americans."[19]

The novel depicts America and India as engaged in a Manichean struggle. Another character in the novel declares that Americans are "fat, loud, thick and divorce all the time." The God character—who, by virtue of being God, speaks what the reader takes to be the universal truth—confirms such a negative judgment, noting that "Americans may have many things, but they are not the happiest people on earth by any stretch. Any country obsessed with war can't

---

[18] Bhagat, *One Night at the Call Center*, 242.
[19] Bhagat, *One Night at the Call Center*, 110.

be happy … many of them have serious issues in the head … they are the most scared and paranoid people on earth."[20] Through these characters, Bhagat asserts that India is the underdog in the relationship between a "developing" country and a global superpower only because Indian men are not living up to their manhood.

> Look at our country, we are still so behind these Americans. Even when we know we are no less than them … I should not have taken up a job just for money. Call centers pay more, but only because the exchange rate is in the favor of Americans. They toss their loose change at us. It seems like a lot in rupees. But jobs that pay less could be better. There could be jobs that define me, make me learn or help my country. I justified it by saying money is progress. But it is not true. Progress is building something lasting for the future.[21]

The answer is for India's men to take up jobs that "define" them but that also progress the national cause. Patriotism becomes one more of the constraints through which Freedom Inc. may be successfully realized by Bhagat's young small-town male protagonists.

Another of Freedom Inc.'s constraints is the necessity of speaking English. For Bhagat, learning English is patriotic because it is the vehicle through which his heroes can achieve the uplift of the nation within a global economy. This is markedly different from the role of English in the public sphere in the past, wherein the language represented colonial domination prior to independence; a language somewhat at odds with the nationalist imagination in the 1980s and 1990s; and then finally a cosmopolitan futurity in the 2000s. Anjaria notes of Bhagat's celebration of English that "idealism has been replaced with utilitarianism, and, consequently, Indian English is now a platform of possibility."[22] Thus, in *Half Girlfriend,* when a professor at St. Stephens denigrates Madhav for not knowing English, he does so on the grounds that "English is no longer a foreign language, Mr. Jha. It's a global language. I suggest you learn it."[23] English here is Indian; it belongs to the world, of which India is a part, and its importance comes from its value as economic capital for India. A personal inability to wield English translates into a flaw as citizen, for without English, Madhav cannot work to uplift rural India by ensuring that poor Indian children

---

[20] Bhagat, *One Night at the Call Center*, 209.
[21] Bhagat, *One Night at the Call Center*, 204.
[22] Ulka Anjaria, "Chetan Bhagat and the New Provincialism," *American Book Review*, 36 (6), January 2015: 6–22.
[23] Chetan Bhagat, *Half Girlfriend*, in *Chetan Bhagat Collection (7 Books in 1)*, Kindle edition (Amazon Publishing, 2018), Location 4942.

get a good enough education to make as much money as Bill Gates one day. One of the constraints of Freedom Inc. here, one of its stipulations, is to master English well enough to prevail in a global economy.

This is why, in *Half Girlfriend*, Madhav's progress in the journey toward achieving Freedom Inc. happens through his struggle to learn English. At the beginning of the novel, his inability to speak English equates to his inability to get the girl, Riya Somani, and to his inability to compete as an Indian citizen with citizens of other nations in a global hierarchy. "I wanted to continue talking to her. I wanted to know her full name and her native place ... However, I didn't know how to ask her in English, the language one needed to impress girls."[24] When Madhav learns that Riya is studying for a degree in English he is disheartened: "A girl doing an English degree would never befriend a country bumpkin like me."[25] The phrase "country bumpkin" identifies the problem: the lack of English signifies a relegation to provinciality, to marginality. Madhav is not yet the kind of youth who can market himself and command an income stream within a global economy so he does not yet deserve the "full" girl. His half girlfriend is justified in playing the field for other men who are more "manly" than he is until he gets his act together. Madhav's own incomplete transformation into embodying Freedom Inc. means that he must be satisfied with being the "half" boyfriend of a "half" girlfriend.

There is also a gender binary at work in Bhagat's novels that takes the form of a zero-sum game. A complete man achieves his freedom by subjugating the woman who once dominated him. Bhagat's idea of masculine freedom relies on the eventual subordination of the woman that brought that freedom into being by accepting the man in question as a sexual partner. When men become free, they are rewarded with the right to "do anything I want," even if this means to be misogynistic and sexually dominating. This is apparent in Madhav's attempt to get Riya to sleep with him. To achieve this goal, he confers with his roommates in a process that he tellingly calls a "panel," a phrase that suggests a businesslike and rational decision-making process along the lines Eva Illouz describes as the rationalization of emotion. This panel tells him to invite Riya to his room in a bid to see whether she will sleep with him, telling Madhav to "Make Bihar proud." The wording here foreshadows that Madhav will be doomed to failure because he is acting to make "Bihar proud" rather than to make India proud. The logic of the novel determines that a real man must reject an inward-looking provinciality,

---

[24] Bhagat, *Half Girlfriend*, Location 5053.
[25] Bhagat, *Half Girlfriend*, Location 5099.

replacing it with a global-facing patriotism that is provincial only in its location but not in its outlook. Since the reader knows that only such a man gets the girl, he expects that Madhav will be rejected. Indeed, Madhav's attempt at alpha-masculinity fails. When Riya rejects Madhav, he turns hostile, even violent, giving her a crude ultimatum: "Deti hai to de, varna kat le," which translates as "Fuck me, or fuck off."[26] Riya chooses the latter option, marries another man, and moves away, leaving Madhav heartbroken. The narrative makes clear that Madhav is a "loser" but not because his masculinity is misogynistic. Rather, he is a loser because he cannot yet get away with his misogyny; he does not yet deserve to use a woman. As he says at multiple other points in the novel: "Losers get words from girls; winners get kisses" and "We are losers. We don't get things easily: Marks, ranks, girls—nothing is easy for us … everyone takes us for a ride. From Kota classes to the bitch back home."[27]

*One Night at the Call Center* confirms these equations between a free alpha-masculinity and sexual domination and between an effeminate masculinity and sexual subordination. Vroom furnishes a masochistic analogy between his demeaning and unpatriotic call center work and sexual subordination and emasculation:

> "Yes, this salary has hooked me. Every night I come here and let people fuck me," Vroom said and picked up the telephone headset. "The Americans fuck me with this, in my ears hundreds of times a night. Bakshi fucks me with his management theories, backstabbing and threats to fire us. And the funny thing is, I let them do it. For money, for security—I let it happen. Come fuck me some more," Vroom said and threw the headset on the table.[28]

The Bhagat logic of masculine freedom as sexual domination and patriotism is once again at work in this novel. Vroom is stuck at the other end of the binary: unfree, effeminate, engaged in a nationally humiliating job, and therefore fucked.

# Freedom Inc. and Love in Reel Life: Netflix's *Indian Matchmaking*

The popularity of Bhagat's novels and of the Bollywood films they become suggests that their notions of Freedom Inc., love, and masculine success are

---

[26] Bhagat, *Half Girlfriend*, Location 6007.
[27] Bhagat, *Half Girlfriend*, Location 10452.
[28] Bhagat, *One Night at the Call Center*, 172.

shared by millions. The novels, in other words, are not only stories. They reflect and construct a powerful discursive imaginary of romantic love and gendered freedoms that has consequences in the real world. This discursive imaginary is also apparent in reality television shows such as Netflix's *Indian Matchmaking* that depict romantic love in the New India. The show aired in Summer 2020, documenting the journey of Indian matchmaker, Sima Taparia, as she helps singles and their families find suitable matches. The show takes viewers into the lives of men and women, including a young Texan professional called Aparna and another called Nadia, as they search for a life partner. As Taparia puts it, in helping them, she is participating in a centuries old and ubiquitous practice, for "In India we don't say 'arranged marriage.' There is marriage and then there is 'love marriage.' "[29] However, as becomes clear, this kind of matchmaking is a far cry from the arranged marriages of centuries past. *Indian Matchmaking*'s "arranged marriage," unlike my parents' character-driven notions of marriage as a communal process, presents love as a consumer choice. *Indian Matchmaking* demonstrates this particular formation of Freedom Inc. through the idea of the self as chooser.

The show's subjects look for a partner via an endless array of selections through which they can exercise particular lifestyle choices and thereby perform their individual freedom. The result is an infinite and shallow illusion of unique individuality produced by what one eats, where one holidays, and the shows one watches. When this evacuated self looks for love, she seeks someone who makes the same specific lifestyle choices, thereby affirming her own. In a telling scene, Aparna rejects a man because he does not know where the Bolivian salt flats are, a place to which she has recently traveled. She rejects a match who "seems to like the outdoors" because "I do not like the outdoors." She grimaces when Sima describes a potential match as "a very nice person who has a good sense of humour," because she "hates comedy."[30] The self here is reduced. Character is replaced by characteristics. Sima seems to confirm the viewers' own feelings when she complains that "Aparna is the hardest type of candidate to match because she thinks finding a life partner is like ordering from a menu."[31] This self is shored up, even co-constituted, by a love interest who makes the same choices

---

[29] Smriti Mundhra and Netflix, Season 1, Episode 1, "Slim, Trim, and Educated," *Indian Matchmaking*, 2020.
[30] Smriti Mundhra and Netflix, Season 1, Episode 1, "Slim, Trim, and Educated," *Indian Matchmaking*, 2020.
[31] Smriti Mundhra and Netflix, Season 1, Episode 1, "Slim, Trim, and Educated," *Indian Matchmaking*, 2020.

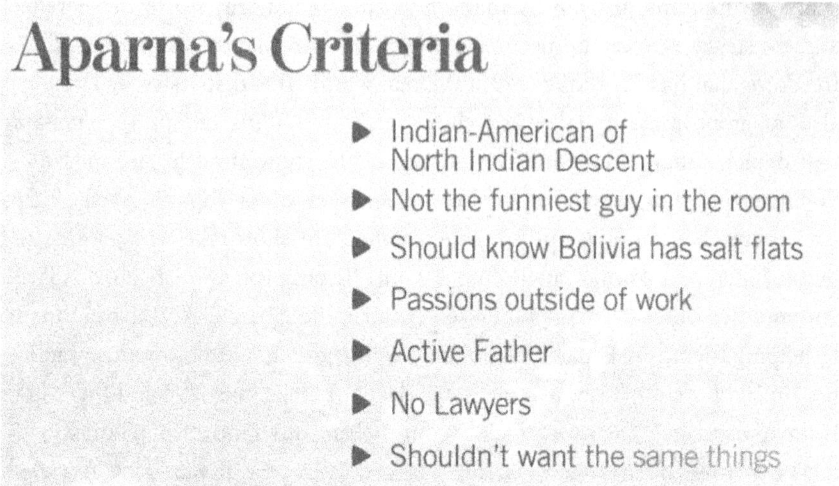

## Aparna's Criteria

- Indian-American of North Indian Descent
- Not the funniest guy in the room
- Should know Bolivia has salt flats
- Passions outside of work
- Active Father
- No Lawyers
- Shouldn't want the same things

**Figure 8** Aparna's criteria.

that the self does. This may be why the show makes much of a scene where Nadia is absolutely delighted at finding out that her date likes ketchup as much as she does. In the scene, a shared choice of ketchup stands in for the absence of any real substantive connection, signaling the potential for "love."

Interestingly, despite Sima's statement criticizing Aparna's method of choosing a partner, *Indian Matchmaking* does not seem to find something lacking in Aparna's model of self as consumer, nor in the fact that Aparna treats matches as dishes. Rather, the problem, according to Sima, is that, as a woman, Aparna should not be so picky. She should accept whatever she gets and acknowledge that love "cannot be tailor made. You have to adjust … compromise."[32] As if to confirm Taparia's viewpoint, the camera moves from close-ups of Aparna's face as she makes dismissive statements about potential matches to a graph listing all of the attributes she desires in her match.

The show juxtaposes this superimposed list, comedic in its extreme specificity, with a snippet of Aparna saying "so I'm not that picky," thereby sarcastically suggesting that she is exactly that. This gendered double standard on the part of the matchmakers, and perhaps of the show's narrative stance, is made obvious when another female candidate on the show, an ambitious professional, is critiqued by both Sima and another matchmaker for not wanting to leave behind her career and relocate to another city where her potential match lives. The show,

---

[32] Smriti Mundhra and Netflix, Season 1, Episode 1, "Slim, Trim, and Educated," *Indian Matchmaking*, 2020.

I am suggesting, represents a particular model of a free self that is reduced to the maker of consumer choices. Rather than critique this model, it genders this kind of freedom in a way that refuses an independent femininity while celebrating male assertiveness.

The show does not just represent Freedom Inc.'s notion of love as consumer choice, it also itself inadvertently participates in it. The form of the show seems to perform this ethos, for it flits between characters in the same way that consumers shop. One reviewer writes of the show that: "the characters are only supposed to represent one trait or idea and the show rarely lets them overflow into fullness, disallowing real intimacy as much as any arranged marriage meet-up. Characters repeat the same lines and thoughts ad nauseum, like MasterChef contestants describing a dish. The viewer too is encouraged to relate to characters as if they are no more than a commodified list of likes and dislikes. We view Aparna with a cynical distance, with the same kind of dismissive judgment that she herself exercises towards potential matches."[33] As in Bhagat's novels, Freedom Inc. reduces individual freedom to consumer choice, to the extent that love itself is commodified and rationalized. Viewers and match seekers are so busy flitting from commodified self to commodified self that they do not see that their freedom to choose is empty; that they have rationalized and commodified their emotions, defining themselves completely through consumer choices rather than through meaningful interpersonal relationships with others.

## Freedom as Character in Vikram Seth and Manju Kapur: An Alternative Model of Autonomous Choice

Bhagat's and *Indian Matchmaking*'s version of Freedom Inc. is the product of particular limiting contexts and conditions, producing some choices while displacing others. In this section, I argue that its cost is that people are not seen on account of their *characters*—those embodied moral referents and values that constitute one's responsibility to other individuals within one's community—but solely in terms of their *characteristics* like personal preferences, economic achievements, or sexual desirability.

---

[33] Paromita Vohra, "'Indian Matchmaking' Wastes the Opportunity to Become a Wonderful Show about Human Connections," *Economic Times*, July 26, 2020, https://economictimes.indiatimes.com/magazines/panache/indian-matchmaking-wastes-the-opportunity-to-become-a-wonderful-show-about-human-connections/articleshow/77171903.cms.

In contrast to this model of *love by characteristics*, Illouz explains her definition of *character-driven love* through the example of Jane Austen's heroines who exercise their freedom in the realm of love by molding their selves to a moral purpose that transcends their desires and interests, thereby confirming their obligations to others. Reading *Sense and Sensibility*, Illouz argues that even though Elinor Dashwood is in love with Edward Farrars, she rejoices when he does not break his engagement with Lucy for her sake because "breaking his promises to others would have made him morally unworthy. Clearly, Elinor's allegiance to her moral principles has precedence over her love for Edward, in the same way that his engagement to Lucy must take precedence over his feelings for Elinor."[34] In the context of love and courtship, self-interest takes a backseat because character designates that both lovers derive their personal sense of value directly from their capacity to enact moral codes and ideals, even if the result is the lovers' potential separation. The self's freedom, then, is performed through one's embodiment of publicly agreed on moral codes, which organize a communally constructed emotional life.

Indian novels in the decades prior to the opening up of the economy often registered a similar organization of selfhood and sensibility that was tied up with a sense of public duty toward one's friends, acquaintances, relations, and love interests. Free actions were those taken when acknowledging the grounds of one's interrelationships and acting in relation to them. Such an organization of subjectivity, and what happens when this subjectivity encounters a vastly different understanding of the "self" shaped by free market capitalism, is represented in the Anglophone novels of the Indian author, Manju Kapur. Kapur taught English literature in Miranda House College, Delhi University, for over twenty-five years. Her first novel, *Difficult Daughters*, was published in 1998 to critical acclaim and won the Commonwealth Prize for best first novel. Despite this transnational recognition, this novel and all her others are written in India for an educated Indian audience who are as likely to converse in the bhashas as they are in English. This is apparent from the fact that, like Bhagat's, her storylines are recreated for local television serials in Hindi and are consumed by mainstream viewers. Unlike Bhagat, however, Kapur's highly accomplished works straddle both the literary as well as popular and commercial spheres.

Manju Kapur's *Difficult Daughters,* published in the 1990s when the project of neoliberal India was just taking off and set in pre-partition Punjab, captures the costs of changing notions of freedom and love, as well as what happens when

---

[34] Eva Illouz, *Why Love Hurts: A Sociological Explanation* (Cambridge: Polity Press, 2014), 25.

they are no longer defined through ideas of character. The novel narrates the love story of Virmati, a teenager who falls in love with her married professor, Harish, and then eventually elopes with him, moving in with his long suffering first wife and family and producing a rift within her own. The outcome of this choice is narrated on the day of her wedding:

> Virmati was tired and depressed. Now that she was actually in Harish's house for the first time, she could see it was going to be difficult to live separately from everybody else … She looked at Harish, her brow wrinkled with unhappiness. "I should never have married you," she said slowly, "and it's too late now. I've never seen it so clearly. It's not fair." … She turned her aching feet obediently towards the gate. They went out and walked silently down the tree-lined road, towards nothing, away from a situation neither could escape. At the end of that road lay Virmati's old house. How far she was from it! Though married, she was dispossessed. Well so be it. She would walk tightlipped, mute, on the path her destiny had carved out for her.[35]

This passage registers the consequences of Virmati's marriage, the outcome of what she once perceived as being a purely self-interested, autonomous choice. However, Virmati quickly realizes that the choice is not in her interest at all, because one's self-interest, in practice, is not separable from one's duty toward others and from publicly agreed on morals. In marrying, Virmati and Harish wronged Harish's first wife and his children and deceived Virmati's own family. Virmati realizes too late that this is "not fair" to herself or to others. The result is that the self whose interests she sought to guard is left "dispossessed," for one cannot survive outside one's network of social relations. Having disregarded the relations that once constituted her "character," Virmati has no choice but to walk "towards nothing." She has rendered herself and her future empty.

I am suggesting that while it is tempting at first to read the novel as a quest for individual freedom and autonomy on behalf of a girl who resists arranged marriage, such a narrative is upended by the end of the novel. Virmati's seemingly free action is revealed to be another form of entrapment that leaves her with no choice in the larger sense; in terms of having the choice of multiple life paths that offer her a degree of self-fulfillment. Kapur tells us that Virmati must "obediently" "walk tightlipped, mute, on the path that her destiny" and notably not that which her free will, "had carved out for her." The novel speaks back to the rethinking of autonomy that I laid out in the introduction. For it reveals the way that an action

---

[35] Manju Kapur, *Difficult Daughters* (London: Faber & Faber, 1999), 196.

is autonomous when it shows "character." Since an individual is co-constituted through her relationships and circumstances within a community and cultural context, an action is only autonomous when it arises out of a process of engaging with and reflecting on these grounds and relationships. For if an individual has not grappled with her situation before acting in relation to that situation, how self-directed, or free, can that act truly be?

This passage from *Difficult Daughters* and its account of Virmati's isolation being the opposite of freedom reminds me of another famous literary wrangling with the idea of what it means to be truly free. Toni Morrison's *Beloved* ponders this question through the eyes of a runaway slave woman, Sethe, who prefers to kill her children rather than see them abused and enslaved by the plantation owners she ran away from. For this assertion of self-ownership and autonomy, Sethe ends up living in isolation, shunned by the Black community she was once a part of. In a moving passage, Sethe ponders the meaning of freedom in relation to her escape to this community:

> Sethe had had twenty-eight days—the travel of one whole moon—of unslaved life ... Days of healing, ease and real-talk. Days of company: knowing the names of forty, fifty other Negroes, their views, habits; where they had been and what they had done; of feeling their fun and sorrow along with her own, which made it better. One taught her the alphabet; another a stitch. All taught her how it felt to wake up at dawn and *decide* what to do with the day ... . Bit by bit, at 124 and in the Clearing, along with the others, she had claimed herself. Freeing yourself was one thing, claiming ownership of that freed self was another.[36]

In other words, Morrison suggests that to be truly free—to own herself—Sethe must figure out who her "self" actually is, but the only way that she can do that is with and through the support of the Black community around her. For without them, she cannot understand the meaning of being able to *decide* what to do with the day. She can only understand herself and the collective experience of slavery that produced her through them, which means that she cannot truly be free without them. It is also telling that Sethe can only rid herself of the ghosts of slavery that haunt her when the Black community that shunned her for her actions finally rallies around her in support.

Vikram Seth's renowned magnum opus, *A Suitable Boy* (1993), hailed as one of the longest novels ever written, is set in the tumultuous years after independence from Britain and also sets out a vision of individual freedom as

---

[36] Toni Morrison, *Beloved* (New York: Vintage, 2004), 112.

constituted through one's interrelationships and communities. As in *Difficult Daughters*, romantic love in *A Suitable Boy* is not an individualist choice but one made on the "foundation"[37] of relational ties, and through one's embodiment of publicly agreed on moral codes.

The novel follows four families in the period leading up to the first post-Independence national election of 1952 and focuses on Mrs. Rupa Mehra's efforts to arrange the marriage of her younger daughter, Lata, to a "suitable boy." Lata is a nineteen-year-old university student who initially refuses to be influenced by her family members about who to marry. Her story revolves around the choice she makes between her suitors: the Muslim student Kabir, the shoemaker Haresh who is of the same community background as she is, and the Bengali poet Amit. Themes central to the Nehruvian idea of India, including Hindu-Muslim antagonism, the status of lower castes, land reforms, and the end of the feudal zamindari system, form a backdrop to this matchmaking.

In what seems like a blow both to the Nehruvian idea of India as a secular multi-faith republic as well as to the idea of individual freedom as autonomous choice, Lata ends up repudiating her relationship with the Muslim Kabir, even though she is in love with him. Instead, she decides to marry Haresh, a more "suitable" match in the eyes of her mother who is horrified at the prospect of Lata marrying a Muslim:

> Never, never, absolutely not—dirty, violent, cruel, lecherous— ... He'll marry you—and next year he'll say "Talaq talaq talaq" and you'll be out on the streets. You obstinate, stupid girl! You should drown yourself in a handful of water for sheer shame.[38]

Lata is repelled by these discriminatory views, pointing to her mother's Muslim family friends, who her mother would never dream of characterizing in this manner: "Like Talat Khala?" demanded Lata. "Like Uncle Shafi? Like the Nawab Sahib of Baitar? Like Firoz and Imtiaz?" Nevertheless, Lata eventually relinquishes Kabir, an action rued by her best friend, Malati. Malati pleads with Lata to: "Look at the danger caused to the world by that sort of attitude" in a reference to the communal riots in Brahmpur, which in previous chapters have resulted in the near murder of dear Muslim family friends. Lata does not agree with Malati's logic here, and she insists on making a distinction between murderous Islamophobic views and her choice to marry within her own

---

[37] Manju Kapur, *Custody* (New Delhi: Random House, 2011), 391.
[38] Vikram Seth, *A Suitable Boy* (New York: Harper Perennial Modern Classics, 2005), 207.

community. Thus, even though Kabir rightly accuses her of making his faith "the basis on which you're acting," Lata insists that it underlies her decision only because marrying Kabir would mean losing her family. As she tells him:

> It's not possible—it never was—Because of my family ... However much they irritate me and constrain me, I can't give them up. I know that now. So much has happened. I can't give up my mother—[39]

Lata's decision is significant because it refuses the idea of romantic love as an individualist choice that is the product of absolute autonomy, for, as Lata realizes, there is no such thing as an autonomy that is absolute. Instead, the self's freedom to choose who to love is performed through a contextual ground of preexisting relations and social ties and through a publicly held morality that individuals embody through their actions. Lata's realization of this truth, unlike Virmati's late epiphany in *Difficult Daughters*, comes relatively early on, through the knowledge that her marriage to Kabir would never be a happy one, for they are constantly rowing their boat

> against the current of society, upstream towards the Barsaat Mahal; but surely there was a solution. Should they row harder, or agree to drift downstream? Should they row in a different river or try to change the direction of the river they were in? Should they jump out of the boat and try to swim? Or get a motor or a sail? Or hire a boatman?[40]

Lata decides not to marry Kabir when she realizes that there is no solution. Having to row against the tide of social norms and publicly agreed on moral values means that their mixed marriage "wouldn't work. No one else will let it work." Indeed, the sheer effort of maintaining a relationship in these circumstances means that Kabir and Lata's interactions "always had a somewhat illogical, incomplete, and insubstantial feel about them. They always met for a very short time, were constantly aware of the risk of discovery, and so, even during the brief while that they were together, seemed extremely awkward with each other. Kabir was straightforward in his conversations with everyone except Lata, and he wondered if she too might not be at her most complex and difficult when she was with him."[41]

*A Suitable Boy*, like *Difficult Daughters*, then, points to a time before Freedom Inc. when individual freedom is seen as constituted by one's interrelationships,

---

[39] Seth, *A Suitable Boy*, 1027.
[40] Seth, *A Suitable Boy*, 1114.
[41] Seth, *A Suitable Boy*, 1422.

social ties, and contexts. Lata's choice to marry Haresh is depicted as the product of a truer autonomy than her previous choice to marry Kabir because it is made on the basis of a communally constructed emotional life. The novel hints that this is the right choice because it is the one that will be the most likely to result in Lata's happiness. At the same time, the novel rues that this is the case, pointing to the tragic reality of a postindependence republic that, despite its status as a democratic secular nation, increasingly succumbs to communal politics and an extremist majoritarian Hinduism. This is why, despite setting up Lata's marriage to Haresh as the choice most likely to ensure her happiness, Seth infuses their wedding with a sense of pathos; for many characters, the reciting of the *gayatri mantra* during the ceremony brings to mind the enraged chanting of a murderous Hindu mob on the rampage. It is a reminder that while Lata's choice to give up Kabir is different from the Islamophobic rage of the mob, they are both products of the same social context of communal strife.

In this moment at the end of the novel, Seth seems to gesture toward an as-yet-unrealized future, when religious minorities are able to live alongside and with the Hindu majority in a vision akin to Dewey and Ambedkar's concept of endosmosis. In this respect, it is significant that Seth names Lata's first love, Kabir, after the medieval saint-poet who preached against religious dogma and insisted that people were not to be judged by predetermined religious identities but by their actions in the world. In a utopic future, the novel implies, perhaps someone like Lata would be free to marry someone like Kabir while not risking her happiness to do so. In its nuanced depiction of individual freedom as constituted by interrelationships, social ties, and publicly agreed on morality, the novel seems to enjoin its reader to work to make such a reality possible for future Latas and Kabirs.

I read *A Suitable Boy* as suggesting that choices made on the basis of one's preexisting contextual relations and ties are most conducive to happiness and to its requisite building block—individual freedom. This means that individual choices cannot bear the onus of reforming those contexts and ties. Rather one must reform social contexts to effect change in individual choices. In other words, Lata cannot fix Islamophobia through the choice of a mixed marriage. Rather, to make mixed marriages a viable choice, social reform must result in an environment within which such a choice can realistically yield happiness and enjoy success.

Manju Kapur's more recent novel, *Custody*, also displays the dangers to happiness of making individual choices that ignore the contextual ground on which those choices are produced. And it does so by depicting the sea change that ideas of individual freedom have gone through in the era of Freedom Inc. The novel tells the story of Raman, his parents, his wife Shagun, her mother, and their two children. Raman's world is upended when he discovers that Shagun has been having an affair with his boss, Ashok, who is manager of "The Brand," a multinational beverage corporation. What follows is a protracted battle for the custody of the two children, with the novel relating the psychological effects of the family's breaking. Set in the 1990s, this story can be read as an account of the personal and emotional effects of the economic changes that were happening in India. As the narrator informs us, "the nineties and economic liberalization meant that rules regarding foreign direct investment were relaxed. The Brand was invited back."[42] Within the logic of the novel's plot, the outcome of this commercial and economic invitation is Ashok's seduction of Shagun. Symbolically, then, the liberalization of the Indian economy stands in for the erosion of family ties. For Ashok, Shagun becomes a commodity to be acquired in much the same way that the domestic Indian beverage market is, and this conquest in turn is responsible for the destruction of Shagun's relationships with her husband, children, mother, and in-laws.

As a representative of "The Brand," Ashok symbolizes Freedom Inc. and its effects. Within this discourse, romantic love remains the reward for the man who has best transformed himself into an income stream:

> Ashok was a corporate man with a strong belief in hard work. As the days went by and his love grew, the effort he put into it became more vigorous … he liked to imagine their encounter to be the hidden purpose behind the two-year assignment that had returned him to his home country. Except for this new interest, The Brand absorbed him completely. With a billion potential customers, sales in India could touch the sky, and he wanted to reach those heights before he was transferred. It would be a spectacular achievement, both in personal and professional terms.[43]

Ashok puts "effort" into his love in the same way that he puts "hard work" into his corporate work. His "two year assignment" does not just refer to launching The Brand in India but to getting Shagun to fall in love with him. Through this paragraph, deliberately confusing in its use of mixed referents, Kapur draws a parallel between the "personal and professional terms" involved in wooing Shagun and launching The Brand. The personal and corporate bleed into

---

[42] Kapur, *Custody*, 3.
[43] Kapur, *Custody*, 2.

each other so that, following Illouz, emotions are rationalized and corporate rationality is sentimentalized:

> Within a few months of arriving in India he saw the woman he knew he had been destined for. In her colouring, her greenish eyes and her demeanour, she was a perfect blend of East and West. A woman so pretty had to be married; besides, she had the look of someone who never had to compete for male attention. To woo her would thus be that much more difficult: he must first create a need before he could fulfil it. But he was used to creating needs, it was what he did for a living.[44]

The passage furnishes an analogy between the logic of global capital and that of romantic love. In the case of global capital, Ashok works at "creating a need" in domestic markets in order to fulfill it, thereby enacting business slogans such as "thinking global, acting local." For The Brand, this involves repackaging and marketing various homemade and locally available Indian drinks for sale: "So many Indian drinks can be packaged—think of kanji, think of all the different types of buttermilk, sweet, sour, fruit-flavoured."[45] Packaging and then selling these drinks for higher profit margins is the definition of creating a need where one does not exist. Kapur refers to what is lost as a result of this packaging, loss that is figured as polluted groundwater, increased waste, and lost domestic livelihoods, and then depicts Ashok's conquest of Shagun through similar ideas of "creating a need" where one did not previously exist. The loss created in this case pertains to Shagun's kinship ties. The effects on Shagun's existing family, or even on her own emotional well-being, do not matter to Ashok. Kapur suggests that this is because Ashok does not love Shagun beyond what she symbolizes: "In her colouring, her greenish eyes and her demeanour, she was a perfect blend of East and West." Within this rationalizing of emotion, Shagun is a commodity to Ashok, a representation of desirable qualities that add up to one more achievement for Ashok, cementing his position as a corporate leader "who saw the world as a marketplace with all its wares for sale."[46]

Ashok's idea of Freedom Inc. is similar to that of Bhagat's protagonists—an individual freedom embodied in remodeling himself via a competitive masculinity into a revenue stream. Raman refers to him as "the man with cutthroat competition bred into his blood and bones"[47] and indeed this competitive

---

[44] Kapur, *Custody*, 4.
[45] Kapur, *Custody*, 45.
[46] Kapur, *Custody*, 354.
[47] Kapur, *Custody*, 354.

edge is what puts him ahead of Raman, who experiences competition only as a "sharp edge, nudging into every idea he had, sometimes to the point of paralysis."[48] This paralysis is why, the narrative implies, Raman loses Shagun to Ashok. Unlike Raman, Ashok realizes that "things never remained static; in business you were always fighting to keep your position, because if you didn't go ahead, you started to decline. And it was turning out to be true of love as well."[49]

*Custody* suggests that this idea of individual freedom as remodeling oneself into a competitive revenue stream relies on Freedom Inc.'s myth of absolute autonomy. Ashok "hates" India, as he puts it, because the country refuses to succumb to this myth in its "obsession with what others think," and because of its "narrow social set up."[50] This is why Ashok thinks absolute autonomy is possible only outside of India. When he encourages Shagun to leave her husband and children behind and move to New York with him, he tells her that she must understand the tension between "traditional versus modern values, individual versus society,"[51] and repackage herself into a modern Western individual who is the opposite of someone who would fit into the category of "Indian Tradition and Society." To convince Shagun, Ashok presents her with the example of Princess Diana:

> let's look at Diana. So much of her identity was bound up with being the Princess of Wales. But she didn't care. She followed her heart. And you must follow yours. Something else will emerge if only you let it. In Diana's case she started saying she was the people's princess—you have to admire the repackaging that went into that.[52]

The word "repackaging" here signals Kapur's intent to alert the reader to Ashok's desire to reduce Shagun to a representation of Freedom Inc., which, for Ashok, is inseparable from "following your heart." Emotion, once inseparable from one's interrelationships, is once again rationalized here as linked to an individualist marketing campaign.

Ashok's views of freedom pit the individual against society and do not recognize that the individual—whether Sethe or Virmati or Shagun—is enmeshed, even constituted by, a particular social set up. Individual freedom, then, can only be achieved through an understanding and navigation of the

---

[48] Kapur, *Custody*, 5.
[49] Kapur, *Custody*, 84.
[50] Kapur, *Custody*, 84.
[51] Kapur, *Custody*, 84.
[52] Kapur, *Custody*, 85.

matrix of relationships and circumstances within which any action can occur. Shagun partially realizes this when she points out that Diana lost her children in her process of rebranding herself and that such a move would have ramifications for her children too: "You will finish and go. I have to stay for my children. How will they like it when they grow up and realize their mother is a divorcee?"[53] Despite this realization, Shagun eventually decides to heed Ashok's advice and give up custody of her children in exchange for a divorce. She moves to New York with Ashok where she pines for her children. In a letter to her mother documenting life in New York close to the approaching New Year, she writes:

> The only thing that upsets me is seeing women with small kids. When the weather is fine, they are all over Central Park, thank God it is getting colder. If I mention the children to Ashok he starts talking of the necessity of my working. I see no connection ... I mustn't grumble. Nobody gets everything, and if I had to do it all over again, I would. Your loving daughter, Shagun.[54]

The narrator juxtaposes this letter with an account of how Raman's family intends to spend the millennium: "The Kaushiks were united in wanting to make sure Raman's party overflowed with warmth and togetherness. The most important thing is family, they declared, when we have each other we have everything."[55] Kapur's syntax suggests that without her children Shagun does not have "everything," while Raman, who has his family, does. The freedom she has acquired is empty because it relies on the myth of absolute autonomy, of an individual who pursues her dreams independently of the existing fabric of her life, which is simplistically referred to as "society" by Ashok. Within Ashok's binaries, children belong in the sphere of society and work in the sphere of the individual. This is why the only way that Shagun can be an individual is to work and forget about her children. Ashok does not recognize that Shagun's children are part of her individuality, so that she cannot be truly free without them. Shagun is left with the painful realization that

> ultimately they are my children not his. That's what hurts ... . Perhaps I was foolish to believe [him], but he did promise to keep me happy for ever. Not that I have reproached him with anything. Our life together would not have been possible if I had regretted my past. Still. What happened to that promise? I guess when you are in love you experience some momentary delusion, then the

---

[53] Kapur, *Custody*, 84.
[54] Kapur, *Custody*, 279.
[55] Kapur, *Custody*, 279.

glow fades and things look ordinary again. Of course, I adore my life here, but sometimes I feel its foundations are fragile.[56]

Individual freedom, the novel suggests, is made up of those actions that are carried out in accordance with a self-will that acknowledges the relationships and circumstances that constitute that self, which Shagun refers to as one's "foundations." For only when one has "foundations" can one's will be accurately discerned and realized; only then can one "claim ownership of the freed self."

The novel posits another idea of individual freedom that relies on the notion of "character" by contrasting Shagun with Ishita, the woman who Raman eventually marries after his divorce, and whose story the novel ends with. Through this juxtaposition of Shagun and Ishita and the ceding of narrative space and perspective to Ishita, the novel elevates its character driven idea of freedom as the enactment of a will that is produced through a careful, conscious nurturing and navigation of one's foundational relationships. But, at first, the novel offers a cautionary tale about what character driven freedom is not. That tale comes to the reader via an account of Ishita's prior life as the wife of a man who rejects her after discovering that she is infertile. Within her initial marriage, Ishita is no more than a reed blown here and there by the wind of other people's inclinations and desires. She lives with her in-laws who dictate her husband's relationship to her. His decision to divorce her for her infertility was one made by his parents, and one that Ishita had no choice but to accept. In that marriage, she is valued not for her personality but for her symbolic value as a gendered reproductive vessel who would bear her husband's children. She is replaceable, and love is fungible, almost in the same way as it is in Freedom Inc. The only difference is that within the gendered economy of arranged marriage, love is evaluated according to the currency of reproductive outcomes rather than through monetary profit. The narrator notes that when Ishita's infertility is discovered:

> it didn't take long for the loving atmosphere around Ishita to grow so thin that it became hard for her to breathe. Was it possible for them all to change towards her? Hadn't they valued her for herself?[57]

Ishita's husband's "love" for her, the narrative suggests, is closer to Freedom Inc.'s version of love than it is to Jane Austen's or that of my parents, because it is similarly expendable, tradeable. The family that professed to love Ishita when

---

[56] Kapur, *Custody*, 391.
[57] Kapur, *Custody*, 68.

she married, she now realizes, does not value her "for herself." Her husband and in-laws violate Ishita's will, her emotional investments in their kinship structures, and the foundational relationships that she built with him and his family. In blindly following his parents' desires to divorce Ishita, her husband negates his own freedom, enacted previously in his love for Ishita.

Kapur contrasts this account of a negated freedom with Ishita's growth into someone whose self-will is carefully and painstakingly realized through an embodiment of "character." The first step is for her to determine what her will truly is through an active process of choosing from a variety of different pathways toward self-fulfillment. The novel represents Ishita's life journey—from arranged marriage to divorce to charity work with children and then to remarriage and step-motherhood—as an array of choices towards self-fulfillment that force her to grapple with what she truly wants. The answer, she finally realizes, is having children and a family, which she obtains after marrying Raman and leading him to a victorious custody battle that wins her the younger of Shagun's two children, the two-year-old Roohi. Ishita's battle for custody of Roohi is the result of Ishita's recognition that her own particular individuality, and therefore her capacity for freedom, is constituted partly through the relational ties that give full scope to the love she has to give. Describing Ishita's love for Raman and Roohi, the narrator notes:

> Even if the relationship were to end tonight she would still be the richer. Not to mention all the love she had received from Roohi. She thought of the little arms around her neck, her weight on her lap, the smell of her breath, the smooth pink lips glistening with a sliver of drool, the baby-white teeth. For those moments in the car she had allowed herself to feel she was the child's mother, with an intimate connection to the man sitting next to her. Well, everybody had to have their few moments in the sun. Those had been hers. She had given herself so easily to Raman to prolong the fantasy. Being with him was like having a taste of what every woman she was ever jealous of had. A man and a child. People to look after and care for, people who loved you in return.[58]

Having realized that her goal is to love and be loved back, Ishita's actions all lead toward this goal. At first, Ishita's work, a job involving working with destitute children, is a way toward achieving that self-fulfillment, for "wasn't it better to devote oneself to many children than to obsess about one little girl?" Ishita decides to quit her job only when she realizes that her new family is in

---

[58] Kapur, *Custody*, 293.

a precarious position because of Shagun's attempts to lure her two-year-old daughter Roohi to New York: "How could she allow herself to miss precious months of Roo's rearing, when so much had already gone wrong in the child's life? In both their lives?"[59] Significantly, Kapur does not present waged work as a simplistic signifier of freedom independently of what that work is. Work is freedom for Ishita only when it strengthens the foundational relationships in her life—that which will lead to the realization of her own will to love and be loved.

Thus Kapur suggests that autonomy is not just an active process of choosing from a variety of different pathways toward one's own version of self-fulfillment. Rather autonomy *also* takes the form of actions taken upon a "foundation"[60] of relational ties. In order to realize her will of having "people to look after and care for, people who loved you in return" Ishita sets out to craft an intricate fabric of relationships upon which this goal can be realized: "On weekends Ishita planned family get-togethers, first checking with Raman whether it should be just themselves or all the grandparents, for now her own parents were included in that category. Raman knew his wife wanted to bind them into a cohesive unit and he did his best to fully participate in these schemes."[61] Ishita's approach to her relationships, then, replete with "planning" and calculation is goal driven and rational.

Significantly, Kapur contrasts Ishita's rational approach to emotion with Ashok's rationalization of emotion. For Ashok, love does not exist independently of rational decision-making processes, which is why it is wholly valued through these processes; Ashok does not fall in love with Shagun and *then* decide that she is the perfect partner for him because her looks represent "a perfect blend of East and West." Rather, this rational evaluation precedes his falling in love with her. Love, within Freedom Inc., is the means to an end. By contrast, the love that Ishita bears for Roohi and Raman comes before the rational actions she takes in order to win and nurture that love. Her love, unlike Ashok's for Shagun, is both the means to an end and the end in itself. It is the basis for, and not just the result of, rational calculation. The novel ends with Ishita's perspective despite the majority of the story being about Raman and Shagun's emotional journey and the breakdown of their marriage. The victory of Ishita's narrative stance at a time when she has just won custody of Roohi is also the victory of a particular model of character driven freedom against Freedom Inc.

---

[59] Kapur, *Custody*, 336.
[60] Kapur, *Custody*, 391.
[61] Kapur, *Custody*, 315.

Previous chapters presented contextual universalisms that rethink how we understand autonomy in the age of Freedom Inc. This last chapter presents novels that, rather than reflect a local structure of thought or a philosophical and ontological idea, seek to guage the effects of differing ways of apprehending love on concepts of individual freedom and vice versa. Chetan Bhagat's version of the local Anglophone bildungsroman, written in a colloquial Indian-English shorn of literary qualities, represents a masculinized Freedom Inc. as the freedom to compete. The competitive self is produced by commodifying components of the self, including one's emotions, through a process of self-evaluation and rational judgment. As Bhagat's protagonists and as Ashok in *Custody* show, within Freedom Inc. emotions exist from the start as purely instrumental components that exist as gendered means to an end. "Love" becomes a means of confirming the self's status as a successful man, as homo economicus, as someone who can compete in a romantic marketplace that is always already economic. This is a model of love and freedom that is vastly appealing to rising numbers of underemployed small-town men in post-1990s India. But, as Manju Kapur's novels testify, what is lost in the process of embodying Freedom Inc. is a collective normative horizon in relation to which the self is generated. Without such a horizon through which to constitute the self and the self's choices, freedom remains unrealized—for one's will remains elusive. Against the myth of absolute autonomy, Kapur's novels present a more nuanced reading of autonomy within which an action or decision is autonomous, first, when it is produced in an environment that offers a rich array of choices for self-actualization. In this sense, Shagun, presented with a binary of children versus work by Ashok, is manifestly unfree, even as she leaves Raman in pursuit of freedom. Second, as *A Suitable Boy* also shows, since an individual is co-constituted through her relationships and circumstances within a community and cultural context, an action is only autonomous when it is character driven, arising out of a process of engaging with and reflecting on the ties through which the self is constituted. Together, these texts offer "lives-in-story" that nuance our understanding of what it means to be free against Freedom Inc.'s simplistic constraints.

# Coda

In August 2021, Prime Minister Narendra Modi sat on a chair in front of a line of women, all waiting to tie a sacred thread around his wrist. The women were there for *Raksha Bandhan*, a popular Hindu festival that literally means "bond of protection." On this day, Hindu sisters of all ages tie a talisman or amulet, called the *Rakhi*, around the wrists of their brothers, enlisting their brothers with the responsibility of protecting them. Brothers respond with gifts. In the years since Modi has been in power, he has used this festival to declare his big brotherly protection for Indian—read Hindu—women. The women lining up to tie a thread around the wrist of their "big brother" were celebrating Modi's gift of funds to rural women's self-help groups as part of an initiative to alleviate poverty in rural areas.

On another *Raksha Bandhan,* Modi opened an accident-insurance scheme for women in his constituency, encouraging brothers to gift their sisters fixed deposit cards that could be put toward that insurance scheme. Addressing Indian women, Modi declared:

> I am happy that you are joining a relationship of security ... If we want to make India prosperous, we will have to integrate this half of our population to the decision-making process. The more the women will be empowered and the more they participate in economic activities, the country will prosper in the same measure.[1]

In this version of Freedom Inc., Modi labeled self-help and insurance as modes of empowerment for women, supposedly gifting them not just insurance schemes but also freedom through participation in a key "decision-making process" and "economic activities." Importantly, both these supposed gifts of

---

[1] Modi quoted in S. Qureshi, "Modi to Gift Women Insurance Scheme This RakshaBandhan," *India Today,* August 22, 2015, http://indiatoday.intoday.in/story/narendra-modi-to-gift-women-insurance-scheme-this-raksha-bandhan/1/460260.html (accessed June 30, 2016).

**Figure 9** Modi and *Raksha Bandhan*.[2]

financial independence were couched in patriarchal benevolence. Women would be free because their brothers, as well as a big brother state, would let them be. Not everyone was convinced. The RSS, a competing Hindu nationalist organization, declared that "measures like pension and insurance schemes would only create business for the insurance companies" under the guise of helping ordinary citizens.[3]

The use of the Hindu festival of *Raksha Bandhan* as a mode of financialization and as an enacting of neoliberal ideologies of self-help suggests that the discourse of Freedom Inc., and the material processes it buttresses, is linked to the Hindu nationalist agenda, Hindutva, of the BJP government. While the term "Hindutva" refers to the state or quality of being Hindu, as a political ideology, Hindutva conflates a geographical, cultural, and national identity with a religious one, claiming that a true "Indian" is one who partakes of this

---

[2] Narendra Modi's official Flickr account, "Narendra Modi Celebrates Rakshabandhan," https://commons.wikimedia.org/wiki/File:Narendra_Modi_celebrates_Rakshabandhan_3.jpg. It is significant that the first women in the photograph are not Hindu yet, as the citizens of a nation that increasingly identifies itself as Hindu, they must join in a Hindu festival to participate in the nation's public life and initiatives.

[3] Quoted in A. Mukherjee, "Pro-poor? Bah!," *Outlook*, March 16, 2015, http://www.outlookindia.com/magazine/story/pro-poor-bah/293611 (accessed June 30, 2016).

*Hindu-ness*.⁴ Hindutva, then, is defined through its exclusion of those groups that do not fit a narrow conception of "Hindu-ness."⁵ And as Modi's reliance on the *Raksha Bandhan* ritual shows, gender roles are a crucial tool in maintaining this idea of majoritarian Hindu-ness, and they work through an ideology of patriarchal benevolence linked to Freedom Inc.

This means that economic liberalization's contracting of freedom into Freedom Inc. is not just discursive; it is implicated in the very real receding of other kinds of freedoms—political, social, and religious under Hindutva. As political scientists like Priya Chacko have argued, Hindu nationalism and economic liberalization have been working hand in hand in post-1990s India. Chacko contends that under Narendra Modi, the BJP has sought to bolster the corporate sector and recreate the middle and "neo-middle" classes as "virtuous market citizens." This virtuous market citizen is different from the self-regulating autonomous individual found in many accounts of neoliberalism because he or she is an entrepreneurial consumer who seems to be absolutely autonomous even while submitting to the regulation of his/her behavior by the cultural framework of Hindu majoritarianism.⁶

A belief in the false promises of Freedom Inc. explains why so many Indians, most of them Hindus, remain ready to submit to the BJP's censorship of the media, its anti-democratic treatment of minorities under the Citizenship Amendment Act, as well as its victimization of non-Hindus, particularly Muslims and lower castes. The latter have repeatedly been targets of violence by Hindu nationalist activists and have had restricted access to government jobs.⁷ Dissenters and protestors, meanwhile, have been labeled as "anti-national" and punished under draconian measures.⁸ The push for a Hindu state alongside the discourse of Freedom Inc. serves as a distraction from the growing inequality brought about by the BJP's pro-corporate agenda as well as from receding social and political freedoms, uniting the Hindu population against an imagined enemy other within.

---

⁴ Arvind Sharma, "On Hindu, Hindustan, Hinduism and Hindutva," *Numen* 49 (1), 2002: 1–36. The founding ideologist of this position is famously Vinayak Damodar Savarkar in his "Who Is a Hindu?"
⁵ See part 1 of Christophe Jaffrelot, *The Hindu Nationalist Movement in India* (New York: Columbia University Press, 1998) and his "The Invention of an Ethnic Nationalism" in *Hindu Nationalism: A Reader* (Princeton: Princeton University Press, 2009).
⁶ Priya Chacko, "Marketizing Hindutva: The State, Society, and Markets in Hindu Nationalism," *Modern Asian Studies* 53 (2), 2019: 377–410.
⁷ Paul R. Brass, *The Production of Hindu-Muslim Violence in Contemporary India* (Seattle, WA: University of Washington Press, 2003).
⁸ *The Wire* Staff, "The Updated List of India's 'Anti-Nationals' (According to the Modi Government)," https://thewire.in/rights/india-modi-anti-national-protest-arrest-sedition-authoritarianism (accessed August 10, 2022).

Githa Hariharan's *In Times of Siege* (2003) and Nayantara Sahgal's *The Fate of Butterflies* (2019) speak to this link between Hindutva and the creation and sustenance of neoliberal economics in India, as well as to the gendered discourse of Freedom Inc. that supports these policies. Both authors write about local realities for a largely Indian audience but their novels have also been taken up by readers of postcolonial writing abroad. Sahgal, the niece of India's first prime minister, Jawaharlal Nehru, is a well-known writer of the Indian Anglophone novel who has been awarded domestic literary prizes like the Sahitya Akademi Award. Hariharan is also a widely acclaimed writer both in India and abroad, whose various works have won the Commonwealth Writers Prize and been nominated for the Booker Prize. She works in the four major South Indian languages as well as in English.

Sahgal's *The Fate of Butterflies* (2019) suggests that regimes like Hindutva are necessary to preserve the balance of power within a neoliberal global economy. In other words, economic liberalization, Freedom Inc., and state-sanctioned religious bigotry work hand in hand. The freedom of those deemed religiously or sexually "other" to the project of the Indian nation-state has to be sacrificed to maintain the edge of dominant groups within the free market. This is confirmed by Sergei, who is an international arms dealer on business in India where a right-wing Hindu regime has begun a widespread and diffused genocide against the country's Muslims. Sergei explains this massacre in the following terms:

> It's not about rights. It's about trade and being in control of it. It's what empires were about. Trade is what makes the world go round. You have to keep the upper hand. You don't need to occupy Asia and Africa to do that anymore. You just stay in control by making sure your kind of people are in power over there.[9]

By Sergei's estimation, right-wing Hindus are the "kind of people" needed to retain "the upper hand," which means that a binary other to Hindus must be created and then obliterated. Sergei reflects that right-wing Hindus propound theories of a "master race" just as Cecil Rhodes once did. While such theories in the past had been "represented by the English upper class" who proclaimed that "the British empire had a divine right to conquer and rule the 'uncivilized world,'" they are also features of the present. Sergei realizes that the economic "sentiments, the language … that sanitized brutality" not only persist but continue to ensure that "a version of divine right still ruled the planet and

---

[9] Nayantara Sahgal, *The Fate of Butterflies* (New Delhi: Speaking Tiger, 2019), 132.

the formula for the capture and control of commerce still relied heavily, if not openly, on arms."[10] Sergei realizes, here, that what was once justified as the opening up of backward markets to development and "free trade," relies on coercion and cruelty.

The title of the novel is derived from the idea of "sanitized brutality" that marks both "free trade" and the crushing of civil freedoms by right-wing regimes like Hindutva. It refers to a cruel method of collecting butterflies that is apparently taught to little children in some schools. The butterflies are trapped in nets, then squeezed and crippled and pinned through their middles to frames. While this method is rationalized as harmless scientific training, for Sahgal it is actually the beginning of a continuum of violence that relies on the supposedly scientific typing of those designated "others." The text thus begins its series of events through an encounter between the protagonist, Prabhakar, and a dead body he sees on the road one day. The man "had suffered the fate of butterflies," but he was not pinned, he was "bloodily axed" through his middle. The only item of clothing that remained on that man's body was his skullcap, which identifies him as a Muslim.

In the novel, such butterflies are created by diasporic organizations such as Voice of Hindu Americans, which is working toward making Hindu Indians in the United States "honorary whites." The sense of entitlement of this particular group involves imagining "an India extending from the Indus in the far north to the Arabian Sea at its southern tip as one unbroken landscape of lustrous gold," with "no Afghanistan, no Pakistan, no Bangladesh."[11]

Moreover, the novel shows that women and sexual minorities often serve as collateral damage within this process of preserving the balance of economic power by dividing the world into "your kind of people" and "others." Hindutva's gender ideology is the weapon used to this end, relying on concepts of sexual purity for Hindu men and women who partake in rituals like *Raksha Bandhan*, and outright annihilation for those who fall outside of these categories. The most notable victims are Muslim women, who in the novel undergo rape as a weapon of war, and gay men who are castrated and lynched.

While *The Fate of Butterflies* connects the crushing of social and political freedoms with the material processes of "free trade," Hariharan's *In Times of Siege* (2003) connects the loss of these freedoms to discursive processes marked by Freedom Inc. The novel is about a middle-aged history professor, Shiv, who is

---

[10] Sahgal, *The Fate of Butterflies*, 137.
[11] Sahgal, *The Fate of Butterflies*, 121–2.

compelled to take a political stance against the forces of Hindutva when a lesson he prepares on the medieval poet and social reformer, Basava, comes under attack by a vigilante group called the Itihas Suraksha Manch (the Society for the Protection of History). The context is the electoral success of the BJP, following which supporters have begun to attack academia in a battle for how the nation is narrated: is India to be depicted as a Hindu nation within which history has to be rewritten to glorify the Hindu heritage and to purge it of any mention of its less-desirable elements? Or is India to be represented as a plural, secular republic full of vibrant difference and debate? Crucially, in the aftermath of the attack on Shiv's lesson about Basava's challenge to caste hierarchies, the novel depicts how Shiv's own academic department refuses to support him, asking him to apologize and retract his lesson so as to keep controversy to a minimum. This is a threat to individual freedom in its fullest sense; for it attacks Shiv's freedom of speech, his freedom to harbor different possibilities in his mind about what it means to be Indian, and his freedom to decide who he will be as a citizen in the new India.

Hariharan suggests that in the new India, the discourse of Freedom Inc. that buttresses the global economy acts as a vehicle for the curtailing of these other freedoms that Shiv seeks to protect. Shiv's daughter, Tara, personifies the forces of neoliberal globalization in her choice of career. Tara has moved to the United States to work at Yahoo!, one of the pioneers of the early internet era in the 1990s, and in that capacity, a company that is one of the leading vehicles of globalization. She also embodies the discourse of Freedom Inc. in her simplistic ontological and sociopolitical stances. In an email to her father, she complains about Shiv's notoriety following the controversy over his Basava lesson:

> I've been getting messages from friends in Delhi and some Indians here. It's sort of weird and embarrassing to explain why you have written something against our temples and priests and all that. It's only after coming to the US that many of us have learnt to appreciate Indian traditions. What does it matter one way or the other? It all happened long ago, didn't it? Only professors are obsessed with details. The rest of us only need to know enough to be proud of our past…. At the bottom of Tara's message is a line that has recently begun to border all her email. The exact words change from time to time, but they are all variations on the same theme: Joy, peace, and love—may these blessings find their way to you. Below this sweet if impractical thought is the ubiquitous question, Do you yahoo?"[12]

---

[12] Githa Hariharan, *In Times of Siege* (New Delhi: Penguin, 2018), 112.

In the Yahoo! era, the only states of being to aspire to are "joy, peace, and love." These are commodities that are to be purchased through a sacrifice of the sociopolitical and personal freedoms that Shiv aspires to. In order to "Yahoo!," one must subscribe to a homogenous Hindu heritage that is to be made synonymous with Indianness, and then traded like a brand within a multicultural symbolic economy. This is why Tara enjoins Shiv to let go of any details that would get in the way of Indians being "proud of our past." The brand of freedom allowed to Indians who participate in this global economy can only be Freedom Inc., through which they are reduced to embodying harmless and attractive cultural difference within the neoliberal discourses of US multiculturalism that accompany globalization. This puts Freedom Inc., or the injunction to "Yahoo!," in direct collusion with the crushing of other freedoms by forces of Hindutva back in India. It is significant that Tara embodies these discourses as an upper-caste Hindu woman in America. She could, in fact, easily be a character in Sahgal's *The Fate of Butterflies*, a representative of the Voice of Hindu Americans whom Prabhakar meets at a high-society party. Through Tara, Hariharan points to how Hindutva's gendered discourses privilege upper-middle-class Hindu women for bolstering the economic balance of power. They do so discursively in their propounding and embodiment of discourses of Freedom Inc. and economically in their roles as employees of large multinational companies based in America.

The links between religious nationalism, economic liberalization, and Freedom Inc. that these novels represent, I suggest, make it even more urgent to recognize the gendered discursive structures that support growing social, political, and economic inequality in the new India. Indian literatures after the 1990s serve as a resource in this respect, representing but also providing the tools through which one can dissect Freedom Inc. and reveal the way that its gendered capitalism curtails the life choices of groups as disparate as Dalit men and women, unemployed young men in the lower middle classes, successful male entrepreneurs, middle-class homemakers, working-class waged women, and religious minorities. Texts such as Adiga's *The White Tiger* represent and satirize Freedom Inc.'s masculinized myth of absolute autonomy, Kapur's representations of its debilitating effects on middle-class women's freedom demonstrate the emptiness of its promises, Dalit life-writing provides other ways of being free for the most disadvantaged—lower-caste women, and Sahgal and Hariharan's novels critique the collusions between Freedom Inc. and the mistreatment of religious minorities. Together, such texts reveal or critique the growing power of Freedom Inc. on various "lives-in-story," while illuminating the buried pathways to autonomy the discourse leaves in its wake. They suggest that free futures for Indians of all genders and religious backgrounds can only be imagined if we understand and dismantle the story structures through which Freedom Inc. acquires dominance, and if we celebrate the story structures through which other freedoms—in the form of contextual universalisms—can be lived and thought.

# Bibliography

## Primary Literary, Historical, and Cinematic Works

Adiga, Aravind. *The White Tiger* (New York: Simon and Schuster, 2008).
Ambedkar, B. R. "Annihilation of Caste with a Reply to Mahatma Gandhi," in *Dr. Babasaheb Ambedkar's Writings and Speeches, Vol. 1*, compiled by Vasant Moon (Bombay: Education Department, Government of Maharashtra, [1936] 1979).
Ambedkar, B. R. "What Congress and Gandhi Have Done to the Untouchables," in *Dr. Babasaheb Ambedkar's Writings and Speeches*, ed. Vasant Moon (Bombay: Education Department, Government of Maharashtra, 1979).
Ambedkar, B. R. "Dr. Ambedkar at the Round Table Conference," in *Dr. Babasaheb Ambedkar's Writings and Speeches, Vol. 2*, ed. Vasant Moon (Bombay: Education Department, Government of Maharashtra, 1982).
Ambedkar, B. R. "Dr. Ambedkar and the Hindu Code Bill," in *Dr. Babasaheb Ambedkar, Writings and Speeches, Vol. 14, Part 2*, ed. Vasant Moon (Mumbai: Education Department, Government of Maharashtra, 1995).
Ambedkar, B. R. *The Buddha and His Dhamma*, annotated and edited by Aakash Singh Rathore and Ajay Verma (New Delhi: Oxford University Press, 2011).
Ambedkar B. R. *Janata*, February 26, 1938.
Ambedkar, B. R. *Janata*, September 15 and 22, 1951.
Ambedkar, B. R. *Janata*, July 26, 1952.
Baby, Jeo. *The Great Indian Kitchen* (Kerala: Mankind Cinemas, 2021).
Barks, Coleman. *Rumi's Little Book of Love and Laughter: Teaching Stories and Fables* (Newbury Port, MA: Hampton Roads Publishing, 2016).
Barry, Ellen. "Young Rural Women in India Chase Big-City Dreams." *New York Times*, September 24, 2016. https://www.nytimes.com/2016/09/25/world/asia/bangalore-india-women-factories.html (accessed June 2, 2018).
Bhagat, Chetan. *One Night at the Call Center* (New Delhi: Rupa Publications, 2014).
Bhagat, Chetan. *Half Girlfriend* in *Chetan Bhagat Collection (7 Books in 1)*, Kindle edition (Amazon Publishing, 2018).
Dutt, Yashica. *Coming Out as Dalit* (New Delhi: Aleph Book Company, 2019).
Ghosh, Amitav, *The Shadow Lines* (New York: Houghton Mifflin, 1988).
Hamid, Mohsin. *How to Get Filthy Rich in Rising Asia* (New York: Riverhead Books, 2014).
Hariharan, Githa. *In Times of Siege* (New Delhi: Penguin, 2018).
Kapur, Manju. *Difficult Daughters* (London: Faber & Faber, 1999).

Kapur, Manju. *Custody* (New York: Random House, 2011).
Mistry, Rohinton. *Such a Long Journey* (New York: Vintage, 1991).
Mistry, Rohinton. *A Fine Balance* (New York: Vintage, 1997).
Morrison, Toni. *Beloved* (New York: Vintage, 2004).
Mundhra, Smriti, and Netflix, Season 1, Episode 1, "Slim, Trim, and Educated," *Indian Matchmaking*, 2020.
Raj, Shilpa. *The Elephant Chaser's Daughter* (CreateSpace Independent Publishing Platform, 2017).
Roth, Vanessa. *Daughters of Destiny* (New York: Cause and Effect Media, 2017).
Roy, Arundhati. *The God of Small Things* (New York: Random House Trade Paperbacks, 2008).
Rushdie, Salman. *Midnight's Children* (New York: Random House Trade Paperbacks, 2006).
Sahgal, Nayantara. *The Fate of Butterflies* (New Delhi: Speaking Tiger, 2019).
Satthianadhan, Krupabai, and Chandani Lokuje (ed.), *Kamala: The Story of a Hindu Child Wife* (New Delhi: Oxford University Press, 2002).
Seth, Vikram. *A Suitable Boy* (New York: Harper Perennial Modern Classics, 2005).
Tagore, Rabindranath. *The Home and the World*. Edited by William Radice. Translated by Surendranath Tagore (London, England: Penguin Classics, 2005).
Umrigar, Thrity. *The Space between Us* (New York: Harper Perennial, 2007).

## Secondary Works

Anderson, Siwan, and Mukesh Eswaran. "What Determines Female Autonomy? Evidence from Bangladesh," *Journal of Development Economics*, 90 (2), November 2009: 179–91.
Anjaria, Ulka. *Realism and the Twentieth-Century Indian Novel: Colonial Difference and Literary Form* (Cambridge: Cambridge University Press, 2012).
Anjaria, Ulka. *A History of the Indian Novel in English* (Cambridge: Cambridge University Press, 2015).
Anjaria, Ulka. "Chetan Bhagat and the New Provincialism," January 2015, *American Book Review*, 36 (6): 6–22.
Anjaria, Ulka. "The New Provincialism," in Ulka Anjaria, *Reading India Now: Contemporary Formations in Literature and Popular Culture* (Philadelphia, PA: Temple University Press, 2019).
Bagchi, Amiya. "Neoliberal Imperialism, Corporate Feudalism and the Contemporary Origins of Dirty Money," *Networkideas.org*, networkideas.org/feathm/may2006/Amiya_Bagchi.pdf (accessed January 10, 2020).

Bardhan, Pranab. "Globalization, Inequality, and Poverty: An Overview," *Eml.berkeley. edu*, eml.berkeley.edu/~webfac/bardhan/papers/BardhanGlobalOverview.pdf (accessed January 10, 2020).

Berlin, Isiah. "Two Concepts of Liberty," in *Four Essays on Liberty*, ed. I. Berlin (London: Oxford University Press, [1969] 2002).

Biswas, Soutik. "Why Are Millions of Indian Women Dropping Out of Work?" *BBC. COM*, May 18, 2017. https://www.bbc.com/news/world-asia-india-39945473 (accessed June 2, 2018).

Blum, Beth. *The Self-Help Compulsion: Searching for Advice in Modern Literature* (New York: Columbia University Press, 2020).

Bogle, Ariel. "The World of Indian Book Piracy," https://www.mhpbooks.com/the-world-of-indian-book-piracy/ (accessed August 1, 2021).

Brass, Paul R. *The Production of Hindu-Muslim Violence in Contemporary India* (Seattle, WA: University of Washington Press, 2003).

Bratman, Michael E. *Structures of Agency: Essays* (Oxford: Oxford University Press, 2007).

Brown, Wendy. *Undoing the Demos: Neoliberalism's Stealth Revolution* (New York: Zone Books, 2015).

Brouillette, Sarah. *Literature and the Creative Economy* (Stanford: Stanford University Press, 2014).

Butler, Judith. "Sovereign Performatives in the Contemporary Scene of Utterance," *Critical Inquiry* 23 (Winter 1997): 233–53.

Chacko, Priya. "Marketizing Hindutva: The State, Society, and Markets in Hindu Nationalism," *Modern Asian Studies* 53 (2), 2019: 377–4.

Chakravorty, Mrinalini. *In Stereotype: South Asia in the Global Literary Imaginary* (New York: Columbia University Press, 2014).

Chatterjee, Partha. "Nationalist Resolution of the Woman Question," in *Recasting Women: Essays in Indian Colonial History*, ed. Kumkum Sangari and Sudhesh Vaid (New Brunswick, NJ: Rutgers University Press, 1990), 233–53.

Cheah, Pheng. *Inhuman Conditions* (Cambridge, MA: Harvard University Press, 2006).

Christman, John. "Liberalism and Individual Positive Freedom," *Ethics* 101, 1991: 343–59.

Christman, John. "Saving Positive Freedom," *Political Theory* 33, 2005: 79–88.

Christman, John. *The Politics of Persons. Individual Autonomy and Socio-historical Selves* (Cambridge: Cambridge University Press, 2009).

Chittick, William C. *The Sufi Doctrine of Rumi* (Bloomington, IN: World Wisdom, 2005).

Craig, Jeffrey. *Timepass: Youth, Class and the Politics of Waiting in India* (Stanford: Stanford University Press, 2010).

Das, Gurcharan. *India Unbound* (New Delhi: Anchor Books, 2002).

Das, Sisir Kumar. *A History of Indian Literature 1911–1956 Struggle for Freedom: Triumph and Tragedy* (New Delhi: Sahitya Akademi, 1995).

Dentsu India, Jet Privilege advertisement, India, https://www.youtube.com/watch?v=gp3BP84tbuw (accessed June 1, 2021).

Dewey, John. *Democracy and Education* (Michigan: University of Michigan Press, 1916).

DICCI. "Developing SC/ST Business Leadership," https://dicci.in/about-dicci/ (accessed September 1, 2021).

Dore, Robert. *The Diploma Disease: Education, Qualification and Development* (Berkeley: University of California Press, 1976).

Eagleton, Terry. *How to Read Literature* (New Haven: Yale University Press, 2013).

Fischer, J., and Ravizza, M. *Perspectives on Moral Responsibility* (Ithaca, NY: Cornell University Press, 1993).

Foucault, Michel. *The Birth of Biopolitics, Lectures at the Collège de France, 1978–1979* (London: Palgrave Macmillan, 2008).

Frankfurt, Harry. "Freedom of the Will and the Concept of a Person," in *The Importance of What We Care About* (Cambridge: Cambridge University Press, 1988).

Fukuyama, Francis. *The End of History and the Last Man* (New York: Free Press, 1992).

Ganguly, Debjani. "Dalit Life Stories," in Rashmi Sadana (ed.), *The Cambridge Companion to Modern Indian Culture* (Cambridge: Cambridge University Press, 2012).

Gershon, Llana. "Neoliberal Agency," *Current Anthropology* 52 (4), August 2011: 537–55.

Gill, Rosalind, and Christina Scharff. *New Femininities: Postfeminism, Neoliberalism and Subjectivity* (Basingstoke, NJ: Palgrave, 2011).

Gokhale, Madhavi. "The Implications of Simplification in 'Inspirational Literature,'" *International Journal of Social Science and Humanity* 2 (5), 2012: 400–4.

Gopal, Priyamvada. *The Indian English Novel: Nation, History, and Narration* (Oxford: Oxford University Press, 2009).

Gopal, Priyamvada. *Insurgent Empire: Anticolonial Resistance and British Dissent* (London: Verso, 2020).

Government of India Ministry of Labour and Employment, "Employment in Informal Sector and Conditions of Informal Employment Vol. IV," 2013–2014, https://labour.gov.in/sites/default/files/Report%20vol%204%20final.pdf.

Greenlees, Donald. "An Investment Banker Finds Fame Off the Books," *New York Times*, March 26, 2008, https://www.nytimes.com/2008/03/26/books/26bhagat.html.

Guha, Ranajit. *History at the Limit of World History* (Delhi: Oxford University Press, 2003).

Hamid, Mohsin. Chicago Humanities Festival, "Mohsin Hamid: *How to Get Filthy Rich in Rising Asia*," https://www.youtube.com/watch?v=0EaIkSNAsWU.

Hill, Napoleon. *How to Sell Your Way Through Life* (Hoboken, NJ: Wiley Books, [1939] 2009).

Himanshu. "India: Extreme Inequality in Numbers," Oxfam International, https://www.oxfam.org/en/india-extreme-inequality-numbers.

Hondagneu-Sotelo, Pierette. *Domestica: Immigrant Workers Cleaning and Caring in the Shadows of Affluence* (Berkeley: University of California Press, 2007).

Illouz, Eva. *Cold Intimacies: The Making of Emotional Capitalism* (Cambridge: Polity Press, 2007).

Illouz, Eva. *Why Love Hurts: A Sociological Explanation* (Cambridge: Polity Press, 2014).

Jaffrelot, Christophe. *The Hindu Nationalist Movement in India* (New York: Columbia University Press, 1998).

Jaffrelot, Christophe, "The Invention of an Ethnic Nationalism," in Christophe Jaffrelot (ed.), *Hindu Nationalism: A Reader* (Princeton: Princeton University Press, 2009).

Jain, Sanket. "How Neoliberal Austerity Stripped India's Healthcare Infrastructure," https://towardfreedom.org/story/admin/how-neoliberal-austerity-stripped-indias-healthcare-infrastructure/.

Jensen, Robert. "Do Labor Market Opportunities Affect Young Women's Work and Family Decisions? Experimental Evidence from India," *The Quarterly Journal of Economics* 127 (2), May 2012: 753–92.

Justman, Stewart. *Fool's Paradise: The Unreal World of Pop Psychology* (New York: Ivan Dee, 2005).

Kamble, Milind, in Polgreen, Lydia, "Scaling Caste Walls with Capitalism's Ladders in India," *New York Times*, December 21, 2011.

Kapur, Devesh, Chandra Bhan Prasad, and D. Shyam Babu. *Defying the Odds: The Rise of Dalit Entrepreneurs* (New Delhi: Random House, 2014).

Kaur, Ravinder. "'I Am India Shining': The Investor-Citizen and the Indelible Icon of Good Times," *The Journal of Asian Studies* 75 (3), August 2016: 621–48.

Kaur, Ravinder. "The Market Hunters: Corporate Masculinity and the Art of Opening the Economy," https://ravinderkaur.net/the-market-hunters-corporate-masculinity-and-the-art-of-opening-the-economy/, August 14, 2020 (accessed May 8, 2022).

Keer, Dhananjay. *Dr Ambedkar: Life and Mission*, Third Edition (Bombay: Popular Prakashan, 1971).

Khilnani, Sunil. *The Idea of India* (New York: Farrar, Straus and Giroux, 1999).

Lears, T. J. Jackson. "From Salvation to Self-Realization: Advertising and the Therapeutic Roots of the Consumer Culture 1880–1930," *Advertising and Society Reviews* 1 (1), 2000, https://muse.jhu.edu/pub/21/article/2942.

Locke, John. *The Second Treatise of Civil Government* (1690), Gutenberg.org, https://www.gutenberg.org/cache/epub/7370/pg7370-images.html (accessed April 2, 2022).

Lowe, Lisa. *The Intimacies of Four Continents* (Durham, NC: Duke University Press, 2015).

Lum, Kathryn. "Why Are There So Few Dalit Entrepreneurs? The Problem of India's Casted Capitalism," *The Conversation*, January 18, 2016.

Maasen, Sabine, Barbara Sutter, and Stefanie Duttweiler, "Self-Help: The Making of Neosocial Selves in Neoliberal Society," in *On Willing Selves*, ed. Sabine Maasen and Barbara Sutter (London: Palgrave Macmillan, 2007).

Mahmood, Saba. "Feminist Theory, Embodiment, and the Docile Agent: Some Reflections on the Egyptian Islamic Revival." *Cultural Anthropology* 16 (2), 2001: 202–36.

Mahmood, Saba. *Politics of Piety: The Islamic Revival and the Feminist Subject* (Princeton, NJ: Princeton University Press, 2012).

McGee, Micki. *Self-Help, Inc. Makeover Culture in American Life* (New York: Oxford University Press, 2005).

Mehrotra, Arvind Krishna. *History of Indian Literature in English* (New York: Columbia University Press, 2003).

Mill, John Stuart. *On Liberty* (London: J. W. Parker, 1859).

Mill, John Stuart. "On the Definition of Political Economy, and on the Method of Investigation Proper to It," *London and Westminster Review,* October 1836, reprinted in *Essays on Some Unsettled Questions of Political Economy*, Second Edition (London: Longmans, Green, Reader & Dyer, 1874).

Mirza, Maryam. *Intimate Class Acts: Friendship and Desire in Indian and Pakistani Women's Fiction* (Oxford: Oxford University Press, 2016).

Mitra, Meghalee. "'Paise Nahin Hai': How Middle Class Mentality Builds Character and Makes You Happy," https://www.arre.co.in/social-commentary/middle-class-mentality-indian-families/, July 23, 2018 (accessed August 2021).

*Monier-Williams Sanskrit–English Dictionary* (Germany: University of Koeln, 2015).

Moretti, Franco. *The Way of the World: The Bildungsroman in European Culture* (New York: Verso, 2000).

Mukherjee, A. "Pro-poor? Bah!," *Outlook*, March 16, 2015, http://www.outlookindia.com/magazine/story/pro-poor-bah/293611 (accessed June 30, 2016).

Mukherjee, Arun P. "B. R. Ambedkar, John Dewey, and the Meaning of Democracy," *New Literary History*, 40 (2), Spring 2009: 345–70, India and the West.

Mukherjee, Meenakshi. *The Perishable Empire: Essays on Indian Writing in English* (Oxford: Oxford University Press, 2003).

Nandi, Swaralipi. 'Narrative Ambiguity and the Neoliberal *Bildungsroman* in Aravind Adiga's *The White Tiger*," *Journal of Narrative Theory* 47 (2), Summer 2017: 297.

Narayan, Uma. *Dislocating Cultures: Identities, Traditions, and Third World Feminism* (London: Routledge, 1997).

National Sample Survey Office, Ministry of Statistics and Programme Implementation, Government of India. "Participation of Women in Specified Activities Along with Domestic Duties," July 2011–June 2012, http://mospi.nic.in/sites/default/files/publication_reports/nss_report_559_10oct14.pdf (accessed May 6, 2020).

NDTV News Desk, "Complete Text of Ivanka Trump's Hyderabad Speech," NDTV India, November 28, 2017, https://www.ndtv.com/india-news/complete-text-of-ivanka-trumps-hyderabad-speech-1781045.

Nehring, Daniel, Emmanuel Alvarado, Eric C. Hendriks, and Dylan Kerrigan, *The Politics of Self-Help: Transnational Popular Psychology and the Global Self-Help Industry* (London: Palgrave Macmillan, 2016).

Nelson, Katherine. "Finding One's Self in Time," in *The Self across Psychology: Self Recognition, Self-Awareness, and the Self Concept, Annals of the New York Academy of Sciences*, vol. 818, ed. Joan Gay Snodgrass and Robert L. Thompson (New York: New York Academy of Sciences, 1997).

Omvedt, Gail. *Buddhism in India: Challenging Brahmanism and Caste* (New Delhi: Sage, 2013).

Organization for Economic Co-operation and Development, "Employment: Time Spent in Paid and Unpaid Work, by Sex," https://stats.oecd.org/index.aspx?queryid=54757, July 2020 (accessed March 18, 2021).

Pateman, Carol. *The Sexual Contract* (Cambridge: Polity Press, 1988).

Pesch, Heinrich. Lehrbuch der Nationalökonomie/*Teaching Guide to Economics*. Vol. 3. Bk. 1. Translated by Rupert J. Ederer (Lewiston, NY: Edwin Mellen, 2002).

Poon, Angelia. "Helping the Novel: Neoliberalism, Self-Help, and the Narrating of the Self in Mohsin Hamid's *How to Get Filthy Rich in Rising Asia*," *The Journal of Commonwealth Literature* 52 (1), 2017: 139–50.

Poovana, Sharan. "In Job Markets, a Higher Education Degree Is Often a Road to Nowhere," *Live Mint*, February 11, 2019, https://www.livemint.com/news/india/in-job-markets-a-higher-education-degree-is-often-a-road-to-nowhere/amp-1549827477203.html?fbclid=IwAR1ANDkpYRgTG30na2q9n_fz3_fgnKoUu-.

Qureshi, S. "Modi to Gift Women Insurance Scheme This RakshaBandhan," *India Today*, August 22, 2015, http://indiatoday.intoday.in/story/narendra-modi-to-gift-women-insurance-scheme-this-raksha-bandhan/1/460260.html (accessed June 30, 2016).

Ray, Raka, and Seemin Qayum. *Cultures of Servitude: Modernity, Domesticity, and Class in India* (Stanford: Stanford University Press, 2009).

Redfield, Marc. *Phantom Formations: Aesthetic Ideology and the Bildungsroman* (Ithaca, NY: Cornell University Press, 2018).

Rhodes, Constantina. *Invoking Lakshmi: The Goddess of Wealth in Song and Ceremony* (Buffalo: SUNY Press, 2010).

Rimke, Heidi. "Governing Citizens through Self-Help Literature," *Cultural Studies* 14 (1), 2000: 62.

Saxena, Akshya, *Vernacular English: Reading the Anglophone in Postcolonial India* (Princeton: Princeton University Press, 2022).

Say, Jean-Baptiste. *A Treatise on Political Economy* (Auburn, AL: Ludwig von Mises Institute, 2008).

Scharff, Christina. "Gender and Neoliberalism: Young Women as Ideal Neoliberal Subjects," in *Handbook of Neoliberalism*, ed. Simon Springer, Kean Birch, and Julie MacLeavy (New York: Routledge, 2016).

Schumpeter, Joseph A. *The Theory of Economic Development: An Inquiry into Profits, Capital, Credit, Interest, and the Business Cycle*, translated from German by Redvers Opie (New York: Oxford University Press, 1961).

Schwartz, B. "Self-Determination: The Tyranny of Freedom," *American Psychologist* 55 (1): 79–88, http://dx.doi.org/10.1037/0003-066X.55.1.79.

Scott, John. "On Rational Choice Theory," in Gary Browning, Abigail Halcli, and Frank Webster (eds.), *Understanding Contemporary Society: Theories of the Present* (London: SAGE Publications, 2000).

Sharma, Arvind. "On Hindu, Hindustan, Hinduism and Hindutva," *Numen* 49 (1), 2002: 1–36.

Sharma, Robin. https://www.robinsharma.com.

Sharma, Robin. *Leadership Wisdom from the Monk Who Sold His Ferrari* (Carlsbad, CA: Hay House Inc., 2003).

Sivaram, Sushil. "(Re)Staging the Postcolonial in the World: The Jaipur Literature Festival and the Pakistani Novel," *Comparative Literature* 71 (4), 2019: 333–56.

Slaughter, Joseph. *Human Rights Inc.* (Fordham: Fordham University Press, 2009).

Smith, Adam. "The Wealth of Nations," in *The Portable Enlightenment Reader*, ed. Isaac Kramnick (London: Penguin Books, 1995).

Srivastava, Prashant. "Job Crisis Clearly Visible in UP," *The Print*, February 8, 2019, https://theprint.in/india/governance/jobs-crisis-visible-up-3700-phds-applied-messengers-police/189339/.

Taylor, Charles. *Sources of the Self: The Making of the Modern Identity* (Cambridge: Harvard University Press, 1989).

Tharu, Susie, and Lalita, K. (eds.). *Women Writing in India: 600 B.C to the Present. Volume 1: 600 B.C to the Early Twentieth Century* (New York: Feminist Press, 1991); *Volume 2: The Twentieth Century* (New York: Feminist Press, 1993).

*The Economic Times*. "Mann Ki Baat: Farmers Will Now Be Masters of Their Own Will, Says PM Modi on Farm Bills," September 27, 2020, https://www.youtube.com/watch?v=FyLz-LAPQ9Q.

*The Economist*. "India's Missing Middle Class," January 11, 2018.

Vancouver, John. *An Enquiry into the Causes and Production of Poverty, and the State of the Poor* (London: Philanthropic Reform, 1796).

Verick, Sher, and the International Labor Organization, "The Paradox of Low Female Labour Force Participation," *ilo.org*, March 9, 2017, https://www.ilo.org/newdelhi/info/public/fs/WCMS_546764/lang--en/index.htm (accessed June 1, 2020).

Verma, Tarishi. "Meet Kalpana Saroj, Dalit Entrepreneur Who Broke Corporate Hegemony," *The Indian Express*, June 12, 2017.

Vohra, Paromita. "'Indian Matchmaking' Wastes the Opportunity to Become a Wonderful Show about Human Connections," *Economic Times*, July 26, 2020, https://economictimes.indiatimes.com/magazines/panache/indian-matchmaking-wastes-the-opportunity-to-become-a-wonderful-show-about-human-connections/articleshow/77171903.cms (accessed July 7, 2021).

Watson, G. "Free Agency," *Journal of Philosophy* 72, 1975: 205–20.

Watt, Ian. *The Rise of the Novel, Studies in Defoe, Richardson and Fielding* (Berkeley: University of California Press, 2001), 62.

World Bank, "Working for Women in India," March 8, 2019, https://www.worldbank.org/en/news/feature/2019/03/08/working-for-women-in-india.

Young, Robert J. C. "Postcolonial Remains." *New Literary History* 43 (1), Winter 2012: 19–42.

# Index

Note: Figures are indicated by page number followed by "f." Footnotes are indicated by the page number followed by "n" and the footnote number, e.g., 20 n.1 refers to footnote 1 on page 20.

"absolute autonomy" 21
Adiga, Aravind 3, 4, 16, 27, 35, 37 n.73, 101, 167
affirmative bildungsroman 61
agency 2, 3, 5, 16, 18, 19, 22, 24, 25, 35, 37 n.72, 46, 48
Algeria 13, 40
alpha-masculinity 3, 115
Alvarado, Emmanuel 100 n.1, 103 n.9
Amazon India 2 n.1
Ambedkar, B. R. 8, 9 n.14, 35, 72, 72 n.1, n.2, 74, 81f
   concept of endosmosis 83
   idea of caste and gender liberation 79–85
American Pragmatism 80 n.19
Anand, Mulk Raj 29
Anderson, Siwan 14 n.29
Anjaria, Ulka 27, 28, 132
Austen, Jane 146
autonomy 8, 10 n.16
   task of recovering 22–3
autotheory 33

Babu, D. Shyam 75 n.7, 76 n.8
Baby, Jeo 42
Bagchi, Amiya 10–11, 11 n.17
Bardhan, Pranab 11, 11 n.18
Barry, Ellen 42, 43 n.10, n.11, 44, 45 n.17, 48 n.23, 49 n.24-6, 51 n.27-8, 56
   bildungsroman 50–2
*Beloved* (Morrison, Toni) 148
Berlin, Isiah 9 n.15, 78 n.14
Bhagat, Chetan 1, 5, 6 n.10, 16, 23, 36, 37 n.73, 102, 131
bhashas 37 n.73, 146
bildungsroman 4, 6, 26, 27–8, 33, 36, 37, 44, 46, 52, 87–8

Biswas, Soutik 40 n.3
Blum, Beth 100, 101 n.2
"Brahminical patriarchy" 71–2
Brand India 14
Brass, Paul R. 163 n.7
Bratman, Michael 10 n.16
Brouillette, Sarah 117
Brown, Wendy 17
Buddhism 9 n.14, 85
Butler, Judith 19, 88–9

capital 11, 13, 15, 16, 21, 32, 50, 51
capitalism 1
capitalist freedom 52
Carnegie, Dale 99, 103, 111
Caste 4
caste and gender liberation
   intertwined freedoms 79–85
caste system 72
   and gender discrimination 72–3
Chacko, Priya 163
Chakrabarty, Dipesh 12, 12 n.23, n.24
Chakravorty, Mrinalini 112
Chatterjee, Partha 45 n.18
Cheah, Pheng 7 n.12
Chittick, William C. 119
choice 2, 5, 16, 18, 21, 22
Christman, John 23 n.50
Clason, George Samuel 99
colonialism 7, 14, 29
*Coming Out as Dalit* (Dutt, Yashica) 27, 35, 74, 85, 86–98
common interest 8, 35, 86–98
competition 20, 53, 108, 153–4
contextual universalisms 6, 35, 36, 75
   freedom as 7
corporate feudalism 10–11
"corporate masculinity" 116

corporation 1, 10, 11, 21–2
Craig, Jeffrey 12 n.22, 13, 13 n.28
*Custody* (Kapur, Manju) 23, 32, 36, 131, 132, 151, 154

Dalit Indian Chamber of Commerce and Industry (DICCI) 73, 75 n.6, 76f
Dalits
  freedom from caste through entrepreneurship 75–9
  entrepreneur 1, 35, 79
  Freedom in Ambedkarite Life-Writing 71
  Freedom Inc. 75–9
  in India 4
  liberation 84
  life narratives 88, 167
  life-writing 9f
  women 35, 74–5, 82
Das, Gurcharan 14, 14 n.31, 16, 17, 22, 25, 133
*Daughters of Destiny* (Roth, Vanessa) 85, 86–98
democracy 83–4
Desai, Anita 28
Dewey, John 72, 81, 82
*Difficult Daughters* (Kapur, Manju) 36, 131, 132, 146
"dissensual bildungsroman" 88, 89
Domestic life 40
domestic servants 32, 57–8
Dore, Robert 13 n.27
dowry 17, 22, 25, 49
Dutt, Yashica 27, 74, 85

Eagleton, Terry 25
*Eat That Frog* (Tracy, Brian) 99
economic liberalization 167
*The Elephant Chaser's Daughter* (Raj, Shilpa) 8, 23, 35, 74, 85, 86–98
empire 164
end of history 11, 12, 13
endogamy 72, 79–80
English 3, 37 n.73, 102, 132, 140
enlightenment 8, 18
"entrepreneurship" 1, 23
equality 7, 8, 9–10, 17, 40, 45, 80, 97, 98
  and freedom 9–10
Eswaran, Mukesh 14 n.29

European liberalism 6
  endosmosis 82–84, 96, 98, 151

*The Fate of Butterflies* (Sahgal, Nayantara) 36, 164–7
*Feel the Fear and Do It Anyway* (Jeffers, Susan) 99
female labor force participation (FLFP) rate 13–14, 40
femininity 6, 15, 36, 44, 45–6
*A Fine Balance* (Mistry, Rohinton) 30
Fischer, J. 10 n.16
Foucault, Michel 19, 20 n.49, 33, 134 n.4
*The Four Agreements* (Ruiz, Don Miguel) 99
Frankfurt, Harry 10 n.16
free market 1–2, 14, 17, 27, 37, 44
  capitalism 73
free will 147
freedom
  as character in 145
  *Difficult Daughters* (Kapur, Manju) 36, 131, 132, 146
  as entrepreneurial agency 109–118
  equality and 9–10
  role of storytelling in 24–8
  *A Suitable Boy* (Seth, Vikram) 36, 131, 132, 148–9
Freedom Inc. 2, 16, 34, 101, 103, 163, 167
  claims and ground realities 4
  development of 17–19
  historical origins 17–19
  and love in reel life 142–5
  in novels of Chetan Bhagat 132–142
  and self-help 35–36, 99–100, 102, 103, 109–10, 117–18
  and waged work 34, 39–40, 42, 50, 52–61, 158
Fukuyama, Francis 11 n.20, 44 n.15

Gandhi, Indira 30
Ganguly, Debjani 87 n.33, 88
Gaza 40
gender 28–34
  equality 1, 40
  and waged work 42
gendered capitalism 6, 98, 128, 167
George, Abraham 86
Gershon, Ilana 107

Ghosh, Amitav 30
Gill, Rosalind 15 n.35
global capitalism 2, 11, 50–2
  with individual freedom
globalization 6, 13, 17, 27, 31, 36, 53, 126, 166
*The God of Small Things* (Roy, Arundhati) 30
Gokhale, Madhavi 117
Gopal, Priyamvada 8 n.13, 29
*The Great Indian Kitchen* (film) 7, 34, 42, 61–9
Greenlees, Donald 132
*Guide* (Narayan, R. K.) 29

*Half Girlfriend* (Bhagat, Chetan) 131, 133, 140–2
Hamid, Mohsin 3, 5 n.8, n.10, 16, 23, 35, 101, 118, 122, 125, 218
  Sufi universalism 6
Hariharan, Githa 36, 164–6
Hendriks, Eric C. 100 n.1, 103 n.9
Hill, Napoleon 99, 103, 108, 111
Hindu nationalism 36
Hindutva 162, 163–7
Hinglish 37 n.73
*History of Indian literature in English* (Mehrotra, Arvind Krishna) 37 n.73
*Home and the World* (Tagore, Rabindranath) 31, 36
homo economicus 19–22
Hondagneu-Sotelo, Pierette 53 n.31
"housewife" 39 n.1
*How to Get Filthy Rich in Rising Asia* (Hamid, Mohsin) 5, 23, 35, 101, 118, 120
*How to Sell Your Way Through Life* (Hill, Napoleon) 108
*How to Win Friends and Influence People* (Carnegie, Dale) 99

"idea of India" 36
Illouz, Eva 130, 135, 146
Incredible India 14
India 6, 40, 102 n.4
  caste discrimination in 71–2
  colonial literature and culture 6
  Dalits in 4, 74

economic liberalization and Freedom Inc. in 10–17
income inequality in 12
liberalization process 10
mega-publicity campaigns 14–15
National Sample Survey (NSS) 41, 41 n.8
post-independence literature and culture 6
post-liberalization literary and cultural scene in 6–7
rural women in 42–4
self-help books in 35
women 41
India Shining 14
*India Unbound* (Das, Gurcharan) 14, 16
Indian literature
  "idea of India" in 28–34
*Indian Matchmaking* (Mundhra, Smriti) 131, 143–5
individual freedom 8–9, 23 n.50, 28–34, 37 n.72, 47, 52, 81, 86–98, 145–159
  in Dalit life-writing 9f
  of Indians 29
individualism 20
individuality 8, 35, 55
individuals 19
inequality 11, 54, 61, 111, 123, 163
  economic 167
  income 4, 12, 14
  structures of 50
integrated education system 74
International Monetary Fund 10
investor citizen 14, 16, 32
Iran 13, 40
Iraq 13, 40

Jaffrelot, Christophe 163 n.5
Jeffers, Susan 99
Jeffrey, Craig 102, 103 n.8, 132
Jensen, Robert 14 n.30, 40 n.2
Jobs, Steve 1
Jordan 13, 40
Justman, Stewart 117

Kabir 9 n.14
*Kamala* (Satthianadhan, Krupabai, and Lokuje, Chandani) 31
Kamble, Milind 73 n.4

Kannada 37 n.73
Kapur, Devesh 75 n.7, 76 n.8, 77, 77 n.11, 79 n.15
Kapur, Manju 23, 32, 36, 131, 132, 146
"karma" 90–1
Kathryn, Lum 4 n.5
Kaur, Ravinder 14, 15, 15 n.32, n.33, 116
Kerrigan, Dylan 100 n.1, 103 n.9
Khilnani, Sunil 28

labor 2, 11, 15, 20, 40, 47
  women's participation rate 14
laissez-faire 43–4, 45, 47
Lakshmi 7, 42, 45–6
Lead India 14
Lears, T. J. Jackson 102 n.5
liberal capitalism 50, 51
liberalization 10, 11, 12, 14, 27, 31, 41, 53, 76, 133, 152, 163, 164, 167
liberty 2, 9, 23 n.50, 74
*On Liberty* and *On Representative Government* (Mill, John Stuart) 12
life in story 4, 33, 52, 62, 69
life-writing 9f
*Literatures of Liberation* (Mangharam, Mukti Lakhi) 8
Locke, John 56 n.39, 57 n.39, n.40
Lokuje, Chandani 31 n.67
love 115, 119, 125–7
  familial loyalty and 112–13
  notions of 36, 130
  and romance 48
  *see also* romantic love
Lowe, Lisa 7 n.12
lower castes 4
Lum, Kathryn 74 n.5

Maasen, Sabine 103
Mahmood, Saba 18, 19, 51 n.29
Marx, Karl 56
masculinity 1, 6, 15, 16, 31, 32, 45
McGee, Micki 107
Mehrotra, Arvind Krishna 37 n.73
memoir 6, 33, 35
"middle class mentality" 102
middle class 12–13, 45, 65, 102
*Midnight's Children* (Rushdie, Salman) 30
Mill, John Stuart 8, 12, 18, 74

Mirza, Maryam 59 n.43
Mistry, Rohinton 30
Mitra, Meghalee 102 n.6
Modi, Narendra 2 n.2, 161, 162f
*The Monk Who Sold His Ferrari* (Sharma, Robin) 101, 103, 104f, 117
Moretti, Franco 26, 87, 88 n.34
Morrison, Toni 148
Mukherjee, Arun P. 82 n.22, 162 n.3
multilingualism 37 n.73
Mundhra, Smriti 143 n.29

Nandi, Swaralipi 116
Narayan, R. K. 29
Narayan, Uma 17
nationalism 31 n.69, 36, 163, 167
negative freedom 78, 81–2, 84, 93
Nehring, Daniel 100 n.1, 103 n.9
Nehru, Jawaharlal 14, 28, 30, 164
neoliberal 41, 53, 73, 75, 108, 117
  capitalism 7
  global institutions 40
  globalization 36
Netflix 143
New India
  Self-Help in 101
*New York Times* (Newspaper) 42–4
novel 1, 3, 6, 7, 16, 24, 27, 29, 30, 31, 33, 36, 37 n.73, 42, 52–3

Omvedt, Gail 9 n.14
*One Night at the Call Center* (Bhagat, Chetan) 5, 131, 133–4, 142
Organization of Economic Cooperation and Development (OECD) 41 n.9

Pateman, Carol 56 n.39, 57 n.41
Pesch, Heinrich 20
pirated books 3 n.3
polygamy 79–80
Poon, Angelia 120
Poovana, Sharan 13 n.26
positive freedom 78, 81–2, 84, 89, 90, 93, 95–6
post-liberalization Indian literature and culture 4
poverty 4
pragmatism 80
Prasad, Chandra Bhan 75 n.7, 76 n.8

precarity 10, 27
public health-care system 11

Qayum, Seemin 54
Qureshi, S. 161 n.1

racial hierarchies 36–7
Raj, Shilpa 8, 23, 35, 74, 85, 92f
Ramanujan, A. K. 37 n.73
Ranciere, Jacques 88
Ravizza, M. 10 n.16
Rawls 57
Ray, Raka 54
realism 4, 24, 25, 26, 27–28, 37
Redfield, Marc 26
reel life
    Freedom Inc.and love in 142–5
religious
    hierarchies 36–7
    nationalism 167
Rhodes, Constantina 46 n.19
*The Richest Man of Babylon* (Clason, George Samuel) 99
Rimke, Heidi 105
romantic love 36
    in popular and literary fiction 129
    *see also* love
Roth, Vanessa 86
Rousseau 57
Roy, Arundhati 3, 30
Ruiz, Don Miguel 99
Rushdie, Salman 30

Sahgal, Nayantara 36, 164
*sangha* (community) 92
Saroj, Kalpana 73
Satthianadhan, Krupabai 31
*satyagraha* ("movement for truth") 80 n.18
Saxena, Akshya 3 n.4
Say, Jean Baptiste 105, 106 n.14
Scharff, Christina 15 n.35, 46 n.20
Schumpeter, Joseph 106 n.16
self-actualization 34
self-help 3, 35–6
    books in India 35, 99–100
*Sense and Sensibility* (Austen, Jane) 146
Seth, Vikram 36, 131, 132
"sexual contract" 57

*The Shadow Lines* (Ghosh, Amitav) 30
Shanti Bhavan 86–9
Sharma, Arvind 163 n.4
Sharma, Robin 101, 103, 103 n.10, 104f, 106
Sivaram, Sushil 5 n.8
Slaughter, Joseph 26, 44 n.16, 77 n.10, 79 n.16, 88
Smiles, Samuel 103
Smith, Adam 44 n.12, n.13, n.14
"social contract" 57, 57 n.40, 58, 59
sovereignty 2, 15, 29, 30, 37
*The Space between Us* (Umrigar, Thrity) 32, 34, 42, 52–61
Srivastava, Prashant 13 n.25
"Start Up India" 2
*The Steve Jobs Way* (Elliot, Jay) 2
story structures 5, 24–5, 33, 37
storytelling 4
*stri dharma* (fulfillment of a woman's duties) 46
*Such a Long Journey* (Mistry, Rohinton) 30
Sufi universalism 5, 6, 35–6, 118
*A Suitable Boy* (Seth, Vikram) 36, 131, 132, 148–9
    freedom as character in 145
Syria 13, 40

Tagore, Rabindranath 31, 36
Tamil 37 n.73
Taylor, Charles 4, 18, 24, 33, 74
thin self 105, 108, 110, 112, 116, 118, 120, 121
*Think and Grow Rich* (Napoleon Hill) 99
Tickell, Alex 28
*Timepass: Youth, Class and the Politics of Waiting in India* (Craig, Jeffrey) 102
*In Times of Siege* (Hariharan, Githa) 36, 164, 165
Tracy, Brian 99
Trump, Ivanka 2 n.2

Umrigar, Thrity 32, 34, 42, 52–3, 54, 55 n.37, 56 n.38
underemployed 4, 23, 35, 98, 99, 159
unemployed 7, 11, 13, 14, 167
universalism 6, 7–8
*Untouchable* (Anand, Mulk Raj) 29

Vancouver, John 57 n.39
Verick, Sher 41 n.7
Verma, Tarishi 73 n.3
virtuous market citizen 163
Vohra, Paromita 145 n.33

waged work 4, 16, 34, 39, 41–2
   and freedom 42, 52–61
*Waiting for the Mahatma* (Narayan, R. K.) 29
Watson, G. 10 n.16
Watt, Ian 26, 27 n.58
West Bank 40 n.4, n.5

*The White Tiger* (Adiga, Aravind) 4, 5 n.7, 27, 35, 101, 109–118, 128, 167
women 4
working women
   as embodiments of freedom in bildung narratives 39
   versus grha lakshmi 45–50
World Bank 1, 2 n.1, 4, 11 n.19, 15 n.34, 40

Yashica Dutt 35
Yemen 13, 40
Young, Robert J. C. 53 n.32

www.ingramcontent.com/pod-product-compliance
Lightning Source LLC
Chambersburg PA
CBHW052121300426
44116CB00010B/1754